W9-ADR-113

TO
COMMAND
THE SKY

Smithsonian History of Aviation Series

Von Hardesty, Series Editor

On December 17, 1903, on a windy beach in North Carolina, aviation became a reality. The development of aviation over the course of little more than three-quarters of a century stands as an awe-inspiring accomplishment in both a civilian and military context. The airplane has brought whole continents closer together, at the same time it has been a lethal instrument of war.

This series of books is intended to contribute to the overall understanding of the history of aviation—its science and technology as well as the social, cultural, and political environment in which it developed and matured. Some publications help fill the many gaps that still exist in the literature of flight; others add new information and interpretation to current knowledge. While the series appeals to a broad audience of general readers and specialists in the field, its hallmark is strong scholarly content.

The series is international in scope and will include works in three major categories.

Smithsonian Studies in Aviation History: works that provide new and original knowledge.

Smithsonian Classics of Aviation History: carefully selected out-of-print works that are considered essential scholarship.

Smithsonian Contributions to Aviation History: previously unpublished documents, reports, symposia, and other materials.

ADVISORY BOARD: Roger E. Bilstein, *University of Houston;* Horst Boog, *Militärgeschichtliches Forschungsamt, Germany;* DeWitt C. Copp, *Author and air historian;* Tom D. Crouch, *National Air and Space Museum;* Sylvia Fries, *National Aeronautics and Space Administration;* Ben Greenhous, *Historian;* John F. Guilmartin, Jr., *Ohio State University;* Terry Gwynn-Jones, *Author;* Richard P. Hallion, *Secretary of the Air Force's Staff Group;* James R. Hansen, *Auburn University;* Von Hardesty, *National Air and Space Museum;* Robin Higham, *Kansas State University;* Lee Kennett, *University of Georgia;* Nick Komons, *Federal Aviation Administration;* William M. Leary, *University of Georgia;* W. David Lewis, *Auburn University;* Air Vice-Marshall R. A. Mason, CBE MA RAF (Ret.); LTC Phillip S. Meilinger, *HQ USAF/XOXWD;* John H. Morrow, Jr., *University of Georgia;* Dominick A. Pisano, *National Air and Space Museum;* Air Commodore H. A. Probert, MBE MA RAF (Ret.); General Lucien Robineau, *Service historique de l'armée de l'air, France;* Alex Roland, *Duke University;* F. Robert van der Linden, *National Air and Space Museum.*

TO COMMAND THE SKY

THE BATTLE FOR AIR SUPERIORITY OVER GERMANY, 1942-1944

Stephen L. McFarland and
Wesley Phillips Newton

Smithsonian Institution Press
Washington and London

GRAND FORKS PUBLIC LIBRARY

Copyright © 1991 by the Smithsonian Institution.
All rights are reserved.
This book was edited by Therese Boyd and designed by Janice Wheeler.

The paper used in this publication meets the minimum requirements of the
American National Standard for Permanence of Paper for Printed Library
Materials Z39.48-1984.

Jacket illustration is from *The Hunter Becomes the Hunted*, by William S. Phillips.
© The Greenwich Workshop, Inc., Trumbull, Conn. From the limited edition fine
art print.

Printed in the United States of America
10 9 8 7 6 5 4 3 2
99 98 97 96 95 94 93
For permission to reproduce individual illustrations appearing in this book,
please correspond directly with the owners of the images, as stated in the picture
captions. The Smithsonian Institution Press does not retain reproduction rights
for these illustrations individually or maintain a file of addresses for photo
sources.

Library of Congress Cataloging-in-Publication Data

McFarland, Stephen Lee, 1950–
   To command the sky : the battle for air superiority over Germany, 1942–1944 /
Stephen L. McFarland and Wesley Phillips Newton.
      p.   cm.—(Smithsonian history of aviation series)
   Includes bibliographical references and index.
   ISBN 1-56098-069-9 (alk. paper)
   1. World War, 1939–1945—Aerial operations.   I. Newton, Wesley Phillips.   II.
Title.   III. Series.
   D785.M39   1991
   940.54′4—dc20   91-9712
                                                                            CIP

To
Maurer Maurer, historian of air power
Carl E. McFarland, survivor of the Hump's "Aluminum Trail"
Connie McFarland and children, Jennifer and Jeffrey
Merlin Newton and children, Linda, Alan, and Brent

CONTENTS

LIST OF FIGURES AND TABLES

Figures

Tables

ACKNOWLEDGMENTS

Many people contribute in essential ways to books besides authors. The authors of this book are especially indebted to a number of persons. Personnel of that great repository of material for the history of air power, the U.S. Air Force Historical Research Center, Maxwell Air Force Base, eased the way with services and valuable advice. They include: Mr. Lloyd Cornett, Jr., former director; Col. Elliott V. Converse, III, USAF, current director; Dr. Richard E. Morse, chief of Historical Reference Division; his deputy chief, Mrs. Lynn O. Gamma; Capt. George W. Cully, USAF, chief of Queries Division; staff historians Mr. Harry R. Fletcher, Dr. Daniel L. Haulman, Capt. David C. Johnson, USAF, Dr. Robert M. Johnson, II, and Dr. James H. Kitchens, III; archivists Mr. Presley Bickerstaff, M. Sgt. Gary C. McDaniel, USAFR, Dr. Timothy D. Johnson, and S. Sgt. Samuel Sheain, USAF; archives assistants Mrs. Nora Bledsole, Ms. Margaret C. Claiborn, and Ms. Essie Roberts; archives technician Ms. Sara Frances Rawlings; and archives specialist S. Sgt. Ed Gaines. Others at Maxwell who assisted us were Dr. Richard Marcus, visiting from the University of Wisconsin, Eau Claire; Dr. Robert F. Futrell, Dr. David MacIsaac, and Dr. Earl Tilford of the Center for Aerospace Doctrine, Research, and Education; Lt. Col. David L. McFarland, USAF (ret.), Air Command and Staff College Foundation; and Mr. Richard Lane, chief of the Air University Library, and his staff.

The archivists, librarians, and staffs of the National Archives, Manuscript Division of the Library of Congress, and the Smithsonian's Air and Space Museum also provided valuable and often essential assistance.

We are grateful to Fritz Ungar, Mary Gill Rice, Starr Smith, Edmond Zellner, Luther H. Richmond, William R. Lawley, Jr., Clyde W. Bradley, Jr., Gerhard H. Kroll, Günther Rall, James H. Doolittle, and Robert L. Salzarulo, for their letters and oral interviews.

Dr. John Wood of James Madison University, whose brother flew a fighter with the Eighth Air Force, and Col. Starr Smith, USAFR (ret.), an intelligence officer with a Liberator group of the Eighth, were instrumental in putting us in touch with American fighter and bomber veterans of the Big Week and Berlin air battles described in this book. Dr. Jim Kitchens of the U.S. Air Force Historical Research Center performed the same service with respect to German veterans of these battles and aided the authors in many other ways deserving of special recognition. Dr. Kenneth P. Werrell of Bradford University and Dr. Lee Kennett of the University of Georgia offered encouragement when it was needed. Dr. Richard Kohn, then chief of the Office of Air Force History, and Dr. Richard Greene Davis of his staff gave us material assistance. The same is true of Col. Capers A. Holmes, USAFR (ret.), who was a navigator with a B-24 group; and Mr. Raymond Toliver and Mr. James Crow, who shared their photographic collections with us. The Auburn University Humanities Fund provided needed financial assistance in the early going and the Historical Research Center funded some of the research. Dr. Gordon C. Bond, head of the department of history at Auburn University, offered departmental resources and facilities.

Besides their families, the authors are most beholden to their colleagues, whose work on the history of flight has made Auburn University the academic center for this scholarly specialty: Professors William F. Trimble, Donathon C. Olliff, James R. Hansen, W. David Lewis, and Robert R. Rea. The authors are also grateful to Felix Lowe, whose vision for scholarship in the history of flight continues to enhance the stature of the Smithsonian Institution Press, and this book's editor, Therese D. Boyd, who has helped turn it into a more polished work.

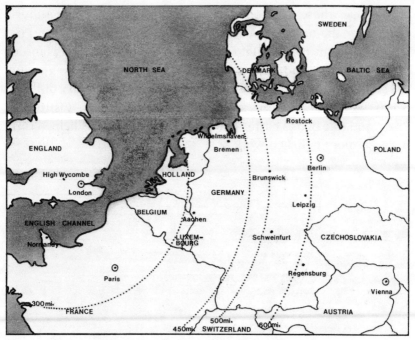

Map of Europe showing distances to German targets from Eighth Air Force
Headquarters at High Wycombe.

INTRODUCTION

The Allies were taking one of the greatest gambles of the war. The assembly of men and equipment on 6 June 1944 was the most concentrated, most vulnerable, and choicest target for German air power of the war. Including 8 divisions of ground and airborne soldiers and 5,000 ships arrayed along some 50 miles of the French Normandy coast, the Allied invasion of France was the penultimate event of 4½ years of British and 2½ years of American endeavor. Never in the war was so much effort concentrated at one point, at one time. Could Allied air forces hold off the savage Luftwaffe attacks everyone expected?

An operation such as OVERLORD was the type for which the Luftwaffe existed. It had been designed to be primarily a tactical air force, acting in support of the German army, and had functioned most successfully in that role. A powerful and prepared Luftwaffe would have meant defeat for the invasion forces. German pilots could hardly have missed. Any bomb dropped and nearly any bullet fired would have found a target, so compressed were Allied forces. Invading forces would have to control the air over the invasion front to have any chance at success.

The British officer who was the chief of the Allied tactical air forces for the invasion felt the best way to defeat the Luftwaffe and control the air over the invasion front was to fight the Luftwaffe in a great swirling air battle the day of the invasion. Most American air commanders, mindful of the capabilities and mobility of air power, had reached the conclusion by mid-1943 that an invasion would require a prior strategic campaign for air superiority—to destroy the Luftwaffe in a war of attrition. They feared, however, that such a campaign might take too long.

The Allied Combined Chiefs of Staff, favoring the more prudent American approach, assigned the U.S. Army Air Forces' Eighth Air Force in the POINTBLANK directive of May 1943 the task of gaining control of the air. Though command of the air (the power to use airspace as desired)—requiring absolute control in all areas at all times—was nearly impossible, Eighth Air Force and its supporting cast would have to win at least air superiority (control of the air at a certain time and place to allow operations without prohibitive losses) or air supremacy (a greater and more extensive degree of air superiority) for the OVERLORD invasion to have a chance for success.[1] Eighth Air Force first had to force the Luftwaffe to turn to defending the Reich, forsaking the plans for offensive air warfare that had been at the root of German successes in the first years of the war. Second, Eighth Air Force had to win air superiority to allow continued strategic bombing, to prevent the Luftwaffe from going back on the offensive, and to permit the OVERLORD landings. The means by which Eighth Air Force completed this assignment is an untold story of World War II.

The need for air superiority stretched beyond the Normandy beaches. Even before Pearl Harbor the Army Air Forces had convinced President Roosevelt and other American leaders that an American strategic bombing campaign against Germany could contribute mightily to Allied victory in World War II. The proclaimed goal of American air power advocates was to destroy German military power through strategic daylight precision bombing to the extent that a cross-Channel invasion would be unnecessary. This idea had developed out of the shock accompanying victory in

World War I. Ten million soldiers and ten million civilians had died of all causes. For the military establishments of the major powers, the challenge was to insure that when the next war broke out, the armies would not get bogged down in four more years of trench warfare—a battle of attrition for which even the winners would be losers.

In the United States a fledgling Army air arm, with no tradition to bind it to the past, developed what it believed to be the answer to such wars—strategic precision bombing by day from high altitudes. By carrying the war to an enemy's civilian population and industrial system, strategic bombers could force a quick end to any war and minimize casualties. America's first air power strategist, William "Billy" Mitchell, had taught that bombers could destroy an enemy's ability to wage war only if they controlled the air with the aid of fighters. A generation of American air leaders, despite Mitchell's lead, came to believe that the bomber could always get through to its target, if properly armed, by fighting its way in, establishing its own local control of the air. Henry Arnold, chief of the Air Corps, made sure that all of his top-level commanders were "bomber" men—disciples of this doctrine. In the airmen's minds, the primary purpose of air power in Europe during World War II would be strategic bombing. It was the only major contribution the airmen could make to the war effort that was largely independent of the Army and the Navy. This is a well-chronicled story.

The doctrine of strategic daylight precision bombing rested on two premises that would not be proven in the war. First, its supporters determined that the civilian population was the weak link in a nation's defense. Unlike soldiers, they could not bear up against the horrors of modern war delivered to their doorsteps by strategic bombers. Still, this premise had to be disguised, for official American policy was against making civilians the targets of bombing. The second premise was the belief that a strategic bombing campaign could eliminate an enemy's ability to wage modern war by destroying its industrial base. Mindful of their desire to win independence for the Air Force after World War II, the leaders of the Army Air Forces were continuously sensitive to the possibility that strategic bombing would not measure up to the enormous investment they had convinced the country to make—over 35,000 heavy and very heavy bombers, over 660,000 tons of bombs on Germany and 165,000 tons on Japan.[2]

So concerned were they that after the war they invested much effort to evaluate the impact of strategic bombing. The U.S. Strategic Bombing Survey, 208 reports for the European war alone, was the result. Though self-serving and designed from the first to justify the strategic bombing effort, the survey revealed the limitations of strategic bombing. Neither the morale nor the will of the bombed populations approached collapse. Physical destruction remained limited and largely ineffective until the second half of 1944, nearly five years after the war began. Germany had sufficient overcapacity to absorb the initial pounding. Dispersal, repair, and expansion compensated for additional bombing. Armies of laborers, free and unfree, insured adequate manpower. Possessing the largest machine-tool industry in the world more than compensated for damage done to machinery. In spite of the bombing, the German economy continued to expand until late in the war. In the words of John Kenneth Galbraith, a member of the Strategic Bombing Survey, "Strategic bombing was designed to destroy the industrial base of the enemy and the morale of the people. It did neither."[3]

Still, the campaign did have an appreciable effect on Germany's ability to wage war. The effort caused a mass diversion of scarce capital and resources to defensive operations, away from the offensive warfare that made German victories in the first three years of the war possible. Though production increased, strategic bombing "placed a ceiling on German war production which was well below what Germany, with skilful and more urgent management of its resources, was capable of producing after 1943."[4] Bombing made the German economy, one of the most efficient in the world, operate with great waste, forcing dispersal, upsetting timetables, eliminating the economies of scale, altering priorities, and disrupting communications.

But again, most of this occurred in the last year of the war, when Soviet armies were pressing on German borders in the east and British and American armies were racing across France. The end of the Third Reich seemed inevitable, with or without strategic bombing. Did strategic air power contribute to Allied victory in World War II? If it did, how?

The answer can be found in the struggle to achieve the air superiority that made the Allied invasion of German-occupied Europe possible. Ground actions such as an invasion were dependent on control of the air. Likewise, the bombing campaign itself, using somewhat slow four-engine bombers, also required control of the air to permit bombing without prohibitive losses. The relationship between the bombing campaign and air superiority was symbiotic—the bombers needed air superiority to permit further bombing, and the battle for air superiority required bombing to make the battle, for the Germans, worth fighting.

Air superiority faced many obstacles. Air power did not seize territory. There were no great battles in the traditional sense in the acquiring of air superiority, just one mission after another until the enemy wore down. The number of missions to achieve air superiority depended on the value of the targets and the enemy's will to defend them. No flags rose over conquered fortresses. Map makers did not change the colors of areas over which the Army Air Forces established control of the skies. Aerial combat was by nature mercurial. Aircrews gained air superiority and then had to regain it repeatedly. It was a truism, but what went up had to come down. The attackers seized control of the air over enemy territory with the right combination of training, technology, and numbers, but gave it up temporarily when their aircraft returned to base for refueling. An unlearned lesson from World War I was the incredible resiliency of air power. There would be no "knockout blow." The struggle had to be continuous, never letting up the pressure.

Air superiority was necessarily the antecedent of bombing warfare—an intermediate stage. Alone it could not win the war. It only permitted or prevented those operations that could: ground campaigns, supported by close air support, aerial resupply, and air interdiction, or possibly strategic bombing. An invasion or bombing offensive had to accompany a campaign to seize air superiority for that campaign to work. The enemy had to be forced to come up and fight in order to be shot down.

In the battle for air superiority the defense nearly always had the advantage. Distances were shorter. German airmen flew over German territory. If an aircraft went down, it could be recovered and repaired. Its crew could be rescued and often healed. Supply was simpler. Morale, that great intangible, played a special role because German pilots were defending German homes.

American airmen faced special offensive handicaps. Air Corps doctrine emphasized strategic bombing to the near exclusion of air superiority. The English Channel, as a protective barrier, convinced political and military leaders in Washington that the strategic effort against Germany from England could be delayed while they diverted resources to North Africa and the Pacific.

The U.S. Army ground forces had long demanded a form of localized air superiority. Its absence would leave the ground forces and air forces providing close air support open to enemy air and ground attacks. This thinking, opposing Air Corps doctrine, called on the air units to concentrate on providing close air support, combat air patrols to protect ground units from attacking enemy aircraft, and battlefield interdiction. If followed, this tactical doctrine would have precluded any strategic bombing to destroy an enemy's industrial structure. It also would have preserved a large and powerful Luftwaffe at the time of OVERLORD, to be defeated, or possibly not defeated, in a great clash with Allied fighters on 6 June 1944. Could air superiority be won in a single day, when the competing air forces involved thousands of aircraft, industries able to produce thousands more, and training establishments able to man them with crews?

In the U.S. Army the strategic bomber advocates believed that this was a question that needed no answer. They had convinced American military and civilian leaders to accept an untried and untested theory of war—that strategic bombing could defeat an enemy by destroying its industrial fabric, with no need for a land invasion. For these bombing advocates, air superiority had little redeeming value because it seemed of use mainly to support ground forces. They misdirected their opposition because air superiority, as the war would prove, was also required for strategic bombing and vice versa.

The bomber barons did not accept this idea until the enemy's control of the air over the continent shocked them with unacceptable losses. Until then they believed that if the gamble of strategic bombing worked, the payoff would be victory in war without a repeat of the horrors of ground warfare and especially of the trenches that symbolized World War I for a generation of Americans. Even if it did not work, the campaign would weaken the enemy and could help to win air superiority, destroying aircraft manufacturing plants and knocking enemy fighters from the skies. In this sense, air superiority would be both the successor to strategic bombing and its antecedent. Many political and military leaders doubted the value of a strategic bombing campaign to destroy enemy industry, but not the necessity for air superiority at the time of the invasion of France.

The two endeavors, to win air superiority and to bomb strategic targets, became necessary means of effecting the same end, although this result was not in the original Allied plans for bombing and for an invasion. In time the bombing of certain targets, particularly the cherished capital of Berlin, would be done deliberately to provoke a showdown for control of the air, with the intention of grinding up the German day fighter force. The Germans would be forced to focus all possible fighter resources to the defense of air space over the Reich, reducing and eventually eliminating almost all fighter resources defending the Channel coast from invasion. The resultant battles on high would wear the Luftwaffe down, in poor shape to move back to the coast when the invasion began. All this helped to insure that, with few exceptions, the aircraft over Normandy on 6 June 1944 would be Allied. The surface forces would bring the invasion off and would be rightly credited with a decisive stroke. Most of the German and Allied troops who grappled on the beaches would be unaware that great air battles had made the landing possible. In hindsight the strategic campaign was the only means for defeating the Luftwaffe and insuring the success of the landing.

The winning of air superiority over Germany in 1944 has yet to be analyzed in its entirety because most observers have recognized it as an intermediate step in the winning of the war. The appeal of the big bomber, the great number of crew involved, and the evident destruction it caused have made the strategic bombing effort outshine air superiority. The U.S. Air Force's official history of World War II covers every aspect of the air war, but the issue of air superiority is lost in the panorama of the entire air war. In addition, this multivolume set is over 35 years old.

Then and now, the appeal of the strategic bombing effort has been dominant. Most of the books on the air war that appear today concentrate on this limited but compelling aspect of the air war, including DeWitt Copp's *A Few Great Captains* and *Forged in Fire*, Ronald Schaffer's *Wings of Judgment*, James Parton's *"Air Force Spoken Here,"* and Michael Sherry's *The Rise of American Air Power*. The battles for air superiority left no blasted factories and no casualty figures running into the hundreds of thousands. They lacked symbols that could compete with charred piles of rubble where great cities used to stand. The battle for air superiority provided no justification for an independent air force after the war. As a key ingredient in winning the war, it deserves more detailed analysis. The battles of air superiority rank in importance with the epic battles of Midway, the Bulge, Pearl Harbor, Stalingrad, and the Normandy invasion and should be treated as such.

How and why the Americans fought for air superiority in Europe from 1942 to 1944 and the significance of the final victory are the subjects of this book. Because air superiority was so tied to strategic bombing, both merge to form a major theme, but only when air superiority became the Americans' paramount objective. Topics such as the morality or effectiveness of strategic bombing will for the most part be avoided. The air superiority role of tactical fighters operating in direct support of the ground forces will be largely ignored. This is not for the usual reason of focusing on one theme, but because the strategic campaign so obsessed Germany that the Luftwaffe chose not to fight the battle for tactical air superiority. The role of the British Royal Air Force in the struggle for air superiority will also be largely avoided. That force could have only a limited impact because of the Spitfire's limited range and because its bombers flew almost entirely at night, downing but few German fighters. Air superiority was the responsibility and the accomplishment of the men, women, and aircraft of the American Eighth Air Force and its supporting units, including Fifteenth and Ninth Air Forces and all the infrastructure of the Army Air Forces dedicated to the efforts of these numbered air forces. This effort is their story, but it also the story or those who opposed them—the German fighter pilots, flak crews, and brass.

The struggle for air superiority became the trench warfare of World War II. It was a battle of attrition. There was no place to hide, except in the clouds. There was little finesse involved. It was kill or be killed, shoot down or be shot down. We stand in awe of those who struggled to create and implement the doctrines, to build the airplanes and other equipment, to train and support the aircrews, and to command the sky in the big planes and smaller ones. The climax of all this was the Normandy invasion and the ensuing successful strategic bombing of Germany.

CHAPTER ONE

THE CHALLENGE

In July 1849 some 200 small, unmanned but armed balloons appeared above Venice. Besieging Austrian troops resorted to this first known episode of aerial bombing in an attempt to crush a Venetian bid for freedom from the Hapsburg monarchy. An Austrian artillery officer, Lt. Franz Uchatius, took advantage of a device developed 67 years earlier to initiate a new era in warfare. A fuse burning in each had been calculated through measurement of air currents and distance to release a pear-shaped iron bomb from each balloon as the flotilla passed over the city. The bombs fell as planned, but apparently did little damage.[1]

Use of the skies for warfare was slow to catch on. Men would not drop aerial bombs again until the early twentieth century, perhaps because of the failure of the experiment over Venice, more probably because balloons were somewhat vulnerable to the influences of wind. Soldiers deployed balloons for observing the battlefield in the American Civil War, the Spanish-American War, the Boer War, and the Russo-Japanese War, but the resumption of bombing awaited a swifter, more stable carrier.

The extension of war into the skies initiated a struggle to control the skies, both to claim superiority in the airspace over enemy territory and to deny enemies the same advantage. The purpose and objective of early aerial warfare was to drop bombs on or shoot bullets at ground targets and to use the vantage point of altitude to gain information about the course of land battles. Control of the air was a necessary first step to allow or to stop bombing and reconnaissance. Air superiority was a means to an end, not an end in itself.

Though used neither systematically nor to any great effect, military forces experimented with this new weapon of war. In nearly all cases it was used in reconnaissance or bombardment. The airplane began to come into its own during the tumultuous and long-lasting Mexican Revolution that erupted in 1910. Though in microcosm, most of the elements of aerial combat developed during this conflict. In 1913 two mercenaries from the United States flying for different factions, Dean Ivan Lamb and Philip Rader, encountered one another and exchanged pistol shots. They were acquaintances and whether the exchange was hostile or feigned is unclear, but it is the first known episode demonstrating the potential of air-to-air combat and the probability of aerial battles for air superiority.[2]

When World War I broke out, no specially designated aerial units existed to carry out bombardment and threaten enemy skies, but the Germans quickly employed Zeppelins and small "Dove" tractor airplanes to bomb French cities in single-craft attacks. The French formed their first bombing unit in September 1914. The British navy's air arm soon began limited raids against German Zeppelin bases. These efforts demanded air superiority, receiving it only because of the weaknesses of defenses, not due to any actions of the offense. In World War II terms, the damage was slight, but the psychological impact was extensive.

Venice, London, Paris, and Freiburg, among others, experienced the horrors of bombing in World War I, temporarily convincing Europeans of the importance of controlling the air over one's own homeland and, in order to gain victory, over an enemy's homeland. The lesson was not wasted on some American military observers. In these places occurred experiences that would become familiar to urban populations in Spain and China in the decade before World War II and to many others around the world during that conflict. The pattern would be repeated, although becoming more complex because of technological advances: from the observers came the first warning; sirens sounded; if it was night, searchlights played across the sky; bursts from antiaircraft guns blossomed darkly here and there; now and again an airship or plane plunged to earth, trailing flame and burning debris. Night or day, the fear was contagious, the terror consuming—the phenomenon of the most modern cities in the world blacked out, their populations hiding. Horrendous sounds and tart smells filled the air and gripped the emotions.[3]

As a leading historian of strategic bombing has noted: "At war's end, the bomber had emerged in the popular mind—with some justification—as the most dangerous weapon the war had spawned." Bombers had spared American cities, though on one occasion a New York City company tested a siren without notice, igniting somewhat of a panic.[4]

In the Great War the most glamorous flier did not ride in a bomber. He was the fighter pilot. At the outbreak of the war there was no such defined role and no aircraft called "fighter" or any equivalent term. Gradually the specialized role, doctrine, tactics, and technology of the fighter evolved from a hodgepodge of primitive actions and innovative thought. Initially reconnaissance was king, most notably when an Allied pilot spotted disarray in the German maneuvering at the Marne or when spying aircraft played a key part in the Germans' overwhelming victory at Tannenberg. The idea was not long in dawning on commanders that something was needed to counter the spies in the sky; the concept of air superiority and air-to-air combat evolved rapidly. The natural hostility between the pilots of the various belligerents soon led to exchanges of gunfire, à la Lamb and Rader, first with pistols, then rifles and awkwardly positioned machine guns. Ten months into the war came the first significant technological breakthrough, the deflector plate of the Frenchman Roland Garros, followed by the interrupter gear of Anthony Fokker for the German air force, which allowed machine guns to fire directly forward through the propeller without shattering the blades. Now pilots could aim their airplanes, not their guns; airplanes became weapons instead of just carriers of weapons. The fighter plane was born.[5] It was, however, known among the English-speaking air forces as a "pursuit plane," or sometimes simply "pursuit," until the name "fighter plane" or "fighter" was substituted in the late 1930s.

As technology became more sophisticated and battle a more demanding teacher, most of the elements of aerial combat involving fighters in that war and future wars evolved: the eight, wingover, falling leaf, split-S, barrel roll, slow roll, snap roll, the wingman concept, the Lufbery Circle, hiding in clouds, using the sun to blind an enemy, other advantageous positions, deflection shooting, and watchfulness—"better a stiff neck than a broken one."[6]

Reconnaissance and bombing airplanes, although they came to perform distinct roles, were at times dependent on the escort fighter. This relationship began to take shape even while the distinctiveness of each type was emerging early in the war. Roland Garros was escorting another plane on a bombing mission in the spring of 1915 when he was shot down. Because British unarmed reconnaissance planes fell increasingly the victims of Fokker's first true fighter, Hugh Trenchard, commanding the British army's Royal Flying Corps, issued an order early in 1916 that reconnaissance aircraft "must be escorted by at least three other fighting machines [and all] . . . must fly in close formation." This was an early case of close escort, a tactic that would prove controversial in World War II.[7]

Because most of the bombers were considerably slower than enemy fighters, they had to have an escort of fighters with speeds able to match that of the interceptors. In 1917 Trenchard mandated that each of his bombers would have two escorting fighters and each reconnaissance plane would have five. In October 1918 formations of eighteen or more DH-9s, a medium bomber, operated in support of British troops breaching German defenses on the Western Front under the escort of at least a third as many speedy SE-5As to take on the still potent threat of the Fokker D.VIIs, perhaps the finest all-around fighter of the war.[9]

During the war the idea of the vital necessity of escort diminished, even for Trenchard. Possibly this was due in part to the short range of fighters that in the main precluded their escorting long-range strategic bombers. When air defenses became effective, the heavy bombers changed from daylight to night operations, again making escort impractical. By necessity, these bombers were self-defending.

To increase the self-defending capabilities of the bombers, commanders usually ordered formation flying. Height was the initial element of self-defense, but interlocking firepower evolved as an equally important tactic. The German Gothas attacking England usually flew in a diamond formation, lumbering along at 75 MPH and an altitude of above 10,000 feet. Altitude and interlocking formation firepower evidently worked, as antiaircraft guns began to cause as much harm to bombers as intercepting fighters, speeding the development of a third tactic to defend the attacking bombers—night bombing.[9]

Besides the implications drawn from strategic bombing in the popular mind and by certain theorists, the most important doctrine to emerge from aerial combat in the Great War was air superiority.[10] From the outset, strategic bombing and air superiority were linked. The first-generation British naval planes that bombed Zeppelin bases in 1914 were attempting to prevent the Germans from winning an early form of air superiority while attempting to exert it themselves. The Zeppelins, Gothas, and R-planes achieved air superiority over England, though admittedly limited in terms of area, duration, and objectives attained. The same was true for the British Independent Force's strategic campaign over Germany in 1918, though it was arguably more rigorously contested by German air defenses.

Air superiority in World War I was connected with the evolution of the fighter plane and its tactics, but the air superiority that the fighter planes strove to win was associated with the ground fronts. Fighters tried to control the air over the battlefields, "a specific operational area," gained through "air fighting."[11] The bombers also played a role in this form of air superiority, bombing rear zones to interdict the battlefields. More rigorous application of bomber efforts by either side against communications and supply might have been decisive.[12]

Fighters in World War I, besides their counterair, escort, air defense, and fighter-bomber functions, took on a strategic role on at least one occasion. The first ship to be refitted with a full carrier deck carried British fighters in 1918 to within range of German Zeppelin sheds; these aircraft inflicted heavy damage. This was a major step in the development of the aircraft carrier, yet it was also the strategic fighter in action, portending future developments in the next world war—using fighters to carry the war to the sources of the enemy's power. How some prophets of air power in the postwar period could downplay the fighter plane remains almost incomprehensible.

Other than American volunteers in the flying services of the Allies and seaplane technology, the United States contributed little to these various developments in aerial warfare until it declared war in 1917. Even then it remained seriously laggard in technology until the end of the war, its Army Air Service using only foreign designs in combat. Because of the time needed to organize and train, most Air Service units did not enter combat under American direction until the summer of 1918. By the Armistice American fliers had participated in most phases of aerial combat, with one notable exception—they received no heavy bombers and so did not experience that precedent for the strategic bombing that a later generation of Army fliers would help to shape and direct in another world war.[13]

In May 1917, shortly after the United States had entered the war, Maj. William Mitchell of the Army's air arm separated the functions of the air forces into a "tactical phase" and a "strategical phase." The tactical phase, he stated, was "basically to insure observation for the fire and control of our own artillery. To accomplish that, airplanes and balloons observe the fire while others fight off hostile aircraft which attempt to stop it." The strategic phase "is being seriously considered by the belligerents . . . To be successful, large combatant groups of airplanes must be organized, separate from those directly attached to the Army units." It was with the latter that Mitchell declared "that the United States may aid in the greatest way and which . . . if properly applied will have a greater influence on the ultimate decision of the war than any one arm." While the Army Air Service did not produce a "strategical" unit, the Navy's air arm did organize such a force, the Northern Bombing Group. It lacked, however, the equipment to conduct operations.[14]

In Mitchell's recommendations can be seen the seeds of the theory that he would promulgate after the war and for which he became increasingly controversial. Meanwhile he became a foremost practitioner of the "tactical phase," appreciating its contribution to the ground campaigns on the Western Front and broadening his view of its possibilities.

In a semi-official postwar history of the Army Air Service in World War I, the terms *air superiority* and *air supremacy* appeared several times. Specifically they referred to British or German air superiority, stressing the former's supremacy for much of 1918, but also noting the U.S. Army Air Service's role in the last campaigns of the Western Front. Mitchell's recommendations and even the statements of nonfliers evidenced this sensitivity to the doctrine of air superiority. On 21 June 1917, Maj. Marlborough Churchill of the U.S. Army field artillery commented, "If the enemy is master of the air, the artillery cannot conquer the ground which the infantry is to occupy." A year later, Mitchell and some of his fliers, with some combat experience under their belts, observed that "ascendancy in the air in any given sector of the front is obtained by the attack, destruction or dispersing of the enemy air elements operating on that sector, and so completely dominating them that they are unable to carry out their missions."[15]

In the two decades after the war, a small group of air power visionaries began the process of turning these practical lessons into doctrine for fighting the next war. They worked in obscurity, with one exception, so that when crews of Boeing B-17s, Consolidated B-24s, Lockheed P-38s, Republic P-47s, and North American P-51s climbed into their aircraft for missions over Hitler's *Festung Europa* in that next war, they had little if any idea of the theories shaping the strategies that had brought them to that moment. These crews were familiar with their aircrafts' accoutrements, characteristics, and capabilities, but were mainly ignorant of the technological developments that had led to the weapons they were trained to operate. Most important for the air battles to come, they knew practically nothing of the finer points of air superiority as a theory—only the consequences of the failure to possess it.[16]

Such was not entirely the case with a few individuals at the group level and some commanders of units echeloned above that level. Some of these had attended the U.S. Army's school for theory, the Air Corps Tactical School, where the ideas of the three most influential theorists, Giulio Douhet, Billy Mitchell, and Hugh Trenchard, had some impact. The most senior commanders, the "Bomber Barons," of the American strategic effort would later testify to varying degrees of knowledge about these theories.[17]

Giulio Douhet (1869–1930) was an Italian army officer in World War I who had begun to theorize about flight and its future impact upon warfare before that conflict broke out. He became a confidant of the Caproni aircraft manufacturing interests, which produced heavy bombers in World War I and which naturally promoted the merits of strategic bombing. An artillery officer, Douhet had some knowledge of scientific principles, which he would later apply in an attempt to validate his ideas. During the war he was so critical of the Italian failure to devote more resources to air power and his government's otherwise inept conduct of the war that he was court-martialed and spent some time in prison. Released and restored to military service before the war ended, he was formally cleared of wrongdoing in 1920 and became a general in 1921. For a time he was a chief consultant on aviation matters to the Fascist dictatorship, but soon retired to advance his theories through literary means. His core work was *Command of the Air*, first published in 1921, revised and republished in 1927.

Douhet postulated that air power was the wave of the future in warfare; it would relegate sea and land forces to secondary holding roles. A winning air force, which must be independent to do its work, must strike swiftly and aggressively in mass area bombings against enemy centers of population, communications, and industry to destroy civilian morale and impair the ability of the enemy's surface forces to function.[19] To achieve these ends, the winning air force first had to "conquer command of the air." When one side had command of the air, it was "in a position to prevent the enemy from flying while retaining the ability to fly oneself." Key to Douhet's theory was air superiority, total if possible. Discounting the plausibility of any effective air defense, he stated, "We must therefore resign ourselves to the offensives the enemy inflicts upon us, while striving to put all our resources to work to inflict even heavier ones upon him."[19] Douhet felt that the most effective way for one air force to defeat another was to strike its bases and sources of production, although air-to-air combat would likely also take place. The air force that possessed the most resources would eventually gain a war-winning victory. The loser would be "at the mercy" of the victor, "compelled to accept whatever terms" the latter might impose.[20]

In the first edition of *Command of the Air*, the Italian theorist gave the major role of conquering command of the air to bombers and assigned a subordinate role to "combat planes," whose primary purpose was to escort the bombers and help defend them against any attacking planes. Douhet mostly discounted the value of speed for such aircraft, arguing they must have only slightly more speed, radius of action, and altitude than bombers. Their equal "carrying capacity," instead of being used for bombs, would consist mostly of extra armor and firepower—characteristics that would enable them to defeat attacking pursuit of the type shaped in World War I. The latter's superior speed and maneuverability could not prevail.[21]

In the 1927 edition of *Command of the Air*, Douhet eliminated any role for fighter-type aircraft. He fused the "combat plane" and the bomber into an all-purpose offensive aircraft, a "battleplane," to conquer command of the air. Yet in his *The War of 19—*, published in 1930, an imaginary account of a war between Germany as one belligerent and France and Belgium combined as the other, Douhet restored a place for fighter-type aircraft in the attaining of command of the air by the winner—Germany. While the losing side entered the fray with a now traditional mix of bombers, reconnaissance, pursuit, and attack, the Germans had a preponderance of battleplanes and fifteen "explorer" squadrons of "very fast pursuit planes." These were not tied to any formation of battleplanes as close escort, yet did on occasion, during the short war, attack the enemy's pursuit that were assaulting certain elements of battleplanes bound for their offensive missions. Douhet devoted much of his account to describing how the battleplanes, in spite of heavy losses, conquered command of the air. The winning side lacked an elaborate air defense system composed of massed antiaircraft artillery and swarms of pursuit such as the losers possessed—in Douhet's view, wasted resources. After a few days of war the French and the Belgians "felt definitely that they had been defeated in the air and that they were hopelessly at the enemy's mercy."[22]

William "Billy" Mitchell (1879–1936) was an enlisted infantryman and Signal Corps officer before he turned to Army aviation after learning to fly in 1916. He had a keen interest in the most modern technology for martial purposes, having previously been associated with the adaptation of the radio and truck transportation for Army use. He commanded U.S. Army aerial operations on the Western Front in World War I. After the war he served as assistant chief of the Air Service from 1921 to 1925, during which time he became increasingly contentious and even bellicose in pushing the cause of air power. When the loss of his general's star and posting to a subordinate command did not quell his zest, he was court-martialed in 1925 for accusing the War and Navy departments of treason in neglecting air power. Convicted and suspended, he resigned from the service. If it broke his heart it did not crush his spirit, and he spent the last ten years of his life writing, testifying, and otherwise propagandizing that air power had arrived and its lessons, as he offered them, must be learned. Whereas after the war Douhet was the dispassionate professional making his pitch to other professionals, Mitchell was a public relations man, trying to inflame public opinion as well as shape official policy.[23]

His belief in the power of strategic bombardment went back to at least 1917 and surfaced here and there in the early postwar years. In 1923 he wrote a document too advanced for the defense-minded climate of America at the time—it did not become official. He entitled it "Notes on the Multi-Motored Bombardment Group Day and Night." It was the first how-to manual on the subject in such breadth, dwelling on both interdiction and deeper, strategic missions against an enemy's heartland. In a sense it was the American counterpart to *Command of the Air,* but with notable differences. It detailed training, unit administration, and actual operations. It was less indifferent toward civilians as targets, but much more definite about the crucial role of fighter planes as the type of aircraft capable of winning air superiority even than Douhet's 1921 edition of *Command of the Air.* "The Bombardment and friendly pursuit must work together," stated Mitchell. "The closest liaison is absolutely essential." He underscored such liaison in daylight operations: "The daytime use of bombardment without the cooperation of pursuit is not contemplated except in rare cases." On these points Mitchell would scarcely waver in the future. But he sounded Douhetian at several places in the document.

Against an enemy not in possession of an adequate air force, offensive aviation, if employed effectively, can force a decision before the ground troops or sea forces could join in battle . . . Anti-aircraft defenses installed for the defense of military objects merely divert that much personnel from actual warfare . . . The whole attack should be conducted in a prompt, aggressive manner.[24]

While he had little use for antiaircraft artillery, Mitchell for a time had to wrap offensive striking power in the cocoon of a defensive role. That role was to maintain air superiority over the United States and protect it from the now feasible attacks by air fleets as well as traditional sea threats from the maritime approaches. Unlike Douhet, he had some belief in an air defense, as his bombing experiments illustrated. The public and official mind of the 1920s dictated this defensive posture that precluded for the United States a strategic bombing force primarily for offensive objectives, such as Douhet insisted upon. Mitchell took an interest in the potentiality of a long-range bomber to ward off enemy sea or air fleets as far from American shores as possible, but also to strike an enemy's heartland—a potentiality Douhet did not emphasize given the proximity of Italy's likely enemies. Always, however, Mitchell remained committed to the necessity of fighter planes for air superiority.[25]

Hugh Trenchard (1873–1956) was a British army veteran of the Boer War who learned to fly in 1912, the first step in his eventually becoming officer commanding-in-chief of the Royal Flying Corps. He nourished the fledgling in the heat of battle and adopted the French strategy of aggressive operations waged over enemy territory to the rear of the front lines. Hesitatingly he accepted the post of chief of the air staff of the newborn Royal Air Force in April 1918, feeling an independent air force was premature and might work against air power in the future. He was still oriented toward tactical air when, soon after stepping down as chief of the air staff over a disagreement with his civilian superior, he was approached to take command of the Royal Air Force's strategic Independent Force.

He was dubious of the worth of strategic bombing, fearing it might detract from the gathering climax on the Western Front. Still, he agreed to take charge of strategic operations in the belief he could get results while maintaining rapport with the senior ground commanders there. A good part of his effort went into counterforce (counterair) strikes against German air bases to seize air superiority. Toward the end he used his force frequently for tactical work. When operations ceased, Trenchard conceded his bombers had not done extensive material damage, but played up the damage to enemy morale.[26]

In 1919 Trenchard again took over the Royal Air Force. Converted fully to the necessity for an independent air force, he adjusted to budgetary restraints, based in part on the belief that there would be no major war for at least ten years, and prevailed against the jealousy of the other services. To solidify independence, he established professional schools for his people based on the army's model. From an organizational standpoint, Trenchard laid the basis for expansion and a long-range strategic force that was not possible during his tenure as chief of the air staff. Even before his retirement in 1929, he began to evolve his prophecy of air power, which he continued later as senior British authority on the subject.[27]

Until 1929 Trenchard keyed upon air superiority as the basic ingredient for successful air power, which would be part of an integrated effort by all the services. The counterforce attacks of his Independent Force in 1918 had the purpose of securing at least a modicum of air superiority. Until the late 1920s he advanced the notion that while it was not possible to seize command of the air (in the Douhetian sense), it was feasible to win air superiority. The opening stages of conflict in the air would be devoted to it. In 1928 Trenchard revised his concept of air superiority. Instead of a clash of air forces at the outset for superiority, the side with the strongest offensive thrust against strategic targets would force the enemy "onto the defensive, and it will be in this way that air superiority will be obtained and not by direct destruction of his forces."[28]

The bomber became central to his theory, as it had for Mitchell

and Douhet. His philosophy was reflected in the famous phrase of
Stanley Baldwin in 1932: "The bomber will always get through."
Like Douhet, Trenchard was inconsistent in his attitude about the
role of the fighter. It was a mainstay of his Royal Flying Corps and
a welcomed escort for the medium bombers of his Independence
Force, but in the 1920s he insisted they were useful mainly to
appease the anxiety of the public and politicians for a defense
against a "knockout blow." In Trenchard's mind, a counter force of
bombers constituted the only defense. In the 1930s, with the possibilities offered by the technological revolution in aeronautics for
both fighters and bombers and with the threat of resurgent German air power, Trenchard expressed his unhappiness when the
fighter pulled ahead of the bomber in the Royal Air Force's scheme
of things late in the decade. He had come to feel that Britain
needed both.[29]

Trenchard, Mitchell, and Douhet were not the only prophets of
air power in the era of its coming of age between the world wars.
They were the ones whom historians have identified persistently as
the figures whose ideas most influenced the development of long-
range strategic air forces by the only two nations possessing them
in World War II. Their legacies continue in the modern era.

It became the duty of the Air Service Tactical School (founded at
Langley Field, Virginia, in 1920 and redesignated the Air Corps
Tactical School in 1926) to formulate an American air doctrine.
Overburdened with other bureaucratic functions, the Office of
Chief of the Air Service delegated to the Tactical School the added
duty of doctrinal development to go with its responsibility of providing professional schooling for air officers. The shaping of any
offensive doctrine for a long-range force such as that Mitchell and
Trenchard would increasingly champion seemed an impossible
task because of several countervailing factors. Foremost was the
isolationist sentiment of the American people, disillusioned by
their World War I experience. The Great Depression heightened
this mood, which condoned only a strategy of defense of the continental area and overseas possessions. Related to this sentiment

was a public and official aversion to strategic bombing that followed in the wake of the war, based in the United States on what was heard, not what was experienced. The defensive attitude began to alter somewhat with the rising tide of Fascist aggression in the 1930s, but mainly with respect to the threat posed to the Western Hemisphere. The antibomber feeling would in time become vague, for it was not subject to the kind of intense and protracted public debate conducted by the British, who were not protected by oceans from an immediate threat from the skies.[30]

The War Department General Staff imposed a role on its air arm in the post–World War I era that stunted the formulation of doctrine and an offensive strategy for any bombing force. This role was principally as auxiliary to help the ground arms. Powerful mossbacks still regarded the infantry as the "Queen of Battles," the arm that won or lost wars. Not only Billy Mitchell but the chiefs of the air arm had to pay at least lip service to this idea. The Army's air arm looked upon pursuit as the dominant aircraft for much of the 1920s, because of World War I experience projecting it as the means of maintaining air superiority against the attacking enemy aircraft of an invader.[31]

These were the barriers that Mitchell, those associated with him, and the chiefs of the Air Corps, Mason M. Patrick, James E. Fechet, and Benjamin Foulois, had to contend with in trying to win a specific strategic offensive role for their branch. Among themselves and with the War Department, there was disagreement on the exact nature of this role and what degree of autonomy the air arm should have. Consequently, offensive doctrine evolved slowly at the Tactical School. Gradually, from about 1926 on, such a doctrine began to take shape. The core of the emerging doctrine would be day, high-altitude, precision bombardment.[32]

Air superiority was to undergo a change that involved a downgrading of pursuit as the achiever and guardian of air superiority and the upgrading of the bomber. Mitchell's bombing manual had pronounced that pursuit and bomber were an integral and almost inseparable team. In the Tactical School, despite Mitchell's undoubted influence, Douhetian ideas began to prevail. In 1930 Maj. Walter Frank, assistant commander of the Tactical School, served as an umpire in the annual Air Corps maneuvers. At the briefing after these war games, he not only cited Douhet as a source of his belief that an air force was essentially an offensive weapon, he observed that the defensive pursuit had a hard time intercepting the attacking bombers.

In the Tactical School's text for 1930, "The Air Force," which listed Douhet's "Il Dominio dell' Area [sic]" as a preparation aid, the definition of air superiority would have for the most part delighted Douhet, who died that year. The air force possessing "such a preponderance of strength in aviation" could attack the enemy's air bases and "other terrestrial objectives, while at the same time the operations of his inferior opponent are so negligible as to be no longer a serious menace." The text concluded that "the relative effectiveness of attack and bombardment on the whole situation is the measure of air superiority." Mitchell's influence could be perhaps seen in the reference to "attack" or special tactical aircraft he had pushed. The text was not ready to dismiss fully the threat of pursuit to attack or bomber formations. Yet, "as victory should accrue to that belligerent who can endure most while striking hardest, air superiority will lessen the hostile blows and will increase the destruction that can be wrought upon the enemy from the air."[33]

The 1930 "Air Force" text was consistent with the dictate from above that aerial bombardment in the final analysis "still hinged on surface strategy."[34] Several individuals stepped forward who were particularly effective in changing this orientation, at first within the School itself, then later in the mission of the air arm. By 1929 two former Mitchell aides, Capt. Robert Olds and 1st Lt. Kenneth N. Walker, led the Bombardment Section while it was still at Langley. In a lecture Walker popularized the Air Corps version of "the bomber will always get through." Arguing that all other forms of military aviation must complement the bomber, the principal strategic offensive weapon system, he stated, "Military men of all nations agree that a determined air attack, once launched, is most difficult, if not impossible, to stop." This idea in the 1931 "Bombardment Aviation" text contended that bombers, by day and night, could by mutual support of their machine guns in close formation persist against enemy pursuit even if unescorted by friendly pursuit.

Olds departed in 1931 and Walker left temporarily for the Army's Command and Staff School. Captain Harold L. George, a recent star student at the Tactical School, now based at Maxwell Field, Alabama, filled the vacuum their absence created. George would rise to become a leader in the unfolding of this doctrine for strategic offensive air power. In 1934 he became the director of a new Department of Tactics and Strategy, which included both bombardment and pursuit. George quickly weighed in with a Douhet-like pronouncement that the only way to stop a swarming bomber attack was to destroy the enemy's force on the ground.[35]

Day bombing seemed to have achieved an almost exclusive place in the doctrine hatched in the Tactical School mainly because of a growing belief that specific targets were not distinguishable at night, the arrival of certain technology to be discussed later in this chapter, and the theory of "industrial fabric."[36] In 1971 a retired U.S. Air Force major general, Donald Wilson, claimed that the "concept of strategic direction of our air effort—first put into practice in World War II—originated in the Air Corps Tactical School (ACTS) in 1933–34." He went on to describe the theory of industrial fabric, which he alleged to have emanated from a course he taught that year at the Tactical School. In summary, the theory was "Future wars for survival would be between industrial nations; continuation of the war would depend upon maintaining intact a closely-knit and interdependent industrial fabric." The new "weapon of precision bombing gave us an instrument which could cause collapse of this industrial fabric by depriving the web of certain essential elements—as few as three main systems such as transportation, electrical power and steel manufacturing would suffice." Although Wilson gave a bow to Douhet, Trenchard, and Mitchell as prophets, especially Mitchell, he denied them any credit for the theory of industrial fabric.[37]

Haywood Hansell, Jr., was a student and later an instructor at the Tactical School while this theory was being formulated and taught. A chief air planner when World War II erupted and postwar historian of the events in which he participated, Hansell discussed industrial fabric in several books, agreeing that Wilson began the work leading to the idea. In 1934 Wilson looked for "specific structures that supported the will and capacity of an industrialized nation to wage war." Lacking detailed information on potential enemies, he turned to the United States industrial infrastructure for "lessons to apply to other industrialized nations," assuming all industrial economies were in the main similar.

When Wilson left for study at the Army Command and Staff School in 1934, George and Capt. Robert M. Webster continued his work by analyzing transportation, electrical systems, and factories producing items for machinery and munitions. They examined New York City and reasoned that precision bombing could hit several essential systems—water, electricity, transportation—and make the city unlivable. Limited by the American perception that bombing civilians was bad, and by the increasing knowledge that darkness did not foster precision, daylight bombing seemed the only way to unravel the industrial web with precision attacks on sensitive spots.[38]

From 1932 to 1936 a battle raged in the Tactical School over whether pursuit or bombers could win air superiority. The intensity of the high-powered personalities involved foreshadowed wartime battles for air superiority. Leader of the pursuit faction was Captain (and later Major) Claire Lee Chennault and carrying the bomber standard were Harold George and Kenneth Walker. The latter were convinced that the long-range bomber should be the centerpiece of offensive doctrine in the Air Corps. The former was equally convinced that pursuit should have the starring role. If properly conducted, George and Walker argued their thesis, with its undertones of the prophets, that a bomber assault could not be checked. Pursuit would not only stop bombers, Chennault countered, but they were more flexible: defensive when combating attacking bombers and pursuit, offensive when giving support to surface campaigns. In these operations, Chennault claimed, pursuit conducted themselves offensively and thus ought to be considered the dominant Air Corps planes. The bomber advocates retorted that in the unlikely event that pursuit were to gain air superiority against bombers, the former could not change the course of a war as bombers could do. While bombers were little more advanced that those of World War I in speed, armament, and bomb load, Chennault had the best of the argument. When the first modern bombers came on line beginning in the early 1930s, aircraft that were as fast and sometimes faster than most pursuit, whose development had lagged, then the bomber reigned supreme in the unfolding doctrine of the Tactical School.[39]

Chennault opposed the use of pursuit as close escort in support of bomber operations. Haywood Hansell recalled that Chennault "rigorously avoided the role of the accompanying escort fighter as part of an offensive strike. He could cite experience in World War I that showed that pursuit . . . tied to the escort role lost the initiative and eventually the combat . . . To him, pursuit was the offensive arm, even though he confined it to local fighting for local air superiority." Martha Byrd, Chennault's biographer, put it this way: he "firmly believed that, with offensive action not tied to close escort, pursuit could seek out and destroy the enemy air force and in this way more effectively provide the protection required."

All this was in vain during his time at the Tactical School and Chennault left the Army in 1937, soon departing for China and fame. In the Tactical School, recollected Hansell, it continued to be "recognized that fighter escort was inherently desirable, but no one could quite conceive how a small fighter could have the range of the bomber yet retain its combat maneuverability." He admitted that "failure to see this issue through proved one of the Air Corps Tactical School's major shortcomings." In a postwar memoir, Chennault blamed the influence of Douhet.[40] Air superiority in World

War II in Europe would ultimately depend upon both fighters and bombers, but largely because of the outcome of the struggle between their partisans in the Tactical School, the Army's air arm entered the war greatly lacking fighter resources.

The Tactical School taught a basic strategic offensive doctrine at the core of which was day, high-altitude, precision bombardment, from 1935 until June 1940, when it was disbanded because both its instructors and its potential students were needed for the Air Corps' expansion. According to this doctrine, heavy bombers were to operate "at high altitude where may be obtained greater surprise, security and relative immunity to anti-aircraft defenses."[41] Repeatedly came the message of the bomber always getting through with irresistible attacks that had the capability of winning a war. "The Air Force" text of 1934–1935 defined what these attacks would lead to: "Loss of morale in the urban population . . . Its disintegration is the ultimate objective of all war." But the prime target was the industrial fabric, not civilians. Its coming apart because of day, precision bombing would lead to disintegration of morale and the permanent breakdown of a system.

The text of "Bombardment Aviation" of 1937–1938 cited Trenchard's final report on the operations of the Independent Force in 1918 for his celebration of what the text called the "offensive spirit." This spirit would prevail in spite of the certainty that "the defenses against bombardment aviation are numerous and their powers are real." In 1939 Capt. Ralph Snavely told students in the bombardment course at the Tactical School that "we believe that a bombardment unit, worth its salt, is imbued with determination that it will penetrate any pursuit force in the world." Captain Laurence Kuter, for the same course in 1938–1939, lectured on the potency of the aerial demolition bomb to destroy any target on land or sea. The bomber with its inspired crew could not only get through, it could eliminate any target.[42]

In a lecture in the 1939–1940 course on bombardment aviation, Maj. R. P. Williams stated, "If unsupported, [heavy] bombardment units must and can perform successfully their own reconnaissance and defense measures." This was the all-purpose battleplane unit. Even Douhet admitted the necessity for separate reconnaissance craft.[43]

In December 1934 the War Department asked the Air Corps for a statement of doctrine meant to define the mission of the soon-to-be activated General Headquarters Air Force. The Air Corps assigned the drafting chore to the Tactical School. "It will be observed," stated the draft, "that, in the following pages, emphasis is placed on the fact that the principal mission of the GHQ Air Force is counter air force." But "it must be realized [this] is applicable only for that period of time during which the radius of action of aircraft is less than that required to reach vital strategical objectives in other parts of the world." An admission of reality quickly tempered this defiant tone: the "high place of priority" given counter air was "at the present time . . . due to a consideration of our national policy of defense which presupposes that initially, at least, our military operations will be restricted to the employment of the GHQ Air Force from bases in this country." Then the statement resumed a defiant note: "There is no intention anywhere in these comments of not conveying the thought that the principal and all important mission of air power, when the equipment permits, is the attack of those vital objectives in a nation's economic structure which will tend to paralyze that nation's ability to wage war," thus ending "the hostile will to resist."

This kind of language was not included in a revision of War Department Training Regulation 440-15, issued in October 1935, which covered the mission of General Headquarters Air Force. Although among the threefold operational aspect of its mission—in addition to direct support of ground arms and coastal defense— was attacking a variety of targets beyond the national coasts and areas of ground operations, the regulation clearly maintained that "air forces further the mission of territorial tactical commands to which they are assigned." Yet for the first time the War Department acknowledged the possibility of long-range strategic offensive operations by its air component, if expressing doubt that an air force could win command of the air and uncertainty on its impact on future warfare.

The Tactical School in 1934 had every reason to anticipate a bomber "with the radius of action . . . to reach vital strategic objectives."[44] In the 1920s, when Douhet was ruminating about command of the air and its consequences and Trenchard and Mitchell seemed to think as much about the strategic as the tactical, bombers were cumbersome and slow, vulnerable to the pursuit of the time that had much more speed and agility. Though in the Tactical School the weight of favor began to shift from the pursuit to the bomber in the latter part of the decade, it was not based on coordinated technological advance. There were in the 1920s innovations emanating from such sponsoring agencies in the United States as the government's National Advisory Committee for Aeronautics and the private Guggenheim Foundation for the Promotion of Aeronautics; from corporations such as Pratt and Whitney and Wright that boosted the United States toward the front in quality engines; and from individuals such as the designer-engineer Alfred Verville and the aviator Charles A. Lindbergh who dramatized nonstop, long-distance flight. However, as the historian of flight Roger E. Bilstein has pointed out, in spite of the innovations of "streamlining, variable-pitch propellers, wing flaps, engine cowlings, a miscellany of engine improvements . . . such trends had not been particularly advantageous when adapted to the standard biplanes, trimotors, and conventional wood/fabric/wire construction of the 1920s."[45] The modern long-range bomber was but an impractical dream until the 1930s.

In that decade, in spite of barriers, the dream for U.S. Army airmen steadily, if sometimes stealthily, became reality. From a technological standpoint, as Bilstein has described it, "in the thirties, advanced designs that featured cantilevered wings, retractable gear, and stressed skin construction made the prior developments highly attractive for the first time." Again in Bilstein's words, a "confluence of technological currents . . . best represented in the trend-setting Boeing 247 and the Douglas DC-3" highlighted this revolution in the area of civil aviation.[46]

Some Army airmen began to concentrate on the acquisition of a long-range bomber, based on this technology, to carry out the unraveling of the industrial fabric in a distant enemy land. The MacArthur-Pratt agreement of 1931, with its implication for long-range reconnaissance, noted Maurer Maurer, historian of Air Corps development between the world wars, seemed to give "plausible justification for long-range bombers to defend against sea attack. One of the significant outcomes of the agreement was War Department approval of projects that led to the development of the heavy bombers of World War II."[47]

In 1933 the War Department solicited designs from major aircraft manufacturers for a "multiengine" heavy bomber that could fly longer distances at a higher altitude with a bigger bomb load than the current B-10. The ultimate winner was a four-engine Boeing design dubbed "Flying Fortress," the first prototype of which was the Model 299 (Air Corps designation XB-17, as the first experimental bomber of the type). Bomber partisans fell in love with the large but sleek craft. It had averaged some 240 MPH on the flight from the Boeing plant in Seattle to Dayton, site of the competition. The fatal crash of XB-17 in October, due to crew error and not design flaw, did little to diminish their ardor. The Douglas entry, a two-engine type, would become for a time the main Army bomber as the B-18. It was only, however, as Air Corps–General Headquarters Air Force classification now reckoned it, a medium bomber and interim while airmen battled the War Department for enough B-17s to give General Headquarters Air Force a heavy hammer.[48]

Major Barney M. Giles flew the first Fortress for operational testing to Langley Field, home of the 2nd Bomb Group, landing on 4 March 1937. In his post–World War II memoir, Gen. Henry H. Arnold—who would command the air arm in that war, with Giles as chief of the air staff—identified the 2nd Bomb Group as the unit that redefined Douhet's theories in its training.[49] Despite bugs to be worked out and improvements to be made, the Fortress was the long-range airplane the bomber advocates had coveted not only because of its size, appearance, and radius of action, but for other reasons as well. No longer were crew members forced to endure exposed cockpits. Bombs were held in an internal bay, reducing drag. The landing gear was retractable. The wheels had a Boeing exclusive—air brakes. The design was aerodynamically clean with a skin of stressed aluminum. The four Wright engines were each capable of about 900 horsepower. The B-17 had five positions for machine guns. It had another marvel—an automatic pilot.[50]

Precision bombing required something more—the Norden bombsight. Originally designed for the Navy by inventor Carl L. Norden, it came with some difficulty by 1935 also into the Army's possession, just in time for the arrival of the B-17. Maurer has succinctly described how it functioned: "The sight solved the problem of ascertaining the angle at which a bomb should be released to achieve a direct hit on the target. Gyroscopic stability kept the telescopic sight on the target despite the plane's roll, pitch, or turn." It also had "a clock-like mechanism [synchronizing] . . . data inserted by the bombardier on ballistics, altitude, speed and drift, and calculated the exact moment for bomb release." These features were not new, but the Norden sight's compactness and superior performance marked the ideal precision mate for the B-17.[51]

While the long-range heavy bomber was climbing to altitude, literally and symbolically, in the United States in the 1930s, the pursuit could barely keep up and sometimes fell behind, literally and symbolically. The latter situation was in contrast to England, where fighter planes were developed in the 1930s that would play a critical part in defending the British Isles in 1940. One great German fighter, the Bf 109, had made its debut in the Spanish Civil War. By the latter part of the 1930s the Japanese would be shaping another great fighter, the Zero, that created such problems for the United States in the early part of World War II.

A biplane relic of the pre-aeronautical revolution, the Boeing P-12, and then from 1933 to 1937 a transitional plane, the Boeing P-26, with characteristics of the old and new technology, were the first-line U.S. pursuit when the modern bomber began to emerge.

No equivalent clique of airmen pushed for modernization of the former as had for the latter. Arnold, who matched P-26s against an advanced version of the B-10 in a mock skirmish in 1934, came away believing pursuit could not stop bombers. Major General Frank M. Andrews, first commander of General Headquarters Air Force, felt the same way.[52]

Belatedly, the War Department sought to repair the neglect of pursuit modernization with the acquisition of the first truly modern types beginning in 1936, namely the Seversky P-35 and Curtiss P-36. Unlike the P-26, these fighter types had enclosed cockpits and retractable landing gear. They were still the first-line U.S. Army fighters when World War II commenced on 1 September 1939. The most advanced P-36 then had far less firepower and considerably less speed than the first-line Luftwaffe Bf 109 and the Royal Air Force Hurricane and Spitfire.[53]

In a bit of irony in 1939, shortly after World War II had broken out, Maj. Gen. Henry H. Arnold, commanding the Air Corps with General Headquarters Air Force now subordinate to him, expressed concern over the neglect of pursuit tactics and technological development. Arnold up to that point had been a bomber partisan, but now with supreme command responsibility over the Army's air arm and with the Spanish Civil War and Poland as evidence, had to consider both sides of the bomber versus fighter issue. In a memo to Maj. Gen. Frank Andrews, former commander of the General Headquarters Air Force, on 14 November 1939, Arnold wrote that "the subject of pursuit aviation—tactics and plane development, has not received the share of attention and interest in the Air Corps it merits." The idea that "fighter craft cannot shoot down large bombardment planes in formation . . . had been proven wholly untenable. It has been demonstrated recently beyond a doubt that the best antiaircraft defense is pursuit aviation."

Arnold went on to suggest that "one or more" factors accounted for the low state of the fighter in the Army's air arm, including "the teaching of doctrine . . . in our tactical schools . . . as to the inefficacy of pursuit aviation." He even named as a possible culprit "new high speed pursuit planes" that had "caused our higher rank-ing officers to avoid service in units of this type and to do little tactical pursuit flying." Related to the latter was a relative lack of experienced commanders of fighter groups and squadrons. "There has been a feeling in many quarters," he stated, "that pursuit avia-tion, being a relative young man's game, does not offer the life time career to an Army officer which bombardment affords." Arnold appeared to point a finger, if not to Maj. Gen. Delos Emmons, commanding General Headquarters Air Force, then by implication at least to Andrews himself, Emmons's predecessor, when he charged, "There has not been an adequate realization by our high command agencies of the role of pursuit."[54]

In a first endorsement to the Arnold memo, Col. C. S. Russell, chief of staff of General Headquarters Air Force, purportedly for Emmons, was even more critical of the neglect of fighters. He ex-pounded at length on the age factor as limiting a career in fighter aviation. He suggested that a clear distinction be made between fighter and bomber pilot requirements at the "very beginning of pilot's career" and persons be encouraged to go into the former and then allowed to transfer into the latter when age became a limiting factor. Russell laid out "vital considerations that appear to have been overlooked by the advocates of bombardment's ability to de-fend itself successfully against pursuit attack." These included "the amount of concentrated fire" a fighter plane with its fixed guns was able to direct against a bomber, whose flexible guns were less accurate; the larger target posed by a bomber; and the protection a fighter pilot, nestled behind his engine, had in contrast to "no protection for the bombardment gunners." He also took a crack at the Tactical School by recommending that "service schools lay emphasis upon the value of pursuit and the necessity for restoring it to its coordinate position among combat units."[55]

More advanced aircraft than the P-35 and P-36 only partially remedied the neglect of the fighter by the outbreak of World War II. One was the Bell P-39 Aircobra, with a single engine placed behind the cockpit. Another was the Curtiss P-40 Warhawk, with a more conventional single engine in front of the cockpit. The U.S. Air Force's official history for World War II summed up their performance: "Especially disappointing was the P-39, whose low ceiling, slow rate of climb, and relative lack of maneuverability put its pilots at a decided disadvantage wherever they fought." The P-40 "proved to be a much better plane. Though a slow climber, it could reach altitudes permitting superior skill and tactics to offset the advantages of the enemy." Chennault especially used the P-40 to advantage against the Japanese.[56]

In May 1939 Arnold appointed a special panel, soon known as the Kilner Board, to make recommendations on research and development priorities. Its third priority, behind liquid-cooled engines and fire-control apparatus, was for a fighter to rank with the best in the world. Eleven months later Arnold felt it necessary to appoint a second panel to help revise research and development priorities. Known as the Emmons Board, this body recommended as fourth priority an escort fighter with a 1,500-mile range, behind a very long-range heavy bomber, a twin-engine fighter interceptor, and a long-range medium bomber. When he received the report, Arnold exchanged places between priorities 1 and 4. The importance of the fighter had obviously come home to Arnold, but his assignment of research and development priority to the long-range escort came late and did not result in a quick technological fix.

From technological and organizational standpoints, the air component of the U.S. Army made substantial progress between 1935 and 1940. This came in the face of continued stubborn opposition from War Department traditionalists, the Navy's jealousy of its prerogatives, the lingering attitude of isolationism, and the internal trauma of economic depression that dictated penny-pinching. While it took Pearl Harbor to sweep all this away, world events and a charismatic and shrewd Franklin Roosevelt combined to open the way for the Army's air arm to move nearer to its goal—a mighty long-range air force with a strategic offensive mission, autonomous if not independent.

World events and the decision of President Roosevelt to boost air power soon overtook opposition by the War and Navy departments. If the Axis threat of bombing cities made at the time of the Munich Agreement in 1938 was a hollow one, it was nonetheless effective. Historian Michael Sherry has contended that the Munich crisis was the great watershed of air power. The Germans used air power as a threat to get their way at Munich, making World War II inevitable. A "war-scarred generation" in Britain and France "welcomed as much as feared the notion of a devastating air attack from Germany, less Europe plunge again into the horrors experienced in World War I." As for Roosevelt, he "had played only a marginal role in the drama of Munich. But he observed keenly, learned quickly, and snatched the promise of American air power out of the debacle."[57]

The story of Roosevelt's role in the expansion and mobilization of American air power from 1938 on and the details of that mobilization are best told elsewhere.[58] From the handful of heavy bombers obtained by the Army up to 1938 the number rose, if not dramatically then steadily, until Pearl Harbor. It represented the beginning of America's massive dedication to strategic bombing in World War II.

The tide of events swept stronger after September 1939. On 9 July 1941 Roosevelt asked the War and Navy departments for "estimates of production required to defeat our potential enemies" or for a "Victory Program" as it became known. In the following weeks, four veterans of the Tactical School—Harold George, Kenneth Walker, Laurence Kuter, and Haywood Hansell—of the War Plans Group in the newly formed Air War Plans Division of the Air Staff drew up a plan that became officially "Annex 2, Air Requirements of the War Department." It would be known to posterity as AWPD-1. This plan at once emphasized production requirements and was a blueprint for unraveling the industrial fabric with long-range heavy bombers. It had little to say about fighters.[59]

As American air power underwent a metamorphosis resulting from the growing menace of another world war, German air power emerged as an especially frightening aspect of that menace. The

Luftwaffe, which was formally introduced to the world in March 1935, had proceeded to show its mettle in the Spanish Civil War and its value to Hitler as a club to be held over those he wished to bully was chillingly revealed at Munich. The great Lindbergh had been much impressed. He, like others, misunderstood the true essence of the evolving Luftwaffe—it became essentially a tactical air force to be the initial bolt of blitzkrieg in support of the developing German armed forces, the Wehrmacht. The bombs dropped by its "volunteers" on Madrid, Guernica, and Barcelona made deceptive its ability to wage a strategic offensive campaign. Few if any thought to wonder whether the Reich itself might be vulnerable to a future strategic air offensive should blitzkrieg reach its geographical limits and the Luftwaffe fail to subdue an insulated enemy, from whose territory a strategic offensive might be launched. As it happens so often, foresight was not nearly the equal of hindsight.

The seeds of a German air defense system had been halfheartedly sown in the creation of seven air war commands (*luftkries kommandos*) shortly before the Spanish Civil War. Territorially stemming from the Weimar Republic's seven defense zones (*wehrkries kommandos*), these commands nominally controlled all air and antiaircraft units in their respective jurisdictions. Gradually they formed a belt of antiaircraft artillery behind the German line of fortifications facing the western approaches. France at that time was considered the only truly continental air threat. Other aspects of Luftwaffe growth quickly outshone air defense.

German air defense doctrine was from the beginning a poor relation of German air offense doctrine, which itself was subject to controversy among the Germans. A point of disagreement that arose before the war was whether the bomber or fighter would be emphasized in offensive operations, paralleling a similar debate at the U.S. Army Air Corps Tactical School. *Luftwaffen Dienstvorschrift*, the Luftwaffe's basic handbook on the principles of aerial warfare, issued in 1935 and revised in 1940, was Douhetian in tone, but somewhat indefinite in defining the prime mission of the air arm. Independent and co-equal with the army and navy, it had the "mission of destroying the enemy's war potential and his air force, to gain air superiority by destroying an enemy's air force, ground organization, and aircraft industry." It appeared as though the Luftwaffe was to be primarily a strategic air force, but in fact ground support became its primary activity. Not only did the *Luftwaffen Dienstvorschrift* specify that all Luftwaffe planes had to have the capability of supporting ground armies, but the Spanish Civil War seemed to validate the primacy of ground support. Generalmajor Wolfram von Richthofen, last commander of the "volunteer" Condor Legion in Spain, concluded from its experience in helping Franco's forces to triumph that the role of the Luftwaffe should be close air support of the army.[60] The major disagreement at this point was whether priority should be given to bombers for offensive action or to fighters for achieving the air superiority necessary for proper bomber usage.[61]

Commander-in-chief of the Luftwaffe Reichsmarschall Hermann Göring advanced a doctrine based on two elements: a tactical air force to support the army directly and a strike force to support the army indirectly by strategic assaults against the enemy's economy. Obviously influenced by Douhet, Göring argued that "the first objective at the beginning of a war must be to destroy the enemy's Air Force, completely disregarding all other targets . . . and only when it is destroyed should other targets be attacked, the priority being dependent upon the economies of the country under attack." Göring thus advocated that preeminence be given to the strategic over the tactical. Future chief of the Luftwaffe General Staff General der Flieger Karl Koller backed Göring in this proposal, but they were swimming against the current of military thought in prewar Germany. The Luftwaffe's manual for tactical training, published in 1938, demonstrated that the tactical was winning out over the strategic: "Attacks on power sources and supply lines are carried out only if they serve as preparation for ground or sea operations." Hitler, Secretary of State for Aviation Feldmarschall Erhard Milch, and Chief of the Luftwaffe General Staff Generaloberst Hans Jeschonnek favored the tactical.[62]

Always, however, the intent was offense. The tactical training manual of 1938 underscored this: "Our armed forces and our own country are threatened by the enemy air force; this danger can never be countered sufficiently by defenses in our own country. The air danger, then, throughout the war, compels offensive action against the enemy air force in his own territory." Prewar planning, dominated by generals who would not look beyond close air support, limited German defensive preparations, mainly if not entirely, to land fortifications such as the West Wall. Even though the *Luftwaffen Dienstvorschrift* had anticipated the allocation of resources such as antiaircraft artillery, searchlights, and fighters for defense of the Reich, it mandated that the latter must intercept enemy bombers over the front lines before they reached the internal defenses.

The fact that the Condor Legion was able to lead Franco's air force in winning air superiority over the Soviet-supported Loyalists convinced the German leadership that an offensive air doctrine was the correct one. In 1938 the Luftwaffe eliminated its old air commands (*luftkriesen*), designed for operations within Germany's borders, and placed all operational aircraft units under several air corps (*fliegerkorps*). It replaced the old commands with ten defense districts (*luftgauen*), subdividing each into Airfield Regional Commands responsible for supply, transport, and administrative functions, airbase housekeeping, the air raid warning system, and control over local antiaircraft units. The defense districts remained nearly perfunctory, for the core of the Luftwaffe was its operational air corps, geared for offense. In April 1939 the Luftwaffe redesignated these air corps as air fleets (*luftflotten*). Four in number initially, the Luftwaffe added other air fleets with the incorporation of new territories into the Reich. Each controlled two to four defense districts. Each air fleet also had subordinate air divisions (*fliegerdivisionen*) that conducted actual operations. In 1940, reflecting its expansion, the Luftwaffe upgraded these air divisions into air corps, one or more of which provided the operational forces for each air fleet. Each air fleet comprised all types of aircraft, but within the air fleets an "air leader" (*fliegerführer*) held tactical control over a specific type of aircraft. A "fighter air leader" or *jafü* (*jagdfliegerführer*), for example, controlled fighter units in each air fleet.[63]

Under Adolf Hitler an odd collection of personalities ran the Luftwaffe, soon considered by many foreign observers the best in the world. Several were World War I heroes and one had an air transport background, but almost all were eccentric. At the head of the Luftwaffe and charged with the responsibility for carrying out its mainly offensive strategy was Reichsmarschall Hermann Göring. Commander-in-Chief of the Luftwaffe, Air Minister, and heir-apparent to Hitler, Göring was a World War I fighter ace with twenty victories to his credit. Inconsistent, pompous, egocentric, often aloof, and fearful to the point of paranoia of challenges to his leadership, he most of all failed to provide leadership. He mistrusted qualified men who performed their responsibilities with skill. Göring liked to be involved in exciting, transitory, tactical details, but had no patience for the somewhat bland, lengthy, and mentally taxing details of strategic doctrine, but especially defensive doctrine.

Generaloberst Ernst Udet was also a World War I ace, claiming sixty-two kills. Between the world wars he established an international reputation as a daring barnstormer. Göring named him to Director of the Technical Department of the Air Ministry in 1936 and Director General of Equipment in 1939. More than any other German official, he was responsible for the technical character of the Luftwaffe in World War II. In many ways he was the image of Göring: irresponsible, flighty, and paranoid. Education and training had not equipped Udet for his technical job. Disliked by most of his colleagues, he lacked administrative skill. Responsible for deciding how the Reichsmarks in the Luftwaffe budget would be spent, he made monumental mistakes in procurement and production. The pressure of his position and criticism of his performance by Göring among others led him to commit suicide in 1941.

Feldmarschall and Secretary of State for the Air Ministry Erhard Milch was an improvement in certain ways over Göring and Udet.

Though he shared the insecurity of these two, he was a workaholic and an efficient administrator, proven abilities that he demonstrated before the war in the air transport industry. He suffered from the knowledge, gained during a background investigation, that his biological father was his mother's uncle. His major flaw, partially of his own creation as a result of his jealousy and insecurity, was his tendency to take on too many tasks. After Udet committed suicide and after failure in the Battle of Britain drove Göring to retreat to his rural estates, responsibilities overwhelmed Milch. In 1942 and 1943, in company with Minister for Armaments and War Production Albert Speer, he succeeded in increasing Germany's aircraft production and switching the Luftwaffe to strategic defense in the West. By 1944, however, Göring had shorn Milch of all but administrative powers, leaving him only limited influence on the battle for air superiority.[64]

The remaining major figure in the early story of German aerial defenses was Luftwaffe Chief of the General Staff Generaloberst Hans Jeschonnek. Professional and a respectable administrator, he was closely associated with and permanently dedicated to the doctrine of offensive close air support. After the invasion of the Soviet Union in June 1941, he kept as much of his force at the Eastern Front as possible, organized into units directly subordinate to the army. He also was aloof to the value of training. In 1943, as one of the foremost advocates of the offensive close air support doctrine, Hitler and Göring made him the scapegoat for Luftwaffe failures and for the seeming inability of the Luftwaffe to turn back the British-American bombing campaign. On 19 August "he did what was expected of him, and committed suicide by shooting."[65]

The triumph of blitzkrieg in Poland in 1939 and in Scandinavia, France, and the Low Countries in 1940 presented no real challenge to Germany's emphasis on tactical offensive air doctrine. The Ju 87 dive bombers, known as Stukas, served as mobile artillery, Bf 109s seized air superiority, while bombers struck at hapless cities such as Warsaw and Rotterdam, as for the most part the Luftwaffe left the Reich undefended by fighter aircraft. Stunned enemies made little attempt to threaten Germany's air space. While the Luftwaffe was learning to rely on, in the words of a postwar U.S. Army Air Forces' study, "short term and ad hoc principles that were inadequate for long campaigns and attrition warfare," the headiness of victory and the absence of intruders influenced German authorities to continue to leave the defense of the Reich essentially to antiaircraft artillery.[66]

Within Germany coordination among the defense districts was decentralized until Milch made Gen. Otto Rüdel Chief of Air Defenses in 1938, replacing him with Gen. Hans Stumpff in 1939. In spite of the impressive title, both men were only chief inspectors of antiaircraft artillery, in keeping with the then-current German defense doctrine. With German air defense organized only on a district level, coordination was generally nonexistent. The Luftwaffe had no sense of strategic defense in mind when it created the defense districts and this continued to be the case when they were assigned to the air fleets.

The Battle of Britain (July-September 1940) and the follow-up Blitz (1940–1941) were the main exceptions to the emphasis on tactical offensive air doctrine. In the Battle of Britain the Germans tried to conquer the British Isles by seizing command of the air, employing many fighters and dive bombers as well as medium bombers. They failed, in part because the tactically oriented Luftwaffe had no heavy bombers or fighters with sufficient range, nor were the fighters allowed to roam away from the bombers. During the Battle of Britain operations had been in the daylight, but during the Blitz most of the bombing was done at night. Both were failures.[67]

In 1940 and 1941 the Royal Air Force began and continued night bombing of the Reich, having learned a lesson from a brief but disastrous flirtation with day bombing in 1939.[68] The early night bombing was ineffective, but it forced the Germans to take initial steps to revise their meager air defense organization. The Luftwaffe began to merge the concept of strategic defense into its air doctrine. The first attempt to deal with the British threat was the establishment in 1940 of the Berlin and Central Industrial Region Air Defense Command under Generaloberst Hubert Weise.[69] Weise's "super" command came to include ten defense districts at its height, but in keeping with prewar doctrine contained at first only antiaircraft artillery.

Ineffective or not, British bombing put political pressure on a German leadership that had promised its people immunity from destruction from the skies. Nocturnal Royal Air Force raids that had begun in earnest in May 1940 forced an additional revision of German thinking to include a regular night fighter organization in the defense of northern Germany. Accordingly, Oberst Josef Kammhuber established such a force with its headquarters initially in Brussels. Within a year Kammhuber, promoted to generalleutnant, had built XII Air Corps, directly subordinate to the Air Ministry, using twin-engine fighters such as the Bf 110 first in coordination with searchlights, then under the direction of Freya and Würzburg radars, and finally under ground control through the Benito system (see below). The Royal Air Force's Bomber Command struck deeper into Germany and with more power in 1942 with the arrival of its great heavy bomber, the Lancaster, and its new and determined Air Officer Commanding-in-Chief, Sir Arthur Harris. The resultant pressure brought strategic defense closer to reality. The Luftwaffe in mid-1941 added Defense Districts VI and XI to Weise's command, renaming it Air Command Center (*Luftwaffenbefehlshaber Mitte*). In the autumn of 1941 Weise received command over three more defense districts and Kammhuber's XII Air Corps, though his command was limited in the later case to training only as Kammhuber continued to answer directly to the Air Ministry.[70]

Allied bombing inexorably increased in the summer of 1942 with the first American bombing missions of the continent. While the American presence remained for some months more shadow than substance, particularly due to the diversion of part of the Army Air Forces strike force from England to North Africa for TORCH, substance became more significant in the first months of 1943 as a result of the Allied decision at Casablanca to mount a "round the clock" strategic air offensive against Hitler's *Festung Europa*. Late in 1942, seemingly in anticipation, the Luftwaffe established four fighter divisions (*jagddivisionen*) in Germany and one in Austria to supervise all day and night fighter operations in their respective operational territories. These came under Kammhuber's XII Air Corps and under the overall command of Weise's Air Command Center, which now included eight defense districts. In actual operation each fighter division acted independently—Air Command Center's control was generally administrative and typically after the fact. From units left in France after the failure of the Battle of Britain and the Blitz, the Luftwaffe created two additional fighter divisions, reflecting the prewar doctrine that enemy bombers be intercepted before they could reach Germany's internal defenses. It was but one more belated attempt to erect an effective air defense. Creation of a third fighter division in southern France was abortive because of a lack of available fighters, especially single-engine fighters.[71]

Despite this array of forces, these units were generally impotent because Göring could find only one fighter wing (*Jagdgeschwader* 1) to equip Air Command Center's daylight fighter defense of Germany. It did have, at least, staff and command organizations that could be fleshed out later.

By January 1943 the Luftwaffe had commenced to build a modern organized strategic defense which would have growing success against the night-flying Royal Air Force Bomber Command. The growth of the American daylight effort, though uneven, combined with British missions to give the Luftwaffe fighter divisions and antiaircraft forces a growing amount of on-the-job training. In the second quarter of 1942, air defense fighters in Western Europe had to deal with 23,000 Allied sorties.[72] Throughout 1942 and into 1943, the largest number of sorties were British and therefore nighttime. Until the Eighth Air Force launched its first missions in the summer of 1942, the Luftwaffe's only real experience against strategic daylight bombing was with the weakly armed, unescorted British bombers of 1939–1940. But it appeared Germany was rapidly making up for lost time.

This defense was more than holding its own until July 1943, when Royal Air Force Lancasters released a lethal combination of incendiaries and high explosives that produced the first aerial burning of a major city—Hamburg. The British used thousands of strips of aluminum-coated paper to confuse German radars and overwhelm German defenses. One casualty of Hamburg was Josef Kammhuber. He had tried to convince Hitler and Göring that a greater commitment of resources to defense was needed, especially for the American day bombers that were joining the British to broaden the bombing campaign. He and Milch proposed the creation of a single, unified organization responsible for all fighter defense in the West and in Germany, but Hitler remained blind and Göring continued to play the lackey. With his system compromised and effective air superiority seemingly imperiled, Kammhuber steadily lost favor and in November was sent packing to Norway to command the only peripherally important Air Fleet 5. The Luftwaffe redesignated XII Air Corps, in operational control of all fighter forces inside Germany, as I Fighter Corps (*jagdkorps*) on 15 October 1943, under the command of Generalleutnant Josef Schmid. It also established II Fighter Corps to direct the fighter operations of Air Fleet 3 in France. Air Command Center tried to unify nonflying activities while providing overall administration for flying operations within Germany.[73]

Despite its ups and downs, the German strategic defense was by the fall of 1943 the most modern and complex the world had seen to that time, including the observer-radar-fighter defense that had saved the British in 1940. This German defense was never standardized from above, but instead was constantly evolving from below, to meet new situations forced on it by the Allies. As it was created in the heat of battle, much of its training was "on the job." Because first night and then day fighters were relatively late additions to German air defenses, for the first several years of the war the ground elements of the system were under the control of the defense districts. When the Luftwaffe added fighters, fighter units merged with a warning and control system in which nonfliers controlled flying operations.

The warning system itself consisted of three major elements supported by four subordinate organizations. The Radio and Radar Listening Service (*Horchdienst*—also known as the H Service) usually gave first warning of an impending Allied attack. This highly professional force (which remained an independent unit throughout the war) intercepted Allied radio and radar transmissions both to assemble long-range intelligence reports and tactical reports of immediate interest.[74] The next warning of an Allied operation usually came from the Aircraft Warning Service (*Flugmeldedienst*), which used both active and passive radars, augmented by the radars of the antiaircraft artillery, to track Allied air forces.[75] The final major warning force was the Ground Observer Service (*Flugwache*). Though they duplicated the function of radar, ground observers were the key early warning source for German defenses until 1943 and thereafter served to fill gaps in radar coverage caused by terrain and Allied jamming.

The aircraft warning system also contained four subordinate groups of lesser capabilities. The Civilian Aircraft Warning Service was a Nazi Party–dominated force assigned the responsibility of announcing air raid warnings to the civilian population; their presence stressed obedience and order in the face of chaos. The Railway Aircraft Warning Service alerted the German railroad network. The Aircraft Warning Service of the antiaircraft artillery used its own radar and observers to supplement the organizations described above. Finally, the Navy Air Warning Service used shipborne and coastal radars to provide additional input to the warning system.

After these major and minor organizations had located and identified Allied attackers, it became the responsibility of the control part of the system to evaluate the threat and bring fighter aircraft or antiaircraft artillery to bear against it. Together, the Aircraft Warning Regiments and the Air Communications and Control Regiments comprised nearly one-third of the manpower of the German aerial defense system. Over 320,000 strong in November 1944, they composed the largest organizations in the aircraft warning and control system.[76] These regiments, usually of three battalions (*abteilung*) each, contained observer companies from the Ground Observer Service, radar companies from the Aircraft Warning Service, technical repair companies, ground control companies, and situation and operations room plotting companies.

The Luftwaffe initially established an operations and situation room at Kammhuber's XII Air Corps Headquarters when it became based in Deelen, Holland, to coordinate the reports of the various warning units with the command of fighter and antiaircraft artillery forces. Later, similar control and operations rooms were established at the various fighter division headquarters in Germany and Western Europe. Each control room contained plotters, meteorologists, controllers, representatives from Signals and the Listening Service, radar operators, and a commander. Large vertical plotting screens up to 30 by 40 feet dominated the rooms. Ground observers would feed their reports to First Order Radar Stations, within the Aircraft Warning Service organization, which would combine their radar and visual intelligence before sending it all to the fighter division control and situation room. All other components of the aircraft warning and control system would transmit data directly to the fighter division. At the latter headquarters intelligence personnel would assemble, synthesize, and evaluate incoming information before creating an "air situation picture" that would be passed to all the lower elements (antiaircraft artillery, civilian authorities, ground observers, radar sites) and sent on to the other fighter divisions and up to XII Air Corps and its successor, I Fighter Corps, and finally to the top echelon, Air Command Center, when it was established in 1942. These headquarters above the fighter division level would consolidate the local air situation reports into a strategic picture covering Germany, France, Holland, and Belgium, transmitting it back to all the subordinate agencies. In this manner, intelligence flowed up, down, and laterally in the system.

Antiaircraft operations were rather simple, relying on radar and visual aiming devices, but fighter control was much more complex. Ground controllers at the fighter division headquarters would notify the flying units under their command of the nature of the enemy threat, how and where fighters were to form up, what weather to expect, and who would be in charge of the mission. Fighter division controllers never had to decide how much of their forces to deploy, because the constant shortage of defensive fighters forced them to scramble all operational interceptors if weather permitted and the Allied effort was a major one.[77] The higher central headquarters would also broadcast to subordinate commands on a single radio channel continuous updates of the course of the battle, including the grid positions of the attacking and defending forces.[78]

Universally an individual sort, fighter pilots, by refusing to use a ground control system, had delayed its development because they resented the use of ground types, who were either unfit to fly or nonflying personnel, to direct them to the enemy. Despite the resentment, British success in the Battle of Britain with ground control led the leadership of the Luftwaffe to adopt the system. Beginning in the summer of 1941 the Luftwaffe installed VHF transmitters in fighters and used direction-finding stations to track its aircraft. For a time, however, there was little actual control from the ground.

It was the night fighter force under Kammhuber that developed the "Y-system" of fighter control, known to the Allies as Benito. A Benito ground radio station (Y-Gerät) transmitted at a set frequency. An airborne Benito aircraft, leading a fighter group, received the transmission and retransmitted it back to a ground station on a different frequency. The ground station measured the phase difference between the two frequencies to determine range. By tracking the single Benito aircraft on the Würzburg-Freya radar system, a ground controller could then vector it by radio to Allied formations up to a distance of 250 kilometers. Because the British night threat was the greater in 1942, the Luftwaffe chose the Y-system as its sole fighter-control organism. It provided the necessary preci-

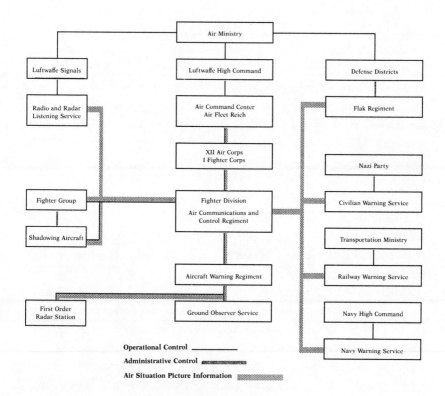

Figure 1. German Daylight Air Defense Network
Source: "Air Staff Post Hostilities Intelligence Requirements on the German Air Force,"
1935–1945, File 519.601B-4, Sec. IVB, vol. 1, HRC.

sion for nonvisual contact at night and did not require the then-scarce VHF equipment.[79]

In spite of serious problems, the German aircraft warning and control system functioned efficiently through most of the war. It was vulnerable to multiple, scattered attacks, but the Allies preferred a few large formations for penetrating German defenses.[80] Its lack of standardization caused serious maintenance problems, yet protected the system from Allied jamming. It was wasteful of manpower (especially after separate night and day warning and control systems were built), yet provided several backup layers of defense if one were to fail. The running battle commentary provided by higher headquarters was an efficient means of passing up-to-date intelligence to the defensive forces, but a serious flaw was that the Allied Y-Service routinely intercepted the transmissions and ascertained the deployment of German forces.[81]

The aircraft warning and control system provided Luftwaffe commanders with an excellent picture of the air situation and allowed them accurate control over their defensive array. With some notable exceptions, such as Hamburg in 1943, they knew when, where, and in what numbers the Allies would attack. The gathering battle for air superiority, however, would be a battle of attrition. Intelligence would be important, but only with sufficient weapons, the antiaircraft gun and the fighter plane, and well-trained and experienced personnel to man them could the battle be won.

Until mid-1943, because of the limited impact of American daylight missions, Germany remained content to leave the daytime defense of the Reich more to antiaircraft artillery than fighters. The former, known popularly as flak (an acronym formed from the German title, *Fliegerabwehrkanonen*), at its height in 1944 numbered some 900,000 men and women, with 14,250 heavy guns (8.8 cm, 10.5 cm, and 12.8 cm), 34,750 light and medium guns (20mm and 3.7 cm), 1,500 barrage balloons, and 6,750 heavy searchlights. At their prime, the flak forces collectively could fire 5,000 tons of shells per minute into the skies over Germany.[82]

The Luftwaffe assigned administrative control of flak units to the local defense districts, though the fighter divisions retained operational control. Each battery contained four to eight heavy guns (and typically several 20mm guns to protect the heavy guns against low-flying fighters) or five to twelve light and medium guns with supporting searchlights, to provide a day and night anti-aircraft capability.[83] The ubiquitous 8.8-cm cannon (the famous "Eighty-Eight") was the primary weapon of these batteries (70 percent of all heavy flak guns). Considering operational limitations, the maximum ceiling of the 8.8-cm cannon was about 20,000 feet— barely adequate for American bombers usually flying between

23,000 and 25,000 feet. The Air Ministry ordered the development of 10.5-cm and 12.8-cm guns to increase the efficiency of its flak defenses, but they never supplanted the "Eighty-Eight."[84]

During the war the Luftwaffe placed flak batteries in rings around cities and important industrial or military targets and in a belt along the West Wall.[85] The rings were 2 miles from the expected targets to insure flak fire at attacking bombers during the last minute of their bombing runs in order to hit bombers before bombs were released or at least to disrupt bombardier aim. All guns in each battery fired at the same target, at the same time, usually as the targets came into effective range. If the guns were radar-aimed, the target was the center of each bomber formation. If visually aimed, the target was the first aircraft in each formation. Each shell was time-fuzed, taking roughly 20 seconds to reach the altitude of 20,000 feet. This 20-second delay required the use of an optical predictor (usually the Kommandogerät 36 or 40), which determined the azimuth, slant range, elevation, and time-setting for the guns.[86]

There was a major adjustment in technique in 1943, from "continuous following," whereby the target for a battery was a single aircraft that had to be led by 20 seconds, to that of a "predicted barrage," in which the battery salvoed at a predetermined "box" in an area through which the bombers were expected to fly. The change improved performance but did not remove certain inherent weaknesses. It was still a case of a more or less static defense against a mobile offensive, some railroad shuffling of guns not withstanding. Flak was still inaccurate. Shells were subject to wind and changing air density no matter in what pattern they were fired. The gunners had to overcome clouds, fog, smoke, and the pressure of hundreds of discharging cannon about. A German general responsible for wartime antiaircraft artillery estimated that it took upwards of 4,000 shells to down one bomber. Radar, used when visual targeting was obscured by night or fog, carried even more difficulties.[87]

Bombers often flew at altitudes that were at the extreme range of most German guns. The addition to the planes of armored padding at critical points reduced the killing radius of the shells, necessitating such expensive countermeasures as bigger guns.[88] The manpower problem overtook flak; the army siphoned away more and more of the able-bodied younger men as time passed and in their place the Luftwaffe was forced to turn to inexperienced women, the elderly, foreign volunteers, and Soviet prisoners-of-war.

And yet, despite these manifold troubles, German flak was effective. Half of American combat losses was to flak. Planes often had to fly higher than the optimum altitudes for precision bombing.[89] Flak interfered with the aim of bombardiers and forced many a bomber out of formation, where it was now the most vulnerable to circling German fighters.[90]

The German day interceptor became by the summer of 1943 the key technology if the Germans were to maintain air superiority over the continent. For various reasons, neither the jet fighter nor the rocket plane then under development would be ready to face the growing American challenge for air superiority in time to thwart the Allied cross-Channel invasion. Both in the summer of 1943 and in May 1944, the month marked on the Allied timetable for a move into France, the Luftwaffe had to rely on the same piston-engine fighter planes. Two single-engine types were in the forefront; the characteristics of the Messerschmitt 109 and the Focke-Wulf 190 made them the best available for assailing the bombers and combating the escort fighters.[91] Both makes were superb aircraft in their own ways and had been periodically updated to keep them competitive with Allied fighters.

The Bf 109 encountered by American bombers in 1943 and 1944 was a far different one from that which had enabled the Condor Legion to establish air superiority in the Spanish Civil War. It was still trim-looking and still used fuel injection for maneuvers that would cause other engines to cut out. Supreme until bested by the Spitfire over Britain in 1940, it was yet, in its improved version, a formidable craft in 1943. The G model of 1943 had a 1,475-horsepower Daimler Benz, over twice as much as had been generated in

1938. The G had increased armor and self-sealing gas tanks. From the original four machine guns of 1938, the G had two higher-caliber machine guns and two 20mm and one 30mm cannon—all needed to bring down the rugged B-17. Speed had increased steadily; in 1943 it was capable of 386 MPH at low altitudes and 406 at high altitudes. But a weight increase from 5,000 to 7,000 pounds had come with the improvements, resulting in greater wing loading that reduced maneuverability, ruggedness, and range.

There were equivalent changes in the FW 190, which had entered combat in 1941. A heavier, more powerful aircraft, it could fly at 382 MPH at low altitudes, its B.M.W. engine producing 1,600 horsepower or over 2,000 with water-methanol injection. The FW 190 could deliver 74 pounds of shells in a 3-second burst from its two 13mm machine guns, two 20mm cannons, and two 30mm cannons.[92] It had in 1943 prodigious capabilities as a bomber killer, but this too was at the expense of maneuverability and range.[93]

In both cases, the use of external fuel tanks would have extended range, but also dramatically affected safety and handling characteristics. In the steep climb to the altitude of high-flying American heavy bombers, the German pilot might well encounter an American fighter and this meant jettisoning nearly full tanks. Besides, the chronic German fuel shortages almost precluded any such attempt to extend range. Generally, a Bf 109 pilot could count on 1 1/2 hours of flight time and his craft had a combat radius of 170 miles. It was somewhat similar in the case of the FW 190. Both planes were exceedingly dangerous to fly if the pilot was the inexperienced product of poorer and poorer Luftwaffe training and tried to run at high power because of the weight.

A number of Luftwaffe fighter pilots interrogated after the war expressed they had awareness at the time of combat of the weaknesses and strengths of their own and the enemy's aircraft. They recalled that they had always been able to outturn and outclimb the P-47, with its air-cooled engine and massive frame, below 20,000 feet. The problem was that most American heavy bombers flew above 20,000 feet, where the later model P-47s were superior in almost all aspects, particularly diving. German veterans tended to dismiss the P-38 as inferior because it lacked all-around visibility, was less maneuverable, and was more vulnerable to cannon fire. The P-51 they adjudged superior to both German types, with the exception of its ruggedness. If the air war had been mostly fought below 20,000 feet, they opined, they would have won. Air superiority, unfortunately for the Germans, had to be maintained at all altitudes.

Based on the relative strengths and weaknesses of enemy aircraft, Luftwaffe rules of engagement were fairly simple: never deliberately dogfight with a P-51 but dive away and live to fight another day; never dive from a P-47 but engage and dogfight below 20,000; attack a P-38 anywhere, anytime. In 1943, before the advent of the long-range American escort, both Bf 109Gs and FW 190As had the speed and firepower even at 25,000 feet to make American bombers pay a price that American sentiment was unwilling to pay. By May 1944, against the long-range P-51Bs and enhanced P-47Ds, the Bf 109G and FW 190A were respectively 50 and 70 MPH slower at 25,000 feet. The Mustangs and Thunderbolts, with some Lightnings, came in relays to protect the bomber boxes practically all along the routes, going in and coming out. Some American fighters went out to hunt their enemy while he was forming up. The P-51 could endure for 7 hours, the two German types still 1½, albeit the latter could land, refuel, and take off for second sorties, although in increasingly dangerous air above. But statistics rarely tell the whole story.[94]

The Luftwaffe developed other weapons in the attempt to counteract the American effort to dominate continental air space. One of these, the dropping of blast, incendiary, and shrapnel bombs into bomber formations from about 5,000 feet above, was a failure. The Germans were never able to solve the problem of coordinating the meeting of the American bombers and their own air-to-air defensive bombers, and when they rarely effected such a meeting, the space they planned to bomb from was often occupied by American escort fighters.[95]

If this technique flopped, another, air-to-air rocketry, had considerable success. Although attempts to mount high-caliber cannons (5.0 to 7.5 cm) were failures, another ploy to give defenders a relatively safe range from which to launch projectiles bore fruit. This entailed the adoption for aerial use of an unguided rocket propelled from an infantry mortar tube attached under the wing. The Luftwaffe attached a 21-cm rocket inside its launcher under each wing of a Bf 109 or FW 190. Two such rockets, each weighing 245 pounds, could be mounted under each wing of the twin-engine Bf 110s and Me 210s and 410s. The 90-pound warheads were bomber killers if they struck a vital spot. The ideal situation for the defenders would be to release their rockets well out of the range of the bombers' arc of fire, causing clusters of explosions from time or contact fuzes, the barrage dispersing a combat box. This was quickly followed by an assault, like a cavalry charge, by fighters flying cover for the rocket-launching planes. These Bf 109s or FW 190s sprayed conventional cannon and machine-gun fire at the scattering and traumatized bombers. By the fall of 1943, Eighth Air Force in England characterized the technique as the greatest threat to massed bombers over Germany. When 1944 dawned, however, neither the rocket-bearing planes nor those flying cover could count on an unobstructed approach to the bombers, even over deep targets such as Berlin.[96]

Essential to any air force's offensive or defensive missions was a stable fuel supply. Lacking domestic resources of petroleum, Germany relied on expensive imports and continued to do so in spite of a master plan initiated by Hitler in 1936 to convert readily available coal into synthetic oil. The Nazi regime used the hydrogenation process to produce the latter, but it cost four times more than the prevailing international price for crude. In the United States during the 1930s, U.S. Air Corps reservist James "Jimmy" Doolittle convinced his bosses at Shell Oil to invest in a pioneering refinery that would produce 100-octane gasoline. It became the model for hundreds more built in the United States during World War II. When the war came in 1939, German synthetic gasoline for its aircraft was in the 87–89 octane range. This degree was attained only by adding 15–18 percent aromatics with tetraethyl lead to the synthetic fuel.[97]

In 1944, when American fighters dueled German fighters for air superiority over Europe, Maj. Gen. Jimmy Doolittle of the Eighth Air Force must have taken satisfaction to know his fighters' engines performed better because of his prewar initiative. The Mustang's Rolls Royce engine produced 1,310 horsepower with 100-octane fuel, whereas the Bf 109's Daimler Benz, burning 87-octane fuel, could only match the Merlin's output with 25 percent more engine displacement.[98]

The United States had shared its 100-octane gas with its allies. As a result of the Battle of Britain experience against Spitfires using 100-octane fuel, the Germans boosted the octane rating of their synthetic fuel to the 95–97 range, but only by increasing the amount of aromatics in the fuel to nearly 40 percent. Additional power came from water-methanol and nitrous-oxide injection. While these kept German fighters competitive in terms of power, it came at a price. First, the increase in fuel quality meant a decrease in quantity, forcing the Luftwaffe to reduce training time so that sufficient fuel was available for front-line aircraft.[99] Second, the increased use of aromatics also resulted in overheated and stalled engines, forcing pilots to run their engines on rich fuel-air mixtures. This in turn caused increased fuel consumption, decreased range, increased fouling, and disintegration of such rubber components as fuel hoses and self-sealing tanks. Even operational flight time had to be shortened and maintenance increased.[100] It was only one of several vicious cycles suffered by the Luftwaffe in its struggle to preserve the air superiority status quo.

Thus shortages and the desperate effort for a quality that the Americans had insured before the war meant problems for the Luftwaffe that affected many facets of its activities. No aspect was more seriously impaired than that of training, the difficulties of which would have been almost insurmountable even without fuel shortages. It should have been axiomatic from the moment the

Luftwaffe emerged from the closet that a rigorous, progressive, and resource-nourished training program went hand-in-glove with the ability of the air force to carry out its assigned missions, whether these be tactical support of a conquering army or strategic air defense of a beleaguered Reich. It was not.

CHAPTER TWO

TRAINING TO DESTROY

Warriors do not spring skilled and fully armed from Mars' brow. They are the end product of a training system that hones them individually and as role players in a team effort. In no other branch of the service during World War II was training more important than in the air arm, with its increasingly complex technology and need for highly skilled specialists.

The training system of the Luftwaffe and the U.S. Army Air Forces developed between the world wars in much the same way that theory, organization, and technology evolved from the seeds planted in World War I. For the Germans it was imperative that an air force defeated in war and then prohibited by the peace settlement be reborn. Planning and training took place more or less secretly for over a decade before the Luftwaffe emerged from the womb of the Nazi state in March 1935. The American Army and Navy air arms did not have to be reborn; their struggle in the 1920s and 1930s was to refocus and expand in an era of penury and inward-looking vision that changed only grudgingly. Training, like all aspects of military aviation, had to adapt to these conditions.[1]

The Treaty of Versailles had dictated that the Germans could have no air force and hence could not conduct military flight training. Led by an aristocratic officer, Hans von Seeckt, a cabal of military, industrial, and political figures was determined that one day their country would regain full sovereignty and an unrestricted military machine, including an air force. The rise of the German phoenix was a part of camouflaged activities within Germany and more openly in hospitable neighbors such as Holland, Sweden, Italy, and the Soviet Union.[2]

Flight training for the nucleus of a future air force had to be conducted in Germany under the watchful eye of the Inter-Allied Control Commission until 1927, when that body terminated, making it easier for the Germans to evade restrictions that were still in force. Because all flight training had to be civilian in nature, the Germans seemingly complied by instituting a group of civil flying schools in 1923, when Germany's air sovereignty was returned, minus the right to have an air force. Purportedly these flying schools offered training only in sports flying. In retrospect the Control Commission should have detected the ultimate military objective. Germany had created a school in each of seven Area Defense Commands (*Wehrkries Kommandos*), with a military air specialist in charge of coordinating the training. That same air specialist was also in charge of coordinating covert theoretical military flight training with the Reichswehr, the small army allowed the Weimar Republic. A former military flier or current Reichswehr officer with flight experience directed most of the schools. Although the government subsidy for the schools ended in 1927 as the result of an international air accord signed that year in Paris that prohibited official support for sports flying, private means were found to back the schools after a short disruption.[3]

That same Paris accord had a positive side for Germany. It permitted the construction of sports planes with the characteristics of current fighter planes, to be used strictly for sports competition, but competition that included challenges to speed records. Directly from these sports designs would evolve the great German fighter plane—the Messerschmitt 109.

Two other areas of German civil flight aided the creation of a cadre for the future Luftwaffe. The Versailles treaty laid no restrictions on glider flight. Germans, especially the young, took to soaring with a zest. The government, upon noting the enthusiasm, encouraged glider training and competitive meets, apparently covertly subsidizing both. In 1926, after the formation of the German state airline Deutsche Luft Hansa, the government sponsored two commercial flight schools, ostensibly to train airline crew members. Students at both of these schools were often Reichswehr reservists or would become reservists after graduation. In the background of most Luftwaffe instructors and commanders of the 1930s was some combination of glider-flying school and commercial flight school training.[4]

Civilian training could only go so far. Experience in military aircraft and flight maneuvers was essential for at least some of the cadre of a future air force. The opportunity for advanced military training came as a result of the rapprochement of the two outcasts of postwar international society, Germany and the Soviet Union. The 1922 Rapallo Treaty made Germany the first European nation to commence normal relations with the Soviet Union and soon led to a military collaboration that was to last to the early 1930s. Collaboration included the production of German tank and aircraft prototypes in factories within the Soviet Union, German training on Soviet soil, and joint limited maneuvers of Germans and the Red Army. At Lipetsk, some 200 miles southeast of Moscow, a military flight school began to receive German students. During the 6-month course, these students trained in the Heinkel HD 17 trainer, faster than any aircraft available in Germany. Guided by World War I veteran pilots, they flew in formations of from two planes to squadron strength, practiced artillery-spotting, and performed simple aircraft maneuvers. They then matriculated to a fighter plane, the Fokker D.XIII, a postwar design of the famed inventor who had smuggled his equipment and stores from Germany to Holland after the war. The D.XIIIs had been smuggled from Holland to Lipetsk via South America.

Wolfgang Falck, who helped pioneer the German night-fighter

organization in World War II, was a Reichswehr officer who had received training at a commercial flight school. At Lipetsk, he recalled, "Our staff was German, but all the mechanics were Russian—Russian soldiers. [The Fokker D.XIII] was a Dutch-designed aircraft, with a British . . . engine . . . and all the technical manuals were in Spanish [apparently from a stay in some unnamed South American country before being transshipped to the Soviet Union]." Each fall the Lipetsk contingent participated in maneuvers with the Red Army, but only in the reconnaissance and antiartillery phases. German fighter and bomber personnel took part only on paper. Even so, the boys from Lipetsk always scored high with German and Soviet judges.[5]

With the advent of Hitler to power, German-Soviet collaboration ended. To fill the vacuum Premier Benito Mussolini allowed a limited number of Germans to train with the Regia Aeronautica. While German authorities did not consider the brief Italian experience worthwhile, one German student, who would go on to become the most famous Luftwaffe fighter leader in World War II, valued it. Adolf Galland, with a background in gliders and commercial flight school training, particularly relished "the tremendous fun with airshooting." His training and his marksmanship would prove valuable in Spain, in the Battle of Britain, and even as General of Fighters during the great battles for air superiority in 1944.[6]

Unlike the German aerial force of World War I, the U.S. Army Air Service emerged from World War I as part of a victorious effort. Although made a combat arm in the National Defense Act of 1920, it was subordinated to the ground arms. Like these arms, it shrank as a result of rapid demobilization and reduced appropriations. The disillusioned American people were ready to turn away from foreign entanglements and the U.S. Senate refused to accept the Treaty of Versailles. The Army Air Service had to limp along. Its principal source of aircrew continued to be the flying cadet program, inaugurated during World War I, which led to a commission in the reserves, or, rarely, in the regular army. The number of cadets in training at any one time was fairly low, kept that way by a shortage of funds, high physical and mental entrance standards, and a high attrition or "washout" rate at the few training fields left over from the sweeping reduction of facilities after the war.[7]

Primary training, which took place at a field in Florida and another in California, consisted of ground school (the theory of flight, navigation, nomenclature of engines, the military way, and other subjects) followed by initial flights in venerable Curtiss "Jenny" primary trainers and Curtiss PT-1s (PT for "Primary Trainer"). The instructor pilot would guide the student through the basics of flight with his dual set of controls and with directions given through a Gosport tube. After soloing, each trainee learned fairly simple acrobatics. If the trainee passed muster during the 6 months of primary instruction, he graduated to advanced training, then containing two phases—basic and advanced. In 1922 the Air Service concentrated all advanced training at Kelly Field, Texas. Basic lasted 12 weeks and its flying training consisted of dual flights in more powerful trainers, principally the light bomber of wartime fame and notoriety, the DeHavilland DH-4. Successful performance led to solo practice in such maneuvers as figure 8s and 180° and 360° turns and formation, night, and cross-country flying. Ground school continued apace. The successful student then came to the final hurdle—advanced training. In this 3-month segment, work continued in the classrooms, while in the DH-4, the Martin MB3A bomber, or the SE-5 fighter students performed the type of formations, dueling, tactics, and gunnery they would encounter in a tactical unit of each man's specialty.

The cadet system of regimentation and discipline in the postwar period was modeled on West Point and it included, especially in the first months of primary, hazing. As long as cadets were limited in number and a true elite, the system seemed to produce a breed of officer who could match the Germans for the type of iron-clad stamina and devotion war called for. Requirements were stringent. In the 6 years of the two-tiered training system, 865 students began the program, though only 480 graduated. Of the remainder, 16 died, 276 washed out, 67 left for other reasons, and 26 were held over for additional work.

In March 1928 the Air Corps divided flight training into three separate stages: primary, basic, and advanced. At the end of the decade, it established the Flying Training Center at a new base, Randolph Field in San Antonio, Texas, which offered both primary and basic training. Advanced training remained at nearby Kelly. Training would be much the same into World War II, though profound changes in technology and tactics loomed. Metal was replacing wood and fabric, the monoplane replaced the biplane, engines were growing, and the elimination of drag was becoming of critical importance—an aeronautical revolution was underway.[8]

Besides active duty training, the Air Service/Air Corps in the interwar era depended to an extent on training offered in the Organized Reserve, the college-based Reserve Officers Training Corps (ROTC), and the air components of the National Guard. The Treaty of Versailles had denied the Germans a reserve, but in the United States air training was subject to frugality. For the most part the Organized Reserve, ROTC, and the National Guard contributed little to a viable air arm. Pay and benefits were negligible and the aircraft they flew were the oldest and least trustworthy available. That these reserves existed at all was testimony to their crews' love of flying.[9]

The Great Depression helped to weaken this already weak training program in the United States, but in contrast contributed to the rise of the Nazis in Germany and the consequent resurgence of the German armed forces. Behind the façade of continued treaty compliance, the Luftwaffe grew secretly until the formal abrogation of the Versailles treaty on 16 March 1935. Until then, sports flying, the flight activities of the Nazi youth organization (Hitler Jugend), the commercial flight schools, the Reichswehr, and the Soviet and Italian training programs provided a fair basis for air force training and organization. Under the overall direction of Hermann Göring, the portly World War I ace, fully trained aircrew joined the semi-official Advertising Squadrons (reklamstaffeln) that participated in Reichswehr maneuvers with reconnaissance and target-marking support while "screening" these operations with commercial skywriting work. These were the lineal ancestors of the first Luftwaffe tactical units.[10]

When Hitler threw off the shackles of the Treaty of Versailles in March 1935 and announced the existence of a Luftwaffe, there were only a few hundred officers available for flight instruction. This small pool had to be augmented by civilian teachers until a new military instructors' school began to turn out a sufficient number of graduates. It took several years for the training system to settle into a normal mold. In the meantime, tactical units took up some of the slack by giving a select number of trainees primary training. By 1938 the system was functioning in a routine manner. All trainees, other than commissioned officers seeking to be fliers, first went to a pilot training regiment for the discipline of infantry drill. The officer candidates then attended one of several air academies for further drill and polishing for commission. Commissioned officers and officer candidates along with trainees who were tabbed to become noncommissioned officer pilots began flight training at one of the flying schools that had been created in 1923.

Now called A or B schools, with some slight difference in curriculum, they had become thoroughly militarized. They were roughly the equivalent of the U.S. Air Corps' primary and basic stages. Students received training in single-engine monoplanes and biplanes, with a lesser amount of instruction in multiengine trainers. The average prewar flight trainee was a volunteer, for supply always exceeded demand in that flight-eager generation. Each new class contained around 200 members. Figures are not available for the attrition rate, but given the spartan discipline, it must have been high. If successfully completing the 7-month course, a graduate received the basic Luftwaffe pilot's license.

Some of the graduates went on to C School for advanced training in more complex multiengine trainers. And some C School graduates then received advanced instrument instruction. Had senior Luftwaffe commanders and training officials but the foresight, all fledglings would have received at least a modicum of this type of instruction. Its general lack was to be one of the Luftwaffe's "Achilles' heels" in the coming world war.

Sooner or later the Luftwaffe assigned all A or B graduates to an ordnance school (redesignated training wing in World War II) for advanced training in their respective combat specialties. The ordnance school was the approximate equal of the U.S. Air Corps' advanced stage. From 1935 to the outbreak of the war, fighter pilot trainees had some 50 hours of specialized flight time. The main advanced trainer was the Arado 65, a highly regarded single-engine monoplane. From 1937 on, the operational type for transitional training was the Bf 109. The latter was rarely available and this chronic lack was to prove another weakness in the testing time of war. Fighter pilot aspirants learned to master the basic two-plane formation known as the *Rotte* (leader and wing man) whose intricate maneuvers had been developed in Spain by Werner Mölders, an alumnus of a commercial flight school. The *Rotten* and larger formations simulated combat, in and out of various thicknesses of cloud. This overcast training, however, would prove inadequate when the defense of the homeland was on the line in winter combat, a situation that was not anticipated in the shaping of a tactical and offensive-minded air force. The Luftwaffe placed special emphasis on gunnery training, from rifle ranges on the ground to towed targets in the air. Classroom work was generally the same in subject matter and hours as those in the American equivalent.[11]

Luftwaffe training suffered setbacks whenever one of the prewar crises occurred, beginning with the Rhineland Reoccupation in 1936 and continuing through the takeover of Czechoslovakia in 1939. The political leadership pressured the Luftwaffe high command to double the rate of expansion of new tactical units. The Luftwaffe sent cadres from the various schools and students from the ordnance schools to form or fill in new units. Already existing tactical groups served as "mother" units to train personnel for recently formed "daughter" units, with the result that the former lost valuable group training and the latter were insufficiently manned. While "volunteers" such as Galland received valuable combat experience in Spain, their tactical units at home lost their services for an extended length of time. As a result of the crisis syndrome, the Luftwaffe had on the average a 10 percent shortage in personnel to fill essential positions in tactical units at the outbreak of World War II.

Another problem that had its origins in training was something that Göring called "the plague." Breaches in flight discipline led to an inordinantly high number of accidents. This reckless or careless flair among fliers contradicted the stress on discipline that was a German trademark. Or perhaps it was a reaction against that discipline. The Luftwaffe attempted to stifle "the plague" using harsh measures, including executions, but the problem continued into the war.[12]

The fighter training program suffered disproportionately from these problems as well as from a low priority among Luftwaffe specialties. Göring had promised the fighter branch equal treatment with bombers and dive bombers. However, like some of the American commanders who came out of a fighter background, he countenanced favoritism of the bombers, for they were the core of a tactically oriented Luftwaffe. In 1936 there was only one fighter ordnance school and it was plundered during the Rhineland crisis for a show of force and became inactive. It was not until the winter of 1937/38 that the Luftwaffe established a second fighter school and not until 1939, in anticipation of a Polish crisis, that the original school was reopened. In all of this, the high command's view was that fighter tactical units could take up the slack in the paucity of fighter ordnance schools.[13]

Adolf Galland, who himself helped to create two new fighter *gruppen* at the time of the Sudetenland crisis, well understood at the time the sacrifice of quality for quantity. In his postwar memoir, he remembered that two bombers, the medium Dornier Do 17 and Heinkel He 111, beginning to come off the production line were faster than the first-line Luftwaffe fighters of the time (the Bf 109 was still a short time away from production). In words that could have described a contemporary situation in the United States, Galland noted, "When it was already believed that the fighter should play a secondary role according to the ideas of air strategy prevailing among the German High Command, this idea was only reinforced by the state of technical development in Germany." Henceforth, until World War II, despite the lessons of the Bf 109s' winning of air superiority in Spain, or because of the ease of it, the high command "believed that [the fighter's] place was local air defense, the winning of air superiority over the front, or if necessary to assist the Army in land operations . . . with ground support planes." Galland himself began World War II as a ground support pilot.[14]

On the eve of the war, young Heinz Knoke of the Hitler Youth applied to become an officer candidate in the Luftwaffe. In July 1939 he was "called up for a preliminary examination. It lasts four days. Psychologists, doctors, teachers, and officers test four other candidates and myself. The first day is filled with medical examinations. The second day we have to write essays, deliver impromptu talks, and answer hundreds of questions."[15]

After two more days of such pressures as being spun around in a "three-dimensional chair" and subjected to a low-pressure chamber and of demonstrating "athletic proficiency," Knoke learned that he was one of two to pass in his group. In November, with the first campaign of the war over, he entered No. 11 Flying [Pilot] Training Regiment for infantry drill and humiliation. "Indeed, my NCO even goes so far as to say that if I am ever commissioned as an officer he will apply for a discharge from the service." In January 1940 Knoke went to an air academy as an officer candidate. At its associated A School he began his flight training in a Focke-Wulf 44 dual-control biplane. In August 1940, during the Battle of Britain, Knoke received his Luftwaffe pilot's license, eager but not nearly advanced enough to fly combat. His next assignment was fighter ordnance school at Werneuchen, where he was fortunate to fly the Bf 109. Knoke endured the advanced training to finish as a fighter pilot. He joined the 52nd Fighter Wing in December 1940 as a cadet. After polishing with his wing, he achieved the rank of leutnant in April 1941 and soon flew a Bf 109 in combat.[16]

United States Army Air Corps' flight training underwent its own changes and crises. Penury and internalization continued to shape the Army's flying service, exacerbated by the Great Depression. The United States evaded international crises as long as possible, while the Germans provoked them, and American training reflected this posture. From 1928 to 1935 twenty-three flight training classes entered 12 months of primary training, with 1,924 trainees graduating, almost four times the number between 1922 and 1928. This was not nearly enough to compete with the air force the Germans were building. On the positive side, the Americans generally avoided any "plague" of dead trainees, losing thirty-eight to accidents from 1928 to 1935, only 1.85 percent of the 2,051 who entered flight training in the twenty-three classes.[17]

Because of the budget crunch in the Depression-haunted years 1929–1935, the Air Corps by 1935 had only 1,251 Regular officers. Most second lieutenants were new, but most first lieutenants had 12 years of service or more. Cadets who graduated from Kelly Field served with tactical units in that enlisted rank for 1 year, then became second lieutenants in the Air Reserve (as it was now known), serving on active duty another year. There were few if any noncommissioned pilots in tactical units, but a good many cadet fighter pilots. Cadet morale suffered as a result, though the opportunity to fly motivated those on active duty as it motivated nonactive duty members of the Air Reserve.[18]

Changes were in the air. Historian Maurer Maurer has cogently described it: "The Air Corps' financial condition began to mend slowly in the mid-1930s, then faster as the end of the decade drew nearer. The period was marked by progress toward recovery from depression; failure of arms limitations; war in Ethiopia, Spain, and China; the menace of Hitler; and the clear need for modernizing and strengthening America's defense." With "these and numerous other developments at home and abroad," the budget picture dramatically improved. The Air Corps' appropriation quadrupled between 1935 and 1939. The advent of the General Headquarters Air Force in 1935 and the resultant need for more men and planes began to elbow penury aside. The need for more commissioned aircrew became so pressing that Congress in 1937 allowed immediate commissioning of cadets serving in General Headquarters Air Force followed by active duty service of 3 to 5 years. Second lieutenants were now eligible for promotion to first lieutenant in 3 years. It was a big step toward a competitive air arm.[19]

First Lieutenant Beirne Lay, Jr.,[20] Air Reserve, on active duty in 1937, wrote an editorial in the monthly newsletter of the cadet battalion at Randolph. A 1933 graduate of Randolph, Lay tried to justify the grind of a flying cadet's existence. "Have I joined the tail end of a bread line with a fatal crack-up at the other end, sooner or later?" Lay answered his own question. "Five years' active duty will give . . . money in the bank and more than the minimum hours necessary for an airline co-pilot's ticket . . . If you're going to be a bombardment pilot, you may get invaluable experience with four-engine equipment. Reserve officers are logging time as co-pilots on the B-17's right now . . . and the chances of getting bumped off? They kill more of them in bathtubs than in Army airplanes." Lay asked another question: "Regular commissions? . . . 310 Douglas B-18s are being delivered to the Service, and an effort made in other categories to bring airplane strength up to the authorized strength of 2,320. Somebody's got to fly them. It looks like regular commissions to me before your five years are up."[21]

It was not coincidence that Lay stressed bombers in his editorial. The day of the bomber's predominant role in Air Corps thinking and tactics had arrived. The silver bomber of strategic dreams, the B-17, was gradually becoming a reality in bombardment groups. And 1937 was the year Claire Chennault gave up trying to push the fighter within the U.S. Army and resigned.

The changing of technology and tactics as a result of the triumph of the big bomber was apparent in Air Corps schools and tactical units. The *Air Corps Newsletter* of 15 February 1938 reported that "the Bombardment Section of the Advanced Flying School, Kelly Field, Texas, was eliminated in order to adjust training methods to the changes in military tactical flying which have resulted [from] . . . the development of the new Bombardment planes." There was no similar reorganization of the Pursuit Section.[22]

After the Munich crisis, and with President Roosevelt's decision to expand American air power, training reflected that growth. Whereas in 1936 primary classes numbered 102 trainees, in 1939 this number was expanded to 400. Randolph and Kelly could not handle such an influx, so the Air Corps contracted out primary training to nine civilian flight schools in Illinois, Nebraska, Oklahoma, Alabama, Texas, and California. Because half of the primary students were expected to drop out, the Air Corps maintained only two basic schools, both at Randolph. Advanced training retained Kelly but added Brooks Field, Texas. More specialized advanced training was now taught in the tactical units, in a partial return to the past.[23]

As a natural consequence of the progress of the age, new training planes offered in design what operational planes had come to be. The Ryan PT-20 introduced in 1940 offered modern design (low-wing monoplane) and skin (metal fuselage). Front (instructor) and rear (student) seats could be adjusted for length and height. Its 125-horsepower in-line, air-cooled Menasco C-4 engine provided the type of stability required for beginning pilots. The most famous primary trainer yet, however, looked as if it belonged back with the "Jennys." Introduced in 1936, the Lockheed PT-13 was a fabric-covered biplane, but was the beloved of several generations of both Army and Navy cadets.[24]

In February 1940 Army Flying Cadet S. W. Bishop gave his impressions in the *Air Corps Newsletter* of what life was like at one of the civilian primary schools, the Spartan School of Aeronautics at Tulsa, Oklahoma.

The size of the classes at Spartan has made it necessary to establish a system of semi-self-discipline for the Cadets, which is based principally upon customs similar to those prevailing at Randolph Field. There is a modified two-class system, viz: Upper and Lower, the Upperclassmen being those who began training six weeks ahead of the "Dodos" . . . The transformation of each incoming group of debonair, if not cocky "Joe Colleges" into eager, militant Fledglings in the short space of six weeks' exposure to the disciplinary measures [a euphemism for hazing, which was to become controversial] of the acting officers and noncommissioned cadet officers is little short of amazing . . . [the Cadets were] eager to climb into the cockpit . . . bent on dusting the cobwebs from Lazy Eights or ironing out kinks in Chandelles preparatory to the coveted day when all will be transferred to Randolph Field for Basic training, another milestone on the road to become one of Uncle Sam's Flying Defenders.

This might have seemed a bit tongue-in-cheek, but Bishop's was not a generation of cynics despite the Depression.[25]

In a little less than two years before the attack on Pearl Harbor, an ambitious expansion program for the Army looked to huge numbers of pilots, navigators, bombardiers, gunners, and support personnel that dwarfed the numbers under training when Cadet Bishop was at Spartan. AWPD-1 projected figures that staggered the imagination, but proved remarkably accurate.

Luftwaffe training deficiencies did not appear critical as the German blitzkrieg crushed Poland and steamrolled over Denmark, Norway, the Low Countries, and France. Trained and shaped for close air support, the Luftwaffe performed awesomely. The bombing of virtually undefended cities such as Warsaw and Rotterdam was no true test of strategic offensive capabilities. When the Luftwaffe attempted a strategic offensive against Britain, it attempted to carry out something for which it was not prepared, and failed. Its training deficiencies could no longer be ignored. From the outset of the war a major barrier to effective flight training was the attitude of Hans Jeschonnek, chief of the Luftwaffe general staff. He believed that the war would be short, therefore all resources, human and materiel, should be devoted to insuring a quick decision. During the Battle of Britain he permitted the resumption of a practice that had taken place each time a prewar crisis occurred— the plundering of training schools for tactical (operational) units.

The fighter branch's inept performance over Britain forced him to permit some small expansion of fighter training, but even after the Royal Air Force stepped up its night campaign in 1942 and some of his subordinates suggested that training should be accelerated to meet the threat, Jeschonnek replied, "Let's beat the Russians first, then we can start training."[26] He and his superiors squandered the best opportunity that the Luftwaffe would have to expand training in both the Reich and adjacent occupied territory, before the American daylight campaign intensified in the summer of 1943 and an invasion loomed, foreclosing that option.

The problem of an adequate number and quality of instructors was constant. Not only did the Luftwaffe general staff permit senior commanders to continue feeding on school cadres, combat veterans were reluctant to exchange the excitement of battle for the routine of instructing, especially because training schools tried to retain them indefinitely. In 1942 the Luftwaffe further drained the pool of instructors with combat experience to help flesh out a Luftwaffe combat ground division, soon to be decimated on the Eastern Front. Tactical units displayed a positive side of the training coin, establishing special personnel replacement groups to give transitional training in areas away from the scenes of action, assuring combat veterans of returning to their tactical units after a tour as instructors. In contrast all too many instructors at the regular schools lacked combat experience with which to inspire and to add a dimension to training.[27]

As serious as the instructor bind was the chronic shortage of training planes, particularly operational models, also a carryover from peacetime. The Luftwaffe never solved the problem. Tactical units in action resisted sparing operational aircraft for training at the schools, thus contributing to ill-trained replacements whose performances weakened the effectiveness of the units they ultimately joined. Training models themselves were often in short supply. The Arado 96, an advanced trainer with characteristics that gave students the feel of a single-engine Bf 109 or FW 190, was frequently not available or sparely distributed. This contrasted with its American counterpart, the AT-6, a powerful, smooth trainer that became so plentiful that it could be exported to the Royal Canadian Air Force and the Royal Air Force.[28]

All this was bad enough, but the gravest problem was one that ultimately affected the whole German war effort—empty or partially filled fuel tanks. From 1941 on it was a bureaucratic headache to obtain the minimum amount of gasoline to operate even a laggard training program. With the expansion of German offensives, operational consumption went up and allotments for training went down. In 1942 Hitler ordered aircraft production stepped up and Göring tried to get the Wehrmacht high command to share its supply, arguing that without more trained crew the increased production would be meaningless. His argument was to no avail and training virtually halted for the last part of 1942.[29]

Steady British night operations and the first appearances of the American day bombers over the Reich early in 1943 led to an opening up of fuel rations as well as a thorough overhaul of the training system. The emphasis on training was for the first time shifted from bombers to fighters. Another positive step was an increase in instrument training for day-fighter trainees, although it was not as intensive as it should have been. A change with positive and negative results was a shortening of training hours in an effort to identify as early as possible which students seemed capable of absorbing fighter training. These were then sent on to fighter training wings after abbreviated training at the now combined A/B schools. The Luftwaffe pared all training, resulting in significant savings in gasoline, materiel, and personnel.[30] But there was no increase in the availability of operational aircraft for transitional training, even for the personnel replacement groups, whose function was to teach neophyte fighter pilots as well as other specialists the particular tactics of the operational units they would soon join.[31] The shortage was now due to two causes: the increase of Allied bombing meant more and more of these aircraft at crash sites or in repair shops; and undertrained graduates of training wings and inadequately oriented crew from personnel replacement groups produced more accidents in the tactical units and hence less new aircraft available for training. It was a vicious cycle that never ceased. As a result of cutbacks in training time in the 1943 reorganization and prior skimping on instruction, a fighter pilot graduate of a training wing had about 160 hours in the air. At a comparative stage in 1943, Royal Air Force fighter trainees had 360 hours and U.S. Army Air Forces advanced training graduates over 400 hours.[32]

United States Army Air Corps training had expanded significantly after President Roosevelt's open push for heightened military air power in 1938, but the number of flying cadets and other trainees did not climb dramatically until after the outbreak of war in Europe. Official estimates grew from 7,000 pilots in 1940, to AWPD-1's 85,000, then to 100,000 eight months after Pearl Harbor. The estimates for other crew climbed proportionately.[33] Until Pearl Harbor swept away the last vestiges of isolationism and congressional miserliness, a scarcity of bases, planes, and instructors limited the number actually in training. While, as for the Germans, the latter would dog the Army Air Forces for much of the war, the number of bases and aircraft soon met the need if not the demand.[34]

In Germany the Luftwaffe had to compete with the elite Schultz-staffel (SS) units of the Wehrmacht and submarines for superior young men. In the United States, the Army Air Forces had to vie with Naval Aviation for the cream of the crop. Both U.S. air arms built up a backlog of personnel to be tapped at the convenience of each. Each used an enlisted reserve and added increments to stretch out the training cycle in order to retain the backlog and protect it from the draft boards, who were authorized to call up eighteen-year-olds in the fall of 1942.[35] The Army Air Forces modified the discipline for aviation cadets (the title changed from flying cadets in 1940) in 1942, perhaps in response to the influx of "citizen soldiers" who had no college once the 2-year college requirement was dropped in 1941 (although several months' college training was subsequently added for aviation cadets). Early in 1942 the Army Air Forces abandoned the upperclassman-lowerclassman system along with its West Point–like hazing. Several veteran officers in the training commands questioned the wisdom of this move. One such officer, Lt. Col. J. M. McAuliff, would later comment: "There was a noticeable change after the outbreak of war. Students I observed were of a very poor caliber . . . Consequently numerous reduction in standards were made and resulted in a poor end product." After several sub-par graduating classes, "we put the squeeze on eliminations in flight training, which resulted in a better end product, but far from the 1941–1942 product." The "squeeze" meant more rigorous applications of standards, particularly at the primary stage, where the majority of the overall 40 percent rate of eliminations between 1939 and 1945 occurred.[36]

Technology over the course of the war changed, but the Stearman biplane remained the most beloved and utilized primary trainer. Charles Watry described in a postwar memoir a war-introduced basic stage trainer, the Vultee BT-13/15: "Spin recoveries . . . were slam-bang affairs . . . Once in a spin the canopy shook and rattled as if it might come off." For the advanced stage, the best trainer was the North American AT-6, with most of the characteristics of a contemporary fighter plane. Richard Turner, who graduated from advanced fighter training in September 1942, recalled it as "beautiful to fly." Once the great industrial complex was cranked up for all-out war production, in contrast to German production, shortages of aircraft tended to fade. The aircraft available for transitional fighter training, however, were obsolete but still operational P-39s and P-40s until toward the end of the war. Charles "Chuck" Yeager was "one of the few who loved the Thirty-Nine and would have gladly flown it off to war." He remembered "whipping through a desert canyon at three hundred miles an hour . . . the joy of flying—the sense of speed and exhilaration twenty feet above the deck—make you so damn happy that you want to shout for joy . . . You feel so lucky, so blessed to be a fighter pilot." German pilots loved to fly in this daredevil way, but it contributed to the "plague." The factors that caused most Army Air Forces training fatalities were more attributed to night flying and the advanced stage's more complicated maneuvers and more powerful aircraft. Two thousand fatalities occurred at the advanced stage, some two and a half times more than in the basic stage and four times more than the total for primary training. The death rate, however, was not a scandal and appeared not to be a crisis approaching that of the Luftwaffe.[37]

Watry would fly transport aircraft in Europe in 1944 and 1945, and Turner and Yeager would fly fighters in the momentous battles there for air superiority in 1944.

For both the Germans and the Americans, instrument training for flying through overcast weather was a serious problem. After the war an American who was involved in bad-weather training called it the "weakest" aspect of all Army Air Forces training. Its training command took, if belatedly, steps to improve the situation, establishing schools that specialized in instruments and bad-weather flying. The graduates of these schools took charge of separate departments of instrument training mandated in 1943 by Training Command for the basic stage. The Luftwaffe also took steps to improve training for day interceptor crews as part of the training reorganization of 1943. It was not until after the disastrous battles for air superiority in February and March 1944, however, that Göring ordered a crash program to train all fighter pilots thoroughly in instruments and bad-weather flying. After the war a former Luftwaffe senior commander commented that American fighter pilots demonstrated that their mastery of "the techniques of bad weather operations and of blind navigation over long distances were of a very high standard . . . It was primarily the high quality of their training which enabled American fighter pilots to execute their unparalleled and difficult . . . missions."[38]

The Germans and Americans took two divergent courses in their respective training systems in the climactic months of 1944 before the invasion of France. These courses were symbolic of the accommodation of each force to reality. In 1944 German aircraft production adjusted to the heavy American bombing of February and began to climb toward record figures. The Luftwaffe had a decision to make: whether to maintain the quality of training, which for fighters had improved somewhat after the 1943 reorganization, or to increase quantity by a further paring of the hours of flight instruction. Under the pressure of getting more planes into the air to cope with the continued American offensive, the Luftwaffe training command chose quantity over quality. At the same time the U.S. Army Air Forces Training Command moved to increase the hours and improve the quality of each stage of its training, albeit not under the same pressure as its German counterpart. Edmond Zellner, an American fighter pilot in the great battles of 1944, summed it up in contrasting American and German fighter pilots: each side had "some real good pilots and some very poor ones, [but] when we got good, they got bad."[39]

CHAPTER THREE

TRIAL AND ERROR—EARLY OPERATIONS

Prewar doctrinal development did not adequately prepare the U.S. Army Air Forces for the kind of warfare that enveloped it in Europe. Ready or not, Brig. Gen. Ira Eaker's VIII Bomber Command began operations on 29 June 1942 with the first of several token raids to the continent using a handful of light bombers borrowed from the Royal Air Force.[1] The designated hammer of Maj. Gen. Carl Spaatz's Eighth Air Force and headquartered at High Wycombe, near London, VIII Bomber Command was primed to operate according to the precepts of air war developed in the 1930s. Indeed, Eighth Air Force in general was thus primed as it took up its headquarters at Bushy Park, England, in June. Mastery of the daylight skies was essential to the planned invasion of Hitler's *Festung Europa*. With the Royal Air Force's Bomber Command mainly a night stalker, the task was left to the Eighth. The big question was whether Eighth Air Force's "self-defending" heavy bombers, when they arrived, could achieve their own air superiority to permit the strategic bombing of Germany.

It was no accident that American fighter aircraft played a limited role in the first 2 years of the Army Air Forces effort over Europe. Prewar doctrine limited them to point defense, support of ground forces, and short-range escort of bombers, much like the role that the Luftwaffe had designated for its fighters when the war broke out.[2] These roles evolved when Army Air Corps leaders believed that any fighter with sufficient range for long-range bomber escort would lack the necessary maneuverability and speed to be able to compete with enemy fighters on anywhere near reasonable terms.[3] During the Battle of Britain the Luftwaffe had tried to use the twin-engine Bf 110 for relatively long-range escort and its disastrous performance appeared to bear out this prewar belief.

This belief was tunnel vision, but it was reflected in the American air war plans for winning World War II—AWPD-1 of 1941 and AWPD-42 of 1942. AWPD-1 envisioned bombers winning the war and long-range escorts as technically improbable. It called for twenty-one American fighter groups stationed in Europe, ten to defend bomber bases and eleven to support ground operations. AWPD-42 raised the number of fighter groups in Europe to twenty-five, but made no reference to the escort function, stating that unescorted bombers could reach their targets "without excessive losses." Haywood S. Hansell, Jr., one of its authors, later was to call this ignorance of the function and possibility of long-range fighter escort the "greatest fault" of AWPD-42.[4]

The problems facing Brig. Gen. Frank O'D. Hunter, commanding officer of VIII Fighter Command, and his staff were legion. Headquartered at Bushey Hall, Fighter Command had to acquire or build suitable bases on a crowded island, polish pilots and tactical units in a crowded sky, and face the technical and logistical tribulations of aircraft indoctrination and performance. But the earliest major problem was the diversion of fighter groups to TORCH, the invasion of North Africa, in the fall of 1942. As various groups passed in and out of the United Kingdom for only short stays, VIII Fighter Command became virtually a training organization. What was soon left for tactical operations was only the 4th Fighter Group, whose nucleus was pilots from the Royal Air Force Eagle Squadrons, the justly famed units made up mainly from American volunteers.[5] The Fourth flew Spitfires, the "hero" plane of the Bat-

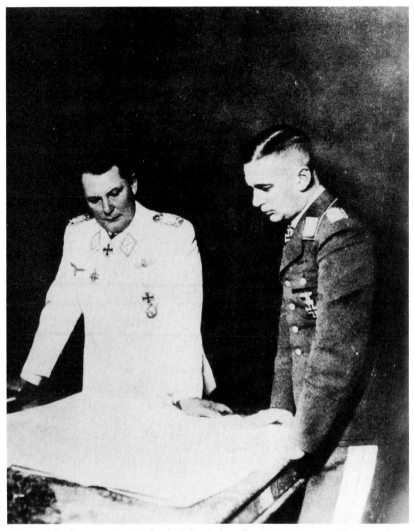

Left to right, Commander-in-chief of the Luftwaffe, Air Minister, and heir apparent to Hitler Hermann Göring with Chief of the Luftwaffe General Staff from 1939 to 1943 Generaloberst Hans Jeschonnek, who steadfastly maintained the Luftwaffe as a close air support air force. (*Source:* USAF Historical Research Center.)

Left to right, Generals Jeschonnek, Korten, Plocher, and von Grief. General der Flieger Günther Korten was Jeschonnek's successor as chief of the Luftwaffe General Staff. In the critical period, 1943 to 1944, he converted the Luftwaffe from close air support to aerial defense. (*Source:* USAF Historical Research Center.)

Generaloberst Hubert Weise, commander of Berlin and Central Industrial Region Air Defense Command in 1940 and Air Command Center from 1941 to early 1944. (*Source:* USAF Historical Research Center.)

Generaloberst Hans Jürgen Stumpff, commander of Air Fleet Reich from 1944 to 1945. (*Source:* USAF Historical Research Center.)

Center, Luftwaffe General of the Fighters from 1941 to 1944 Adolf Galland. *(Source:* USAF Historical Research Center.)

Generalleutnant Josef Schmid, commander of the Luftwaffe's I Fighter Corps from 1943 to 1944. (*Source:* USAF Historical Research Center.)

Right, the Luftwaffe's Egon Mayer, who in late 1942 perfected the head-on attack that proved so deadly against the "self-defending bomber." He gained 102 aerial victories, but failed to survive the battles for air superiority. *Left* is Hermann Graf. (*Source:* Toliver Collection.)

Center right, Günther Rall, Germany's third-ranking ace of the war with 275 victories, being congratulated upon his return from a mission. Rall represented one of many experienced Luftwaffe pilots moved to the defense of the Reich from the East in an attempt to regain air superiority. Though shot down and wounded, Rall survived the battles for air superiority. (*Source:* Toliver Collection.)

Bf 109 fighter. Despite being overloaded and lacking range, it was the Luftwaffe's mainstay during the battles for air superiority. (*Source:* National Air and Space Museum.)

Fokker D.XIII over Lipetsk, Russia. One of fifty used to train German fighter pilots secretly in the Soviet Union before the war. (*Source:* USAF Historical Research Center.)

Bf 110 fighter. When equipped with heavy cannons and 21-cm rockets, it became the major cause of the "Fall Crisis" facing Eighth Air Force in 1943. (*Source:* National Air and Space Museum.)

FW 190 fighter. Heavier and more powerful than the Bf 109, the FW 190 was armed with two 13mm machine guns, two 20mm cannons, and two 30mm cannons, but at the expense of maneuverability and range. (*Source:* USAF Historical Research Center.)

Maxwell Field's Air Corps Tactical School, where advocates of the "self-defending bomber" determined that escort fighters were not essential for gaining air superiority. (*Source:* National Air and Space Museum.)

Major Claire Chennault (here a major general), who at the Air Corps Tactical School led the futile attempt to give fighter aircraft preeminence in Air Corps doctrine. (*Source:* National Air and Space Museum.)

General Henry "Hap" Arnold, commanding general of the Army Air Forces throughout the war. His 1943 decisions to assign Eighth Air Force priority over all other units in acquiring long-range escort fighters and to shuffle the leadership of the air war against Germany were keys to winning air superiority. (*Source:* National Air and Space Museum.)

Brigadier General Ira Eaker, commanding general of Eighth Air Force from 1942 to 1943. Eaker's lukewarm support for long-range escorts contributed to his being transferred from command of the Eighth Air Force. (*Source:* National Air and Space Museum.)

Right to left facing camera, beginning with second from right, Brigadier General Curtis LeMay, commander of the 3rd Air Division and responsible for bomber formation tactics; Lieutenant General James "Jimmy" Doolittle, commander of Eighth Air Force and responsible for "freeing" the fighters; unidentified colonel; Lieutenant General Carl Spaatz, commander of U.S. Strategic Air Forces in Europe and the person with whom the buck stopped; and Major General Frederick Anderson, chief of staff for operations, U.S. Strategic Air Forces in Europe, and major force behind the attrition warfare that defeated the Luftwaffe. (*Source:* National Air and Space Museum.)

A scene typical of the struggle within, extending to the Officers' Club, after hours. Lieutenant General "Jimmy" Doolittle (*left*) and Major General Frederick Anderson (*right*) compete for Commanding General Carl Spaatz's attention. (*Source:* National Air and Space Museum.)

Major General William Kepner (*left*), commanding general of Eighth Air Force Fighter Command, 1943 to 1944, the man behind "unorganized air guerrilla warfare," and Francis S. Gabreski (*right*) of the 56th Fighter Group, an ace with twenty-eight victories. (*Source:* USAF Historical Research Center.)

tle of Britain, whose possession ensured that replacement pilots would get the best advice from the ex-Eagles and the Royal Air Force. The Spitfire was a short-range fighter, however, deficient for the long-range bomber missions the Eighth was brewing up for the future.

Prewar doctrine called for the bombers to make the major contribution in the war effort, bombing the sources of German power. Wartime experience would prove this impossible without first at least a semblance of air superiority. Orthodox Army Air Forces thinking envisioned two means of achieving air superiority. First bombardment forces would attack Luftwaffe power on the ground, including airfields, aircraft manufacturing, ball-bearing industries, and various support activities. Most of these were beyond the range of possible fighter escort. Second, bombardment forces would meet Luftwaffe power in the air head-on, reducing the enemy's strength with the defensive fire of 100 half-inch bullets per second from each B-17 or B-24, multiplied by hundreds in their massed formations. But VIII Bomber Command had also suffered diversions to TORCH.

These factors kept the arrival of fighter pilots, bomber crew, and support personnel to the United Kingdom throughout the first year of aerial warfare for the Army Air Forces in Europe at a trickle. As American training facilities geared up for total war, crews began to arrive in England to join with the slowly mounting strategic bombing effort of 1942–1943 against the German-held continent of Europe. This effort faced three great challenges, any of which could mean failure for the daylight campaign. First was quantity of aircraft. Ira Eaker, after he succeeded Carl Spaatz as commanding general of Eighth Air Force late in 1942, determined he would need 250 heavy bombers per mission to penetrate German air space successfully. He was not able to launch such a large force until 29 May 1943—the buildup, because of diversions, was excruciatingly slow. Indeed, Eaker felt diversions were a greater danger to the bombing offensive than the Luftwaffe.[6] The second challenge was the sheer size of the task. The German aircraft industry, prime target of the offensive, was an immense, complex sector of the German war economy. The Luftwaffe would not suffer from an actual aircraft production diminution until 1945. The third challenge was the Luftwaffe itself, which the Army Air Forces would have to defeat in battle to permit the strategic bombing calculated to pave the way for the invasion of Western Europe.

The general officers initially assigned the duty of achieving air superiority were Eaker and Frank O'D. Hunter. Eaker was born in Field Creek, Texas, in 1896, 7 years before the dawning of manned, controlled, powered flight. After graduation with a B.S. in science, he joined the Army in 1917, serving first in the infantry before transferring to the Air Service. He did not see combat in World War I. Eaker rose slowly in the ranks, relying on his own skills as a pilot and especially on his skills as a writer and unofficial public relations man for the Army's air arm. In 1933 he earned a bachelor's degree in journalism at the University of Southern California. During the interwar period he participated in several "firsts" in aviation, including the record-breaking endurance flight of the *Question Mark* in 1929, with a crew that included Carl Spaatz. Influenced by a year at the Air Corps Tactical School, he wrote two books on air power with his close friend Henry H. Arnold, who did not have a stint at the Maxwell Field facility.[7] Promoted to brigadier general on 17 January 1942, Eaker was sent by Air Corps chief Arnold to England to prepare the way for Eighth Air Force. Although he came to the Eighth from service in fighters, Eaker took charge of VIII Bomber Command. Arnold wanted him to inject the aggressive spirit of the fighter into his bombers. Promoted to major general, Ira Eaker became the commander of Eighth Air Force on 1 December 1942 when Spaatz moved to the Mediterranean in order to command American air units in North Africa.[8]

Frank O'D. Hunter was born in 1894 in Savannah, Georgia. Selling stocks and bonds in New York when the United States entered World War I, he joined the Army Aviation Section in 1917, shooting down eight enemy aircraft while flying with the 94th Aero Squadron. A "handsome, swashbuckling" playboy who liked "snappy" clothes and cars, "cocktail parties, women, and fishing," and handlebar mustaches, "Monk" Hunter was in France in 1940 as assistant military attaché. Evading advancing German forces at the last minute, he observed the Battle of Britain firsthand. Promoted to brigadier general on 20 April 1942, he took charge of VIII Fighter Command on 17 May 1942.[9]

But it was the activities of VIII Bomber Command under the three officers who successively commanded it during the early period—Eaker, the least able Newton Longfellow, and the great bomber strategist Frederick L. Anderson—that drew the most attention. Throughout the period of early Eighth Air Force operations, the Army Air Forces constantly upgraded the B-17 to maintain its currency. Many of these modifications involved attempts to increase forward firepower and armor for the crews. The single .50-caliber machine guns mounted on either side of the nose of the initial B-17E and F models proved inadequate in combat and difficult to aim. Early in 1943 Eighth Air Force added twin .50s to the B-17's nose, mounted over the Norden bombsight, but by spring dropped them in favor of a single .50 because of poor azimuth travel and handling. The problem of forward fire would not be adequately solved until the addition of a Bendix chin turret mounting two .50-caliber machine guns in the late spring and early summer of 1943, bringing armament to a formidable thirteen .50-caliber machine guns in the B-17G.[10]

Other modifications were less noticeable. The Army Air Forces ordered both waist guns moved out to a position nearly level with the fuselage to extend their field of fire and increased their ammunition supply from 200 rounds to 600 rounds each. It installed plexiglass windows to prevent frostbite for these gunners. The tail position received a new optical gunsight. Nine auxiliary gas tanks ("Tokyo Tanks") installed in the wing tips increased range. The rate of crew casualties made necessary the addition of 14 millimeters of armor plate to the instrument panel, to the navigator/bombardier floor, pilot's compartment, and waist gun positions. Crews began wearing light flak suits consisting of a steel helmet and steel strips in a flexible canvas apron. Finally, in late 1943 and early 1944, Eighth Air Force removed the 14mm armor plate to save weight and replaced it with hanging flak curtains using elasticity to absorb the impact of flak shrapnel.[11]

The result was a heavily armed bomber with gunners scanning all areas of the sky, which was divided into quadrants each designated by an hour of a clock according to whether it was above or below or level with an aircraft (12 o'clock high, 6 o'clock low, etc.), the "hour" position of a threatening enemy fighter called out over the intercom as a quick and handy way of pinpointing an attacker. The Eighth organized its bombers into formations designed to bring the greatest amount of defensive fire to bear against enemy attackers. Such formations had the disadvantage of disposing individual bombers in a poor position for precision bombing and making formation maneuvering difficult.[12]

From the first VIII Bomber Command heavy bomber mission of 17 August 1942 until the suspension of deep penetration raids into Germany in October 1943, the Eighth experimented with different formations, discarding this one, altering that one, in an effort to strike some sort of balance between defense and offense and in reaction to changing enemy tactics. The initial six-plane squadron formations, flying several miles apart, were adequate so long as they flew within range of Royal Air Force Spitfire escorts, but changes had to be made when strikes against German submarine pens in France in September took them beyond the range of the escort fighters. What ensued was a variety of aircraft clusters: "vees" on line; Javelin with a lead element and two others above and below in column; Five Group Wedge with a lead group in the center, two groups above and stacked in echelon, and two groups below stacked in the opposite direction. The size of these various formations was and continued to be limited by available aircraft until the spring of 1943. They also had problems of thin firepower at one place or another, being strung out, or blocked fields of fire. Compressed or tight clusters had better mutual fire support and were more easily controlled with less straggling, but these took longer to assemble and were more vulnerable to flak. Bombing improved with tighter formations, but there was always the risk of a bomb or bombs from one plane above striking another below.[13] These were the risks of combat, but much of what was learned here could not be taught in training until transmitted from experience gained the hard way.

Training, in fact, came under criticism from some of the first group commanders to serve with the Eighth. Colonel Charles B. Overacker, who had commanded one of the B-17 groups, the 306th, to remain with the Eighth, told a member of the Air Staff in a debriefing session in Washington in March 1943 that inadequate training caused aircraft to bomb poorly in the attacks on the sub pens. "We didn't have the proper training," he claimed. "I know this is true in the case of the combat crews we received as late as December." These crews, of course, were in part composed of members from the training classes of 1941–1942, later so touted by Lt. Col. J. M. McAuliff. Overacker also complained that additional training in England was virtually impossible because of bad weather, limited air space, and the lack of bombing and gunnery ranges. When informed of his remarks, Eaker, who had removed Overacker from his command of the 306th Group, commented that the colonel had lacked the "stamina for the hardships and rigors of war" and was "broken mentally by the experience." Overacker was not far off the mark, however, and the Army Air Forces soon confined training mainly to the continental United States and based it on experience gained in battle.[14]

Yet, in spite of problems with training and formations, and rising casualty figures, the idea continued to prevail that the heavy bomber could "penetrate existing German defenses to the limit of their radius of operations without excessive losses."[15]

The other force engaging the Luftwaffe, VIII Fighter Command, was having its own difficulties, some similar, some different. Its major problem was acquiring an air superiority role. The bombers never had such an identity problem. They were to fight their way

GRAND FORKS PUBLIC LIBRARY

through enemy defenses and drop bombs on the sources of the enemy's ability to wage war.[16] The purpose of the fighters was to intercept enemy attackers before they could do damage to bases in England and to engage enemy fighters to gain air superiority over the continent. The Royal Air Force's Fighter Command had been doing a superb job of the former for 2 years before the American arrival. The trouble with the latter function was getting the enemy to fight.

The World War I notion of dogfighting ("swirling jousts" or "furballs" of group-size formations over the battlefield)[17] to achieve air superiority would not be the style of this war. There would be no battlefield over which to gain air superiority until June 1944. Lacking the range to provide escort beyond Paris, Allied fighters concentrated on defensive operations and on brief forays into France in search of at least fleeting combat with German fighters. Underequipped German forces in France, Belgium, and Holland were under orders to fight a defensive war, while the bulk of the Luftwaffe fought its essentially ground support war in the Soviet Union and the Mediterranean. The Germans would therefore limit air-to-air combat, the kind that the Allies hoped would help win air superiority, to a few engagements where the defense would have the advantage. Combat would be brief and fleeting—evidence indicated that 90 percent of all aircraft shot down never saw their enemy.[18] Some special inducement was needed to bring Luftwaffe day fighters up in force.

The air space over Europe had to be made sufficiently valuable to make it worth fighting for. In time it became obvious that the battle for air superiority would be fought in the vicinity of the bomber formations. Curiously, however, the struggle did not begin there for VIII Fighter Command. In 1942 and early 1943, dictated by the sizes of the forces available, the Royal Air Force provided short-range escort for American bombers, while VIII Fighter Command flew shallow sweeps into France and the Low Countries, attempting to bring Luftwaffe fighters into battle while building up its strength and experience.

Beginning on 8 April 1943,[19] VIII Fighter Command would rely on the Republic P-47 exclusively for the next 6 months, until P-38s and North American P-51s appeared late in 1943. Deficient in climbing ability and speed, the P-47 would rely on the firepower of its eight .50-caliber machine guns, its ruggedness, and its outstanding diving ability to compete with German fighters. It would only barely hold its own against the Luftwaffe, however, until the latter force began to concentrate on American bombers, giving the P-47 the advantage of being able to attack without being attacked itself. The addition of a paddle-blade propeller and water injection would later improve the P-47's performance substantially. In any case, its lack of range in the meantime would limit its impact through the spring and summer of 1943.

These early months were a period of trials as Eighth Air Force felt its way into its mission. The first Eighth Air Force heavy bomber mission (twelve B-17s of the 97th Bomb Group) came on 17 August 1942 to the Rouen-Sotteville area under heavy Royal Air Force Fighter Command escort. While Eaker, who flew on that mission, soon came to believe his bombers were destroying the sources of German power, the Royal Air Force believed that a more restricted objective, that of attriting the Luftwaffe, was the likeliest possible outcome of these early daylight missions. The bombers were along to attract German fighters, which explains why the Royal Air Force would typically launch 400 or more fighters to accompany several dozen American bombers. The initial Allied agreement covering fighter escort for American bombers called for the Royal Air Force to provide all escort with American fighter reinforcements until sufficient Army Air Forces fighters were in England. Eighth Air Force would then take responsibility for escort duties, freeing British fighters for sweeps and withdrawal coverage. Eventually the Eighth was to assume all responsibilities, but be able to call on the Royal Air Force for assistance when operational conditions required.[20]

In the meantime, VIII Fighter Command was free to carry out prewar fighter doctrine: shallow sweeps into conquered Europe to seek out the Luftwaffe. The first mission (by the 31st Fighter Group), a joint British-American fighter sweep on 26 July 1942, set the tone for VIII Fighter Command operations for the next 6 months.[21] After 2 months of such on-the-job training, three groups transferred to North Africa, leaving the 4th Fighter Group as the only Eighth Air Force fighter group from October 1942 until the first missions of the 56th and 78th Fighter Groups in April 1943.

Yet it was not wasted isolation. VIII Fighter Command used the Fourth to refine the tactics of fighter air-to-air combat learned from the British. These included the Circus, a large-scale combined fighter and bomber operation intended to bring Luftwaffe interceptors into action. The Circuses included a powerful fighter force with a small bomber force. This was the essence of offensive, air superiority combat. The Ramrod was its counterpart, using fighters to escort large bomber formations with the principle aim of destroying a ground target through bombing. The fighters were along to defend the bombers and not to engage enemy aircraft unless absolutely necessary—the antithesis of air superiority warfare. Missions also took the form of Rodeos, the most numerous type flown by the Fourth, which were offensive sweeps without accompanying bombers, and Rhubarbs, which were small-scale harassing operations against ground targets.[22]

Unfortunately an unproductive pattern set in—uneventful sweeps with few losses, but also with few claims of enemy aircraft destroyed. Squadron and group unit histories told an uneventful tale. "Our casualties nil. Enemy casualties nil." "Jerry is apparently in hiding." "More convoy work and it's pretty dull." "Nothing to report." The 335th Squadron historian summed up the frustration that not only the 4th Fighter Group but the Eighth Air Force high command was experiencing: "An uneventful sweep to Rouen today. With all our sweeps, France should be a tidy place soon." On the few occasions where combat was possible, VIII Fighter Command ordered its pilots to avoid action if Luftwaffe fighters had an altitude or numerical advantage and to avoid going to the deck.[23]

With this atmosphere surrounding early fighter operations, it is understandable why after nearly 9 months of operation, VIII Fighter Command could claim only fifteen Luftwaffe fighters as destroyed, against losses of seventeen, hardly enough action to inspire the offensive spirit needed to win air superiority.

Nevertheless, the VIII Fighter Command learned lessons for the future. These lessons became the clichés, almost homilies, which thousands of American fighter pilots committed to memory during the war:

Beware of the Hun in the sun. Always turn into an attack. Keep your head out of the cockpit. Eye search to the rear nine times to once forward. Wait until you see the whites of his eyes. Fools rush in where angels fear to tread. Altitude gives you the advantage. Know your airplane.[24]

The most valuable lesson learned during this period was that the place to find the Luftwaffe was near the bombers. VIII Fighter Command's Frank O'D. Hunter remained dedicated to the sweep, despite its apparent lack of productivity. One major reason for this conviction was the American experience in North Africa, where the Allies had achieved air superiority through fighter sweeps. Escorts, Hunter felt, were a waste of limited resources.[25] The evidence worked against him, however. Of the fifteen aerial victories claimed by VIII Fighter Command in its first 9 months of operations, eleven came while on its few escort missions.[26] In any case, no effort was made to concentrate on escort duties, for VIII Bomber Command was operating mainly beyond the range of the P-47 in its attacks on German submarine pens in France.

The bombers pursued their objectives alone. Losses, though still relatively low, continued to rise and forced the constant evolution of tactical formations to maximize the firepower of massed bombers. This was especially important in preparation for Eighth Air Force's first penetration into Germany on 27 January 1943 against Wilhelmshaven. Such long missions left the bombers exposed to German fighters for more than 4 hours, seriously challenging the ability of the "self-defending" bombers to defend themselves. On that mission the Eighth lost three of the fifty-five B-17s and 24s credited with sorties, a loss rate of over 5 percent. As before, the only apparent solution until the arrival of long-range fighter escorts was to improve combat formations.

To escape the threat of flak, the Army Air Forces used various tactics, including evasive action, multiple flight paths, and increased altitude. These were the early recommendations of Col. Frank Armstrong, Jr., who was as close as the Army Air Forces had to an expert on flak, having flown the first several bombing missions against flak-defended targets. He predicted that flak would make any mission impossible if the flight path were not altered every 10 seconds over the target. Such maneuvers during the bomb run would have made precision bombing impossible. The newly arrived Col. Curtis LeMay, commander of the 305th Bomb Group, evaluated the threat of these German flak defenses using ballistic charts for French 75mm guns. He calculated that the odds were in favor of the attacking aircraft—a flak gun would have to fire 372 shells to down a high-flying B-17. American formations would from then on fly in formation, straight and level over the target for 10 minutes, to insure the best bombing accuracy possible and the best defense against German fighters. Generally American forces ignored flak, having determined the best defense against it was to get over a target quickly and to saturate flak defenses with large numbers of planes.[27]

That left German fighters as the major threat to Eighth Air Force bombers. LeMay and Brig. Gen. Laurence S. Kuter, commanding general of the 1st Bomb Wing, an alumnus of the Air Corps Tactical School, and a co-author of AWPD-1, coordinated the development of the combat box and wing to maximize firepower and bombing accuracy. Each group formed a combat box of eighteen to twenty-one bombers and three groups then formed into a combat wing. One group flew above and echeloned to one side of the lead group and the other group flew below and echeloned to the other side of the lead group, both flanking groups flying slightly in trail of the lead group.[28] The increased forward firepower and mutually protecting fields of fire more than compensated for the unwieldiness and inaccuracy of bombing from this formation. As the lead group or squadron turned from the initial point to the target, the two flanking units had to fly their own bomb runs, arriving at the target obscured by dust and smoke resulting from the lead unit's strike.

With these lessons and forces at hand, Ira Eaker flew to the Casablanca Conference in January 1943 to make the American case for daylight strategic bombing to a skeptical audience led by British Prime Minister Winston Churchill. One of the arguments he made was that the bombers could defend themselves successfully and that in the process could destroy quantities of German fighters, which would help to pave the way for the cross-Channel invasion. He did not mention American fighters in the battle for air superiority, except as a means to quell British fears that heavy bombers could not reach Germany without heavy losses. Eaker promised the British military chiefs that he would have 240 fighters to accompany his bombers to Germany by 1 March 1943, though he probably knew he would not have that many and those that he did have (P-47s) would lack the range to accompany bombers to Germany.[29] He told the American chief of the Air Staff that his bombers had achieved a 6-to-1 kill ratio against German fighters and could therefore achieve air superiority if the Air Staff sent him the bombers he needed to do the job. He boasted that his bombers were "knocking the ears off the German day fighter," though he based his boast on the dramatically exaggerated claims of Eighth Air Force bomber crews.[30]

In spite of the fact that he had come directly to VIII Bomber Command and Eighth Air Force from a tour in fighters, Eaker remained a bomber man, perhaps influenced by his earlier stint at the Air Corps Tactical School. He believed victory would come only from a strategic bombing campaign. But he also correctly saw that any such campaign and any cross-Channel invasion would depend on defeating the Luftwaffe. He argued that if Eighth Air Force switched to night bombing, as the British advised, then the Allies could not achieve air superiority. Given the performance of American fighters to that time, Eaker had every reason for believing VIII Bomber Command's day bombers were the only Allied means at hand for confronting the Luftwaffe. He played down the escort role for American fighters, but correctly concluded that the Luftwaffe would not challenge American fighters over Europe unless the bombers were present.[31]

Eaker and the Army Air Forces won Allied support for the Eighth's daylight strategic bombing campaign at Casablanca.[32] The Royal Air Force's Bomber Command would strike at Germany by night and VIII Bomber Command by day, "'round the clock." Eaker's presentation at Casablanca impressed Winston Churchill, himself one of the most grandiloquent statesmen in modern history.[33] The Army Air Forces established the Committee of Operations Analysts, a group composed of American industrialists, bankers, and Army Air Forces personnel, which suggested the targets for American bombing. The Committee, like Eaker, understood the importance of reducing the Luftwaffe's strength, but unlike Eaker, pointed to the importance of escort fighters in protecting the bombers. The Committee's report, however, included no specifics about the battle for air superiority. It nonetheless became the basis for the Combined Bomber Offensive, codenamed POINTBLANK, the plan that established priorities and missions for Eighth Air Force for the next year, still influenced by the assumptions of AWPD-1 and 42. Approved by the Combined Chiefs of Staff in May 1943, it set the Luftwaffe as the "intermediate objective second to none in priority." The document reflected Eaker's view that the bombers were the key (it was the Combined BOMBER Offensive). Army Air Forces chief Arnold, however, foreseeing a much expanded role for fighters, appended his opinion: "At all times there is a need for an extensive U.S. fighter force both to protect the bombers and to assist in the reduction of the German fighter strength."[34]

To implement POINTBLANK the Eighth had to fight with less force than was necessary and than had been promised. Its bomber force

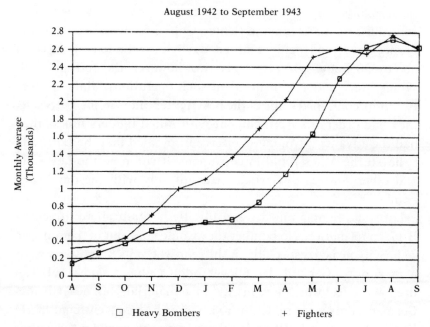

Figure 2. Eighth Air Force Buildup
Source: USSBS, Report No. 2a, Chart 2.

included only six B-17 and 24 groups (91st, 303rd, 305th, 306th, 44th, and 93rd Bomb Groups) and three P-47 groups (4th, 56th, and 78th Fighter Groups). Eaker's continuous plea was "Please rush replacement aircraft and combat crews as fast as you can." Still, there was room for optimism. Losses remained acceptable, the Luftwaffe was bleeding, and new American groups were arriving in England at a quickening rate.[35]

The Army Air Forces based this optimism, however, on a misunderstanding of the activities of the Luftwaffe. It appeared as if Eighth Air Force had little to fear from the Luftwaffe through the spring of 1943. German fighter strength was weak and unorganized because of the decision of the German high command to concentrate its air power on the Eastern and Mediterranean fronts. The Luftwaffe was just beginning to organize day fighter defenses in Germany under the five newly formed fighter divisions loosely controlled by Air Command Center. Only three wings remained in France to defend against Allied daylight incursions, a force of about 330 fighter aircraft. Only two, however, the 2nd and 26th Wings, were actively involved in such operations. Though these two units contained some of the best fighter pilots in the Luftwaffe, they had orders to avoid combat with Allied fighters unless they had the advantage. An ULTRA intercept revealed that the Luftwaffe believed the Allies could force ruinous attrition on the Luftwaffe and other sources of German strength only with the day heavy bomber.[36]

Luftwaffe fighter pilots were initially hesitant about attacking B-17s in formation. No bomber they would confront in the war was so heavily armed, especially in the rear where its firepower was at a maximum. General der Flieger Adolf Galland said the B-17's firepower effect was "more mental than material," but nevertheless German pilots were reluctant to attack. Their conventional tactic had been to attack Allied bombers from the rear. In November 1942 Major Egon Mayer of the 2nd Fighter Wing, the "Abbeville Kids," as the Eighth Air Force knew them, perfected the head-on attack. German fighters would fly a parallel course to an American bomber formation, but beyond the range of the bombers' guns, until they were about 5 kilometers ahead, would turn into the path of the bomber formation, and make a head-on attack at the same level as the bombers. The psychological impact of such attacks on B-17 crews was understandably chilling. They not only had to endure the drawn-out tension from enemy fighters flying parallel for several minutes, but then had the trauma of these planes suddenly turning directly into their faces with guns blazing at a closing rate of over 500 MPH.[37]

This was not Eighth Air Force's only cause for alarm. The effectiveness of German flak increased noticeably, largely because the Luftwaffe ordered flak units from Italy and the Eastern Front back to Germany, organizing two or three batteries into "great batteries" under one controller.[38] The Luftwaffe also established a new fighter wing, the 11th, to defend the Reich along the North Sea coast. Fighters in the 2nd and 26th Fighter Wings near the Channel coast began delaying their attacks until after American and British fighters had turned for home, allowing them to concentrate entirely on the heavy bombers. Most threatening of all, the Luftwaffe began attacking in group strength, overwhelming heavy bomber defensive fire.

These actions, though threats to POINTBLANK, also revealed flaws in the Luftwaffe's defense of the Reich. Lacking lengthy experience in daylight defense, the Germans were forced to improvise in reaction to Army Air Forces pressure. The nature of this improvisation indicated a growing anxiety that German possession of air superiority was truly challenged and a showdown was in the offing. They had become aware that it took group-sized formations to meet the growing mass of heavy bomber firepower, but such formations also involved more time to form up and hence their fighters had less endurance. Galland tried to solve the dilemma with wing tanks, but these impeded the climb to bomber altitude and the idea was abandoned. Early in 1943, even before the inauguration of POINT-BLANK, Galland sensed what was coming and informed Hitler that not only would the Luftwaffe need three or four interceptors to down an unescorted bomber, but should the Americans extend the range of their fighter escort, additional interceptors per bomber would be required. Having ordered an increase in aircraft production in 1942, Hitler was certainly angry and perhaps a bit fearful, but as in the case of the flagging submarine campaign, he did not have the resources to alter the situation. On its current footing, his industry could not produce the suggested numbers.[39]

For the Allies the most detectable German measure was the expansion of its defensive zones along the coast and back into Germany, creating a "defense in depth" against American attacks. By moving back, the Luftwaffe hoped its forces would be beyond the range of American fighters and therefore able to concentrate on the bombers. This occurred, but concurrently, because VIII Fighter Command's planes no longer had to worry about German fighters once they crossed the coast, American fighters could reduce their power settings and thereby gain an increase in range. Like most tactics used by both sides, there were advantages and disadvantages. From initially assigning each group a specific area along a narrow coastal front in 1942, the Luftwaffe developed a unified system of five defensive zones stretching 125 miles inland. Each zone came under the direction of a single controller, a "fighter air leader" (*jafü*), at a fighter command center, and stationed at a fighter division, who was responsible for concentrating all Luftwaffe fighters in that zone against American bomber formations. As the American assault expanded and as the fighter command center network showed promise, the Luftwaffe extended the system back into Germany and Austria, adding two districts to the original five. The fighter command center system by the early summer of 1943 covered a zone up to 480 miles deep. To extend the range of German fighters and to allow aircraft to fly two or more missions per day, the Luftwaffe established auxiliary bases all over western and central Germany with ammunition, fuel, and ground crews to simplify emergency landings and provide a quick turnaround.[40]

German efforts to create new units and to expand pilot training were not up to the challenge of the attrition warfare that the air war in the West was becoming. Because of the tardy effort to expand the Luftwaffe, in the short term it had no choice but to begin withdrawing units from Norway, the Soviet Union, and from the Mediterranean to expand its defenses in the West and in Germany.

Unaware of the troubles the Luftwaffe faced, Ira Eaker's Eighth Air Force continued to develop the combat box formation as more bomber groups arrived. Eaker remained committed to the heavy bomber: "There is still not the slightest question but that we can continue effective daylight bombing with large well-flown formations at a loss ratio of 5% or less." He felt the newly arrived P-47 was a match for the FW 190, but remained convinced, as most were at the time, that fighters lacked the range to accompany bombers on long-range missions.[41]

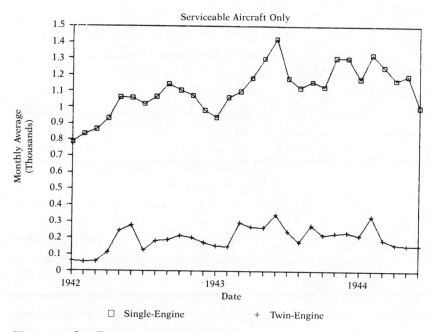

Figure 3. Luftwaffe Fighter Order of Battle
Source: Quartermaster General, German Air Ministry, "Luftwaffe Strength and Serviceability Tables," August 1938–August 1945, File K512.621 VII/107, HRC.

"Monk" Hunter continued to rely on independent fighter sweeps. He told Eaker the P-47 was not an effective close-escort fighter and was unwilling to send his P-47s to the limit of their range until he had the aircraft to neutralize the Luftwaffe "by sheer weight of numerical superiority."[42] Eaker, for his part, made no effort to change VIII Fighter Command policy, despite the Luftwaffe's continued avoidance of combat with Hunter's fighters to the end of the summer of 1943. Mission report after mission report contained the same observation: "Nothing was encountered. No bandits sighted. Nothing was seen except a smoke screen." Sometimes the frustration was worse: "Many Huns were scared into the sky, but none attacked our planes." More often, however, the message was "No enemy aircraft seen."[43]

Bare statistics showed the need for a change in tactics. By May

1943, the heavy bombers of Eighth Air Force were experiencing losses averaging 1.6 percent when under complete fighter escort, but 7 percent without escort. Eleven of VIII Fighter Command's fifteen claimed victories had come during bomber escort missions, which comprised fewer than 10 percent of all missions flown.[44] Eaker decided as a result to shift VIII Fighter Command tactics to close escort in the summer of 1943.

Until that time, the U.S. Army Air Forces in Europe had learned many lessons and had some significant accomplishments to their credit. For the VIII Bomber Command, it had successfully committed the B-17 and B-24 to battle; the Luftwaffe had been unable to turn back a single heavy bomber mission. With its refined combat formations, the Eighth was ready to begin the struggle for air superiority. VIII Fighter Command was still a long way from making a significant contribution to this effort but, with more planes and pilots and a new mission, seemed headed in that direction. Perhaps the best measure of the Eighth's success through the early summer of 1943 was its impact on the Luftwaffe. Eighth Air Force had forced the German high command both to withdraw fighter units from other theaters to defend the Reich and to form larger formations with more heavily armed fighters, thus reducing their efficiency against American fighters.

Defeated in North Africa and at Stalingrad, the Germans were now clearly on the defensive. The urgent construction of defenses along the English Channel in expectation of an invasion and the production priority for fighters over bombers to cope with the American campaign to wrestle away air superiority were German acknowledgments of that reality.[45]

Yet despite its training and other problems, German defenses were increasingly efficient, so the size of Eighth's bomber force alone (by September nine more bomber groups had arrived) would not achieve air superiority without rising losses. Through the fall of 1943 the P-47 lacked the range to accompany the heavy bombers into Germany. The solution seemed obvious: to improve the firepower of the heavy bombers while working to extend the range of

American fighters. The former revolved around an old idea—the battle cruiser aircraft or bomber-destroyer (Douhet's battleplane). Because the conventional wisdom held that a fighter aircraft could not have the range of a bomber and still maintain superior speed and maneuverability, the Army Air Forces concentrated on using existing bombers. The scheme was to equip B-17s and B-24s with extra armor and augment their defensive firepower to serve as flying antiaircraft batteries.[46] The program began in June 1941 at the Army Air Forces Materiel Center at Dayton, Ohio, as part of a broad investigation to improve escort protection for American bomber formations. After Pearl Harbor the Center determined that the B-17 was the most promising aircraft for conversion and contracted in January 1942 with Vega Aircraft Corporation for the design and conversion of a B-17F into an XB-40 battle cruiser. Initial tests indicated the practicality of the aircraft and in the fall the Army Air Forces ordered thirteen converted B-17Fs from the Douglas Tulsa Modification Center.[47] Testing at Eglin Field showed promise and resulted in a contract for Douglas to produce two YB-40s per month (the YB-40 was the production designation of the experimental XB-40).

The original design called for a Bendix turret with two .50-caliber machine guns in the chin position, a Martin turret with two .50-caliber machine guns in the radio compartment, and two .50-caliber machine guns in the waist positions added to the standard armament of the B-17, with reserve storage for some 8,000 rounds of ammunition. Over a ton of armor plate protected the crew and the engines. To make room for these additions, Vega removed the bombsight and bomb-dropping equipment.

In early May 1943 Arnold ordered all thirteen YB-40s to the 327th Bomb Squadron of the 92nd Bomb Group in England for operational testing. In England Eighth Air Force added two more .50-caliber machine guns to the nose. VIII Bomber Command at first positioned the YB-40s in the "coffin corner" of its combat boxes, later ordering them used to escort the aircraft of the lead bombardier in each combat box. The results were not promising.

Crew morale suffered because YB-40s experienced the same dangers as regular bombers, but had no bombs to climax the perilous journey. Their additional firepower seemed impressive when compared with a standard B-17, but when compared to a combat box of B-17s the increase in firepower was negligible. The YB-40 had different flight characteristics. It was slower and forced the formation to throttle back. It was no solution to the escort problem.[48]

The entire YB-40 project cost the American taxpayer $9 million for twenty-five aircraft, including the cost of the converted B-17s. The project was not an absolute loss, however, because Eighth Air Force found the Bendix nose turret of the YB-40 to be the answer to the increasingly numerous frontal assaults of the Luftwaffe. At Eaker's request, Air Staff chief Barney Giles gave production priority to equipping all new B-17Gs going to Eighth Air Force with Bendix nose turrets. Manufacturers complained about the last-minute change in specifications and resulting delay, which cost hundreds of bombers in lost production. Giles's response was appropriate: it was "a hell of a lot better to lose 100 airplanes on the production line, than to lose 100 airplanes from the Eighth Air Force with 10 hand picked officers and men in each airplane." He cabled Eaker, "So much for that—the turrets are coming."[49]

The failure of the battle cruiser left the development of the long-range fighter as the only solution to the escort problem.[50] The quest for greater range for aircraft was a component of the natural evolution of human flight. Part of the process of improved performance was to increase the distance aircraft could fly before refueling. Beginning in the 1920s, American aeronautical engineers tried to extend fighter range by hanging auxiliary fuel tanks from bomb racks. Because such tanks limited maneuverability and speed, builders intended them to be either jettisonable or for ferrying use only. In the 1930s the Aeronautical Revolution's drive for high performance in fighters led designers to incorporate auxiliary fuel tanks inside the aircraft, but succeeded only in placing a severe restriction on aircraft maneuverability. Reflecting this limitation, at the Air Corps Tactical School endurance was deemed the least important characteristic of a fighter aircraft. The tendency of drop tanks to catch fire reinforced this belief and motivated the Air Corps in May 1939 to order tactical planes not to carry such tanks.[51]

With the outbreak of World War II, distances to Europe and a shortage of shipping renewed interest in external tanks.[52] After a meeting on 20 February 1942,[53] Army Air Forces' chief Arnold ordered the all-out development of auxiliary tanks for the P-51, P-38, and P-47 in response to demands from his field commanders and his own growing doubts over the invincibility of the bomber. Progress was slow. Under the pressure of events in Europe, in June 1943 Arnold gave Barney Giles 6 months "to get a fighter that can protect our bombers. Whether you use an existing type or have to start from scratch is your problem. Get to work on this right away because by January '44, I want fighter escort for all of our bombers from U.K. into Germany." Assistant Secretary of War for Air Robert A. Lovett added urgency to Arnold's demands in June after an investigative trip to England revealed the need for long-range escort.[54]

As in most cases of technological advances, conventional wisdom was a stubborn barrier: "No fighter plane can be designed to escort heavy and medium bombardment to their extreme tactical radius of action and there engage in offensive combat with enemy interceptor fighter types on equal terms. In order to have the range and speed of the aircraft it accompanies [the fighter escort] may be as large and at least as expensive as such aircraft."[55] The British gave up on extended range in favor of short-range high-performance fighters. The Germans had twin-engine fighters large enough to carry sufficient fuel to accompany bombers, but at the cost of poor fighter performance. In the American case common wisdom had delayed the eventual development of the long-range fighter and was, according to the official historians of the Army Air Forces in World War II, "the most serious flaw in the Army Air Forces' program."[56]

By 1943 the Army Air Forces was committed to extending range and performance. In the words of the Pursuit Project Officer, the technology was based on

efficiency (the ratio of lift to drag) and the percentage of the gross weight devoted to fuel. Consequently, the effort to reduce drag to attain high speed also improved basic efficiency. By overloading the maneuverable fighter, the heavier structure and power for maneuvering in combat became a smaller portion of the total weight, and the increased fuel raised the percentage of the total new weight to approximate that of bombers.[57]

Combat experience proved that external tanks would have to be dropped before combat, which meant a fighter aircraft would have to be able to return to home base on internal fuel. For the P-51 and P-38 Maj. Gen. Barney Giles[58] and Maj. Gen. William Kepner, commander of the stateside Fourth Air Force, and James H. "Dutch" Kindelberger and Clarence L. Johnson at North American and Lockheed, respectively, worked to increase internal fuel storage. They gave the P-51 an 85-gallon self-sealing fuselage tank, raising total internal capacity to 265 gallons. Additional tanks in the leading-edge of P-38 wings gave the P-38 an additional 120 gallons, raising its total internal capacity to 420 gallons. When combined with jettisonable external tanks, the P-38 and P-51 gained the range necessary to accompany B-17s and B-24s to the limits of bomber endurance. Testing and adjustments delayed production until Giles ordered Brig. Gen. B. W. Chidlaw, chief of the Material Division, on 9 September to eliminate all service tests and expedite the range extension project.[59] By the time of the critical battles for air superiority in early 1944, the resulting increases in fighter range were impressive.

The major problem in the meanwhile was the availability of external tanks. In January 1943 the Army Air Forces had attempted to contract with British firms for the drop tanks, but the Ministry of Aircraft Production claimed such production was beyond British means. Eighth Air Force ordered 60,000 metal 200-gallon tanks from the United States in February. The Ministry of Aircraft Pro-

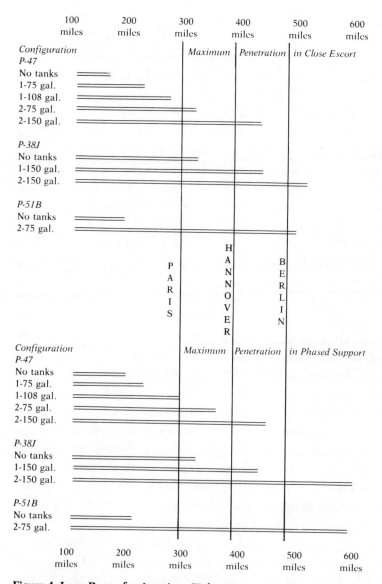

Figure 4. Long-Range for American Fighters
Source: VIII Fighter Command, "Achtung Indianer," 24 July 1944, File 168.6005-54, Plate xii, HRC.

duction gave way to American pressure and agreed in March to produce them. Eighth Air Force commander Ira Eaker, however, assigned the project only a number 4 priority. Additional delays resulted from shortages of steel in England. In June tests indicated the superiority of British-manufactured 108-gallon paper tanks, which Hunter of VIII Fighter Command approved for purchase on 1 July 1943. Anticipating British production, he and Eaker requested that all new American tank production be cancelled. Eaker's failure to give the British Ministry of Aircraft Production a clear order for large-scale tank production until the first week in October caused additional delays. Total British production of the essential 108-gallon tank amounted to only 7,554 units in 1943. In the fall of 1943, VIII Fighter Command had to rely on American stocks shipped to England at great cost and at great delay.[60] Tanks were "borrowed, begged, stolen, and improvised."[61]

Before the fighter range extension program produced results, Eighth Air Force had only the "self-defending bomber" and what escort the short-range P-47 could provide. Despite the Combined Bomber Offensive's injunction in May 1943 that "at all times there is a need for an extensive U.S. fighter force both to protect the bombers and to assist in the reduction of the German fighter strength," conventional wisdom and unnecessary delays contributed to a serious crisis in the American daylight POINTBLANK offensive.[62] From April to June 1943 only 37 percent of the missions flown by American P-47 fighter groups were escort for heavy bombers. Half were generally "Monk" Hunter's favorite, unproductive fighter sweeps. Bomber losses were rising: from 3.5 percent in 1942 to 5.8 and 6.5 percent in the first and second quarters of 1943. With escort, loss rates were 1.6 percent for the total period. By the summer of 1943 losses were seven times greater without escort than with. A postwar interrogation of Adolf Galland revealed that before effective escort his fighters averaged a loss of one fighter for every American heavy bomber they claimed. After the initiation of effective escort, the Luftwaffe lost two or three fighters for each heavy bomber shot down.[63]

VIII Fighter Command continued other missions, but generally after 4 May 1943 its primary function was to provide escort for VIII Bomber Command formations, Eaker now having some notion that perhaps bombers could not do it alone. Although Luftwaffe day interceptors would occasionally depart from their habit of not engaging American fighters on sweeps, the bombers usually had to be present to do damage to ground targets for the Luftwaffe to rise automatically and challenge the attackers. The symbiotic relationship of Eighth Air Force fighters and bombers ("Big Friends and Little Friends") became fixed in the summer of 1943. Not only did bomber losses drop under escort, but fighter claims nearly quintupled while escorting heavy bombers.

Initially fighter escort was of the "umbrella" type, patterned after the Royal Air Force practice of placing escort above the bombers. This tactic had been born of necessity while British fighters were escorting Wellington bombers, which lacked overhead firepower. But when Luftwaffe fighters began concentrating their attacks on American heavy bombers from the side and the front, at the same level of the bombers, bomber crews demanded that fighters fly close escort, generally within 50 to 75 feet beside and in front of bomber formations. In this "Spread V" formation, fighters had to limit their speed to stay close to the bombers, putting themselves in a vulnerable position when German fighters appeared. By July 1943, however, Eighth Air Force ordered escort "opened up somewhat," because close escort had covered up some of the defensive machine guns of the heavy bombers. With this limited flexibility, VIII Fighter Command began the practice of weaving in order to maintain combat speeds and yet still stay near the slower bombers. Fighter escort range was so limited that VIII Fighter Command had to order its groups to avoid German fighters while on the way to rendezvous with bomber formations. The latter restriction allowed the Germans to form up and approach without impediment and the weaving tactic would limit the protection American fighters could provide for American heavy bombers to fewer than 30 minutes. Both severely restricted VIII Fighter Command's contribution to winning air superiority.[64]

On escort missions the Combat Operations Section of VIII

Fighter Command controlled fighter operations through fighter radio channel A. Eighth Air Force assigned fighter radio channel C for fighter-heavy bomber intercom to insure close cooperation between the Little Friends and the Big Friends.[65] Groups flew with their squadrons arranged to provide top, front, and side cover. Within squadron units, Training Command had trained its fighter pilots to fly in three-ship "V" formations, but Eighth Air Force adopted the battle-tested Royal Air Force two-ship formation consisting of a leader and a wingman and this battle wisdom was soon imparted to stateside training.[66]

Because of limited P-47 resources, Eighth Air Force also compressed its combat wing formations of fifty-four bombers to reduce the area fighter escort would have to protect. It tucked in the high and low squadrons, reversing the echelon of previous formations. Another advantage of the new combat wing formation was the uncovering of more bomber defensive machine guns. The disadvantage was the increased difficulty of maintaining formation and the increased vulnerability of stragglers.[67]

With these improved bomber tactics and this fledgling but expanded escort, Eighth Air Force intensified its attacks on targets in Germany during the summer of 1943. It concentrated mainly on Luftwaffe-related targets, including airfields and aircraft manufacturing plants. This was in keeping with the Combined Chiefs of Staff's POINTBLANK directive that made the Luftwaffe the "*intermediate* objective second to none in priority."[68] The Blitz Week missions of 24-30 July best typified these raids. On 6 days out of a week over 1,000 Eighth Air Force bombers struck at some fifteen targets all over Germany. Impressive was the number of bombs dropped and the damage wrought. American claims totaled 330 German fighters downed. If accurate, air superiority would have been nearly at hand. American losses, however, suggested that Eighth Air Force was a long way from achieving aerial domination over the Luftwaffe. Despite the first two instances of P-47s using drop tanks to extend their escort range into Germany, on the missions of 28 and 30 July, the week's missions had cost the Army Air

Forces ninety-seven aircraft—a loss rate for the week of 10 percent. Losses were exceeding the rate of replacement. Worse, there were no signs of a weakened Luftwaffe. American claims were obviously exaggerated. Eighth Air Force would have to recuperate for 2 weeks before returning to the skies over Germany.

The new commander of the VIII Bomber Command beginning 1 July 1943, Frederick L. Anderson, had been upbeat about the potential of American strategic bombardment before the Blitz Week attacks. "The VIII Bomber Command is destroying and will continue to destroy the economic resources of Germany to such an extent that I personally believe no invasion of the Continent or Germany proper will ever have to take place, with the consequent loss of thousands and possibly millions of lives . . . This Bomber Command will be the greatest striking force the world has ever known." The sobering effect of the Blitz Week effort, however, brought home the importance of air superiority to Anderson. His somber assessment of the condition of his command stands as a watershed in the gradual recognition by top officials of the Army Air Forces of the importance of air superiority to the Allied war effort. As a result of the July losses, Anderson believed that VIII Bomber Command was now capable of no more than five "full-out missions against Germany." He told Ira Eaker that he "should be well aware of the critical situation on replacements facing us."[69]

Evidently the Blitz Week attacks also had a sobering effect on the Luftwaffe. On 28 July 1943, during a meeting to evaluate the damage Germany had suffered, Göring ordered Milch to give the defense of the Reich the "main emphasis" in Luftwaffe planning. This order was less significant than at first apparent because in actual experience if not policy the defense of the Reich had been receiving priority since the spring. The 28 July decision was perhaps more of a reflection of the failure of a Luftwaffe organizational change begun on 10 June 1943. Göring had ordered an expansion of the strength of German squadrons from twelve to sixteen aircraft as a way of increasing the size of forces defending the Reich. Blitz Week demonstrated the failure of the effort. Operational strength did not increase because no contingency was made to increase the number of service personnel. More pilots and planes were available, but the squadron aircraft operational rate dropped to 58 percent.[70]

Combat fatigue had been a negligible factor when viewed with the other problems the Eighth faced, but the intensification of attacks during the summer of 1943 forced commanders to begin paying attention to the anxieties and morale of their flying personnel. Flight surgeons discovered, to their surprise, that weather and mechanical problems had as much impact on the mental competence of their patients as enemy defenses. After Blitz Week, 80 percent of Eighth Air Force flight surgeons reported "undue fatigue" among their charges, 16 percent reported an increase in ordinary illnesses, 68 percent reported crew weight losses, and 67 percent reported that four successive days of flying was the limit of operational effectiveness.

These flight surgeons were able to identify three distinct phases in the tours of bomber crews. The first ten missions were the most difficult for the fliers, typified by extreme anxiety based on fears of the unknown. Reports of airmen fainting during operations were at their peak during this period. A sense of hopelessness was the common complaint. Cases of "combat neurosis" usually developed during the first five missions.

After the initial period flying personnel reached a "period of stability." Those unable to deal with the ardors of combat had been removed from combat and the remaining fliers adapted to the routine and familiarity of operations, founded on the recognition that they were part of a crew and not alone. This "team spirit" was the most important factor in fighting combat anxiety. An additional factor was the tendency of personnel to report "blacking out" while under enemy attack—doing their jobs, but remembering nothing. Returning crews reported little panic, paralysis, or confusion during these times. Everyone did as they were trained, despite the danger. Medical observation indicated that nervousness was highest during the briefings before missions. The regularity of flying helped to calm crews upon takeoff. Combat served to relieve tension.

Nevertheless anxiety continued as a problem during this second phase, manifested in irritability, nervousness, insomnia, and temper outbursts. This irritability was most clearly identifiable in the increased use of profanity, "almost entirely based on excretory products and transactions." Crews turned to the excessive use of tobacco and alcohol as an escape. Weight loss was common.

During the last ten missions, fatigue, nervousness, and irritability reached a maximum. Flight surgeons recorded dangerously decreased appetites verging on anorexia and inability to sleep. According to a flight surgeon who flew the requisite twenty-five missions, the force that drove the crews to complete their required number of combat missions was "the burning desire to complete the combat tour with a respite . . . far from the rigorous routine and the perils of combat flying." During the first year of operations, only 29 percent of officers completing their twenty-five missions reported that hatred of the enemy drove them to finish their tours.

The "burning desire" was evidently quite strong: of only seventy-four forced reclassifications among officer flying personnel in Eighth Air Force from May 1943 to August 1944, fourteen were due to stress, twenty-two to selection failures, and thirty-eight to insecurity. All but one reclassification came during the first ten missions.

Emotional disorders were never "a threat to operational activity." During the entire war, including officers and enlisted men, the Eighth Air Force Central Medical Board reported 2,102 "emotional casualties" among heavy bomber crewmen, many of whom eventually returned to duty. The board discovered also that the number of cases was directly proportional to the number of aircraft lost during action. "Emotional casualties" were not concentrated in any particular flying job: 49.5 percent were pilots and co-pilots, 26.9 percent bombardiers, and 23.3 percent navigators.[71]

In the midst of the horrors of combat and the accelerating

daylight air battles over the continent there came to England in July 1943 some troops requisitioned a year before. They would not fly aircraft in combat—the law forbade it. They were the officers and enlisted women of the Women's Auxiliary Army Corps, soon to be fully militarized as the Women's Army Corps (WAC). Some of the members of this female battalion, which was under the command of Capt. Mary A. Hallaren, served in various headquarters-level positions in Eighth Air Force. One of the enlisted WACs, Mary Gill, for example, became the personal secretary of Maj. Gen. Frederick Anderson of VIII Bomber Command. Most served as secretaries and clerks. Some of the WACs, however, came to occupy slots not considered traditionally "feminine." General Eaker prized their work in intelligence, decoding, and, especially, interpreting photographs. Others became weather observers and forecasters. A few were mechanics, some were aircraft warning and mission plotters and tellers; but whatever each WAC did, it was exhilarating to be even that close to the air battles.[72]

By the end of the summer Arnold and other leaders in Washington were apparently exasperated with the performance of the Eighth. In the late spring of 1943 Arnold's staff had determined that the "self-defending" bomber was incapable of defending itself against German attacks. Combat formations, YB-40s, and increased firepower were only interim and partial or failed solutions. The key to continuing the strategic bomber offensive was fighter escort and yet Eighth Air Force showed little sense of urgency in this regard. The Air Corps Tactical School's successor, the Army Air Forces School of Applied Tactics at Orlando, Florida, was teaching its students that escort was essential to successful bombardment as early as March 1943, while Eaker and Hunter were at that point still committed to unescorted bomber formations and fighter sweeps.[73]

Eaker as late as October 1943 still believed the key was in the size of the bomber formations. He told Carl Spaatz that 300 was the magic number. The great firepower of these massed bombers would prevent "excessive or uneconomical loss." Eaker stuck to this belief while high-ranking officers such as Chief of the Air Staff Barney Giles and commander of the VIII Bomber Command Fred Anderson had determined that escort was the key to victory. Major General Jimmy Doolittle in North Africa, commanding the Northwest African Strategic Air Force, told Arnold in May 1943 that fighter escort was "critical" to the continued success of bombardment, if for no other reason than the Luftwaffe was arming its planes with cannon, which would allow it to fire at American bombers from beyond the range of bomber .50-caliber machine guns.[74]

Eaker and Arnold were prewar friends and evidently this restrained Arnold from pressing Eaker too hard on the issue for a time. But other members of the Air Staff urged Arnold to increase his pressure: "fighters are not escorting our heavy bombardment to the full extent of their capabilities . . . Fighters to date have given them no real support . . . the Fighter Command in U.K. must be made aware of this fact that it is not fully executing its mission."[75] Arnold's June cable to his old friend in response to this encouragement did not equivocate.

"Of grave concern to me is the employment of your fighters [emphasis in original]. I cannot comprehend what value is derived from the frequently reported so-called offensive fighter sweeps in which the enemy is rarely sighted. Except as a means of consuming gasoline I can see no purpose in this practice . . . I can't help but compare the excellent results accomplished with the P-38, an airplane with small internal tankage, and the meager results accomplished by your Fighter Command equipped with our best high altitude escort fighters [P-47s] . . . I feel that a vigorous escort can successfully be accomplished if the fighters are less cautious. Higher fighter combat losses than those now reported may result from this policy but will be more than offset by reduced bomber losses . . . give this subject your personal attention."[76]

Throughout the war fighter losses had trailed significantly behind those of the heavy bombers. Arnold was aware of this fact. He had read the operational narratives Eaker had sent him: on 15 August, 373 P-47s swept France and Belgium but claimed no results; 95

P-47s on a sweep on 4 September saw no German aircraft, while Royal Air Force Spitfires escorting B-26s claimed 19 Luftwaffe aircraft; and 395 P-47s flying sweeps and diversions on 22 September claimed only 2 enemy aircraft. On 27 September while escorting 3 combat wings to Emden, 262 P-47s claimed 21 enemy fighters.[77] In his cable Arnold proposed without ordering that the fighters should cut their power and fly slower to extend their range. Such tactics would make them more vulnerable, but Arnold saw low fighter-loss rates as evidence that they were not taking necessary chances. Neither Eaker nor Hunter heeded the suggestion. In hindsight, the fighters would not have been much more vulnerable because the Luftwaffe was concentrating on the bombers. But even if a reduction in power would have allowed better escort for bomber formations, whether sacrificing additional fighters for the sake of reduced bomber losses would have won air superiority for the Army Air Forces earlier is a matter only of speculation.

Unfortunately Eaker did not know of the shock his P-47s with drop tanks had caused the Luftwaffe. General der Flieger Galland had a special meeting with Göring and Hitler to inform them that American fighters were now appearing over Germany. Some, he said, had been shot down. Göring refused to believe it, claiming the P-47s must have glided into Germany after being hit.[78]

Not willing at that point to take stern action against Eaker, Arnold decided at least Frank Hunter had to go. During June 1943 Assistant Secretary of War for Air Robert Lovett visited England to observe Eighth Air Force operations. He spent considerable time inspecting the VIII Fighter Command and especially the problems of escort. At an Eighth Air Force commanders' meeting immediately after Lovett's visit, Hunter told Eaker that he feared Lovett would insist on the use of P-38s for escort. Hunter identified the P-38 as a "wonderful ship," but preferred to give the P-47 a "complete trial." In doing so Hunter revealed his misunderstanding of the basic issue confronting Eighth Air Force in the summer and fall of 1943. The bombers needed fighter escorts with range, not superior fighters. The P-47 was a better dogfighter, but it did not have the legs to fly long escort missions.[79]

Hunter knew his mission was to support day bombardment, but wanted twenty fighter groups that could fly into the continent and defeat the Luftwaffe in a series of swirling dogfights. He preferred the rugged and powerful P-47 to the longer-range P-38 and P-51, which he evaluated as having inferior fighting capabilities. Left alone, Hunter would probably have developed a powerful fighter force capable of defeating the Luftwaffe in a series of pitched battles. But in the words of VIII Fighter Command's chief of staff a year later, the Luftwaffe had become "allergic" to American fighters. There would be no pitched battles unless the "Little Friends" accompanied the "Big Friends" into Germany. The end came when Hunter wrote Washington on 8 August that "heat had been applied" for him to throw his fighters totally into escort. He refused, claiming he lacked sufficient fighters and that the fighters he had lacked sufficient range. Three weeks later Arnold replaced him with Maj. Gen. William Kepner. Eaker opposed the change, but Arnold had made up his mind—Kepner would take over at VIII Fighter Command.[80]

Hunter was a carryover from an earlier age of aerial warfare. The Army Air Forces was on the verge of a revolution in fighter operations and Hunter could neither see it coming nor see the need for it. He served the remainder of the war in New York as the commanding general of First Air Force.

CHAPTER FOUR

TO THE BRINK—THE FALL CRISIS

U nlike Frank O'D. Hunter, William E. Kepner had made his reputation as a fighter, not as a dashing airman. He worried little about doctrine, but demonstrated a single-minded dedication to defeating the enemy. The B-17 and B-24 could be self-defending or not self-defending—it mattered not to Kepner. His job was to kill German pilots and to destroy German aircraft, which he knew, however, would be found swarming around American bombers. Kepner helped merge the two major assignments of Eighth Air Force into one. In Operation POINTBLANK the Combined Chiefs of Staff had assigned Eighth Air Force the responsibility of both overcoming German air resistance to allow the invasion of France and destroying Germany's industrial capability to wage war. Under Kepner, VIII Fighter Command would try to defeat the Luftwaffe during the course of the bombing destruction of German industries.

Born in Miami, Indiana, in 1893, Kepner joined the Marines at the age of sixteen, later serving in the National Guard, the Army cavalry, and the Air Service. He fought on the Western Front and was wounded as an infantryman during World War I. An Army balloonist of some renown, he flew Explorer I to a world record

60,613 feet in 1934. At the Air Corps Tactical School, Kepner avoided the bomber-fighter controversy. Prior to assuming command of VIII Fighter Command on 29 August 1943, he served as the commanding general of Fourth Air Force. His most important assignment before going to England, the one that won for him the job of leading Eighth Air Force's fighters in the struggle for air superiority, was spearheading the program to increase the ranges of the P-38 and the P-51 in the spring and summer of 1943.

Of medium height, heavyset, with a neat, trimmed moustache, he was a fighter and an innovator. He held a deep concern for his warriors, spending many hours touring the units under his command. Unmarried, he had a fatherly way of offering solace to the families of his missing or dead pilots. Once, at a high-level conference, he used the term "son-of-a-bitch." He quickly turned to a Women's Army Corps secretary who was present and apologized. The secretary, Mary Gill, later recalled that two of the generals of the European theater were especially courteous and compassionate men—one was Kepner and the other, the man for whom she was long a secretary, James "Jimmy" Doolittle.

A true pilot's general, Kepner ate, and drank, with his men. He never missed an opportunity to fly, although his rank precluded him from deep missions over the continent. But unlike other commanders so close to their men, Kepner never allowed his regard for his men to interfere with the job of defeating the Luftwaffe.[1]

The leaders of the Luftwaffe, including Kepner's opposite number, Josef Schmid, felt the urgency of the air superiority battle. Six months of steadily increasing American daylight bombing had clearly demonstrated the weakness of German defenses and the vulnerability of German industry. On 18 August 1943 Chief of the Air Staff Jeschonnek committed suicide. His death marked the end of the Luftwaffe's emphasis on offensive close air support. His successor, Günther Korten, shifted Luftwaffe priorities to defensive operations in the West and the Reich.

By the fall of 1943, in addition to increased numbers, the Luftwaffe had strengthened itself with a highly centralized organization for the defense of the West and of the Reich. In the West, Air Fleet 3 under Feldmarschall Hugo Sperrle directed II and IX Air Corps, responsible for anti-invasion preparations and operations; X Air Corps responsible for cooperating with the German navy in the Battle of the Atlantic; and II Fighter Corps, responsible for day and night fighter operations over France and Belgium. Under the latter, two fighter divisions headquartered in France directed the aerial defense of the West. During combat operations, several fighter command centers (*jafü*) controlled the airborne fighters of both divisions against Allied air forces operating in their respective areas of responsibility. This chain of command insured Air Fleet 3's limited forces could be concentrated at the point of greatest Allied threat.[2]

In Germany proper, the Luftwaffe's defense had grown from a single fighter wing (1st Fighter Wing) with less than 100 aircraft in January 1943 to eleven fighter wings (1st, 3rd, 11th, 26th, 27th, 53rd, 54th, 76th, 101st, 104th, and 108th Fighter Wings) with twenty assigned groups, totaling 342 single-engine and 139 twin-engine operational aircraft at the end of 1943. Most of the additional units had come to Germany at the expense of Luftwaffe forces on the Eastern, Southern, Northern, and Western fronts.[3] These forces were under the overall command of Generaloberst Hubert Weise's Berlin-based Air Command Center, which also controlled antiaircraft forces in Germany. On 27 January 1944, reflecting the rise to preeminence of fighter defenses over antiaircraft defenses, the Luftwaffe replaced artilleryman Weise with airman Generaloberst Hans Jürgen Stumpff, formerly commander of Air Fleet 5 in Norway. It renamed his organization Air Fleet Reich so that Stumpff would have a command status equal to that of other air fleets.[4]

Under Air Command Center/Air Fleet Reich, Generalleutnant Josef Schmid commanded I Fighter Corps, headquartered at Zeist, Holland, with responsibility for all fighter aircraft in Germany, except for those of Fighter Division 7 in southern Germany and Austria.[5] Schmid distributed his fighter forces among Fighter Divisions 1, 2, and 3. These divisions now controlled the early warning system, feeding an assembled air situation picture to I Fighter Corps and Air Command Center/Air Fleet Reich, but more immediately using the gathered intelligence to direct fighter operations. Putting all fighters under one controller and one radio frequency allowed the Luftwaffe to concentrate its fighter forces in swarms of fifty aircraft or more.

Antiaircraft defenses had also undergone significant expansion. At tremendous effort and at a great diversion of scarce resources and manpower the Luftwaffe had created an enormous flak force. Considering the relative successes of the fighter and flak forces, Göring would have been more successful if more of an effort had been made to build the fighter forces instead of concentrating on the flak forces.

By the fall of 1943 fighter aircraft production had finally achieved priority in German war planning. In late July, in direct response to the British attacks on Hamburg, Göring ordered Milch to concentrate on defensive fighter production at the expense of other aircraft production. He did not, however, order a concurrent expansion of the fighter pilot training program.[6]

Other adjustments also contributed to the defensive capabilities of the Luftwaffe. Allied bombing raids on German airfields close to the coast forced the Luftwaffe to withdraw its units into eastern Holland and western Germany. The first such move took place in June 1943 and involved the transfer of the 1st Fighter Division to eastern Holland, headquartered at Deelen. The 26th Fighter Wing, the most experienced fighter wing in the struggle against American day bombing, moved back to the Reich in July and August. The decision to withdraw, however, was actually more the result of the need to move German fighters beyond the range of American escort than an attempt to escape Allied bombing. Though itself a sign of weakness in the face of expanding American fighter activities, the withdrawal had the effect of eliminating the advantages close escort brought to American bomber formations because German fighters withheld their attacks until American fighters turned for home. It had the side effect, however, of allow-

Table 1. German Antiaircraft Strength: Number of Batteries

Battery Type	13 January 1943	9 January 1944
Reich Heavy	629	1,121
Reich Medium	538	439
Navy Heavy	162	144
Navy Medium	66	58
West Heavy	0	245
West Medium	258	351
Total	1,653	2,358

Source: Grabmann, "German Air Force Defense Operations," 1956, File K113.107-164, HRC.

ing American fighters to cut the power settings needed to climb to tactical altitude and thereby extend their range closer to Germany. Another plus for the Luftwaffe was the extra warning time the withdrawal brought, which allowed the Luftwaffe to assemble for group-strength attacks able to overwhelm bomber defensive fire. The movement included the construction of back-up airfields throughout Germany equipped with fuel and ammunition to allow German fighters repeat sorties. The central controller at Air Command Center/Air Fleet Reich headquarters in Berlin broadcast a continuous battle commentary (*reichsjägerwelle*) that allowed the pilots of these repeat sorties to locate the battle.[7]

American bombing in the summer of 1943 had limited the planned expansion of the Luftwaffe's forces. This expansion had begun in mid-1941 when Göring ordered Milch to increase aircraft production sufficiently to quadruple front-line strength. Hitler accelerated the effort with additional demands for greater aircraft production in 1942. Milch merged existing factories into larger complexes in order to increase production. Though efficiency of scale helped raise output, it also made the American bombing effort easier by concentrating production in a few large complexes. Eighth's bombing efforts in the first half of 1943 were small by later standards, but they forced the Air Ministry to request the dispersal of Germany's aircraft manufacturing industry in May 1943.

Little was done until Hitler gave Minister for Armaments and War Production Albert Speer power to order plant dispersal in August 1943. This dispersal and American bombing caused output to lag in the fall of 1943.[8] Speer and Milch planned to reach a production level of 2,000 fighters per month by the summer of 1944, but the intensity of the Blitz Week attacks of late July 1943 convinced Milch to try to reach a production level of 2,000 per month by the end of 1943. Continued bombing frustrated Milch's venture and he reduced his production goals to 1,000 Bf 109s per month by December 1943 and 1,000 FW 190s per month by March or April 1944.[9]

But production was not the problem. In 1943 the Air Ministry planned to produce 3,288 single-engine and 435 twin-engine pilots. Though the products of this training lacked sufficient instruction, especially in front-line aircraft, the system nevertheless met 99.6 percent of the single-engine goal and 85 percent of the twin-engine goal. The fault was in the planning. Goals were entirely insufficient for attrition warfare. Luftwaffe plans called for a force expansion of 904 new single-engine pilots in 1943. In that year, however, Germany lost 2,967 single-engine pilots plus 446 twin-engine pilots. The bottom line, one of the most critical statistics of the war for air superiority, was that the Luftwaffe fell 516 single-engine pilots and 76 twin-engine pilots short of planned needs in 1943.

The disparity between aircraft production and pilot training revealed the key difficulty the Luftwaffe faced in the fall of 1943. Whereas German industry did the job of providing the Luftwaffe with sufficient aircraft to defend German skies, producing a monthly average of 937 single-engine fighters in 1943, the Luftwaffe's training establishment was unable to keep pace, due to both the lack of fuel for training and poor planning. The 273 single-engine fighter pilots graduating each month on average over the same period barely filled the empty spaces in operational units left

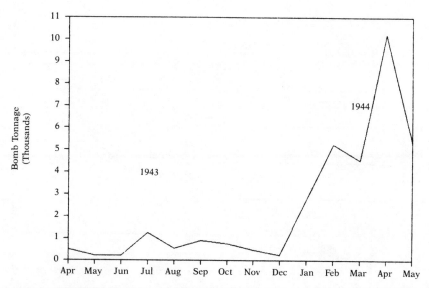

Figure 5. AAF Bombing of German Aircraft Industry
Source: USSBS, Report No. 4, Table V-2.

by the average monthly loss of 247 single-engine pilots. The net increase of only twenty-six pilots per month were all the Luftwaffe had to reinforce the five fronts on which it was engaged in 1943, forcing it to cannibalize other aerial units to meet defensive needs.[10] During the same period Eighth Air Force grew by an average of 193 fighter aircraft with pilots and 210 bomber aircraft with crews per month.[11]

The Luftwaffe also employed new tactics to defeat the American bombing offensive. Milch had equipped Bf 109s with Daimler Benz 605A high-performance engines and armed them with light machine guns and cannons. Göring through Galland ordered these to drive American escort fighters away from the bombers. This would allow Bf 109s and FW 190s, modified into bomber killers with additional 20mm cannons, to attack the bombers, now in group and larger formations. They equipped Bf 110 and Me 410 twin-engine "destroyer" fighters (*zerstörer*) with additional cannons and

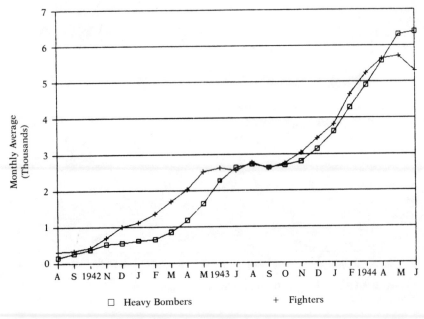

Figure 6. American Buildup, Eighth and Fifteenth Air Forces
Source: USSBS, Report No. 2a, Chart 2.

four 21-cm air-to-air rockets to enhance their bomber-killing abilities. Launched from beyond the range of bomber defensive fire,
they broke up American combat boxes.

The initial success of these tactics encouraged Göring to expand
this force, ordering twin-engine night fighter units to fly day missions. These crews, some of the most highly trained and skilled
airmen of the war, were accustomed to flying alone and unac-
customed to fighter escort and heavy bomber defensive firepower.
Results were mixed. Their ability to down American bombers was
proven, but they also proved especially vulnerable to American
defensive fire. In April 1943 Göring had ordered that no night
fighter crews with more than twenty kills were to fly day missions,
but the needs of daylight defense in the fall forced the Luftwaffe to
violate that restriction.[12]

In an attempt to compensate for past training deficiencies that caused pilot shortages, Göring ordered the organization of factory test pilots into factory defense squadrons, to provide point defense of the critical aircraft manufacturing industry. Like many German decisions in the war, the immediate tactical needs of the air war had taken precedence over long-term strategic planning.[13]

Despite these improvements, the Luftwaffe had reason to be anxious about the future. With dispersal well under way and with most of the damage caused by the Blitz Week attacks repaired, fighter production picked up. Göring, however, remained committed to the idea that the key to German success was not more aircraft, but "more dashing and determined tactics." Spirit and morale, the spirit of National Socialism, would overcome American numerical superiority.[14] Increased production meant more airplanes, but the Luftwaffe had not made plans for increased replacement parts production nor for many more service personnel. By late 1943 fighter units in the West and in the Reich maintained only a 60 to 70 percent operational rate. Though it was inflicting heavy losses on American forces (an average monthly loss in 1943 of 34 percent of Eighth Air Force's heavy bombers and 6.5 percent of its fighters), its own monthly single-engine fighter losses on the Western Front were averaging 45 percent of effective strength.[15] And the force the Luftwaffe faced was growing rapidly.

Critical to German success against American bombers was the "destroyer" twin-engine fighter, yet it lacked the maneuverability and speed to operate in areas where enemy fighters were present. Readily apparent to the commanders forced to operate with heavily armed twin- or single-engine fighter aircraft was the loss of performance such firepower brought. I Fighter Corps commander Schmid ordered one of his fighter squadrons in Holland to reduce its FW 190 armaments to only one cannon and two machine guns, using that squadron to attack American fighter escorts. The problem, Schmid admitted, was that the effort was too slight and the light fighters in general lacked the firepower to shoot down American bombers.[16]

The actual key to Schmid's new tactics, weapons, and organization was the presence or absence of escorting American fighters. On 1 October 1943 the Luftwaffe used only sixty-eight fighters to engage unescorted Fifteenth Air Force bombers attacking Weiner-Neustadt in Austria. German losses were two Bf 109s. American losses were twenty-seven heavy bombers, four by antiaircraft artillery fire. Missions over the next week, however, demonstrated to Schmid the growing menace of fighter escort and the weakness of German defenses in the face of fighter escort. On 2 October, over Emden, in the presence of continuous escort, Schmid's forces could down only eight bombers and one American fighter, losing ten of their own fighters. On 4 October (Frankfurt) with escort most of the way, the score was eight American bombers at the price of ten defending fighters. And on 8 October (Bremen), despite launching 453 sorties, using every fighter he had, including many with more than one sortie, Schmid paid a high price of twenty-eight losses to claim thirty-five American bombers and six fighters.[17]

Apparent to Schmid was the weakness of Germany's bad-weather flight training. Shortages of fuel and the danger to trainees had led the Luftwaffe to deemphasize bad-weather flying in its training program. In the miserable flying conditions of the last two months of 1943, the time Americans had devoted to bad-weather practice paid dividends, even though they were far from perfect at it. American commanders complained constantly about the weather, but were able to launch missions regularly in weather that severely hampered German fighter units. As General der Flieger Kammhuber saw it, Americans were able to fly above the weather; the Germans had to fly through it.[18]

On 13 November Schmid's command lost nineteen fighters to icing. On 29 November Eighth Air Force attacked Bremen in conditions of complete cloudcover and severe icing. Schmid launched nearly 300 fighters, claiming fourteen bombers but losing thirty-three of his own aircraft, most to weather-related causes. On the 13 December American mission to Kiel, Hamburg, and Bremen under extreme fog, I Fighter Corps kept its aircraft on the ground, as it would continue to do for the remainder of the war unless the situation appeared sufficiently critical to force a bad-weather launch. This decision did not solve the problem, because the situation was becoming more and more critical. On a 22 December mission I Fighter Corps lost twelve fighters to icing in opposing a daylight mission.[19]

Another cause for concern was the short amount of time, 70 minutes, German fighters had after takeoff to assemble into combat formations, climb to 25,000 or 30,000 feet, attack the American bombers, and land. Drop tanks were no solution because they degraded the climbing ability of German aircraft. Few pilots wanted to use them anyway because on 7 October Göring ordered that drop tanks could be dropped only if they had been struck first by enemy fire or if necessary to achieve maximum aircraft performance. General der Flieger Galland called this situation "intolerable," but neither he nor anyone else in Germany had an answer to the problem.[20]

Eighth Air Force's late summer and fall campaign began a short two weeks after the Blitz Week attacks. On 17 August 1943 it launched its most important mission of the war to that point. Deploying the largest force yet, 315 heavy bombers, carrying the heaviest bomb load yet, 724 tons, Eighth Air Force attacked the German ball-bearing plants at Schweinfurt and the Messerschmitt aircraft complex at Regensburg, deep in southern Germany. The chosen targets represented the essence of American prewar doctrine—choke points in the German industrial fabric, the destruction of which would insure air superiority by destroying aircraft production and the ball bearings critical to modern aircraft. The mission was part of a joint effort with Ninth Air Force in North Africa, which bombed the Ploesti oil refineries and aircraft production at Wiener-Neustadt in Austria.

Using every tactic it had developed in the summer, the Luftwaffe rose up en masse to challenge the American air fleet coming from the United Kingdom. The air battle was the largest in the war to that time. German fighters waited for escorting American fighters to turn for home at the limit of their endurance. For 6 hours the Luftwaffe slashed at the bombers in the air over Germany. In the chaos of battle, Allied pilots and gunners reported downing over three hundred German fighters. The Luftwaffe recorded the loss of only twenty-seven. American losses were over 19 percent of the attacking force—sixty heavy bombers shot down.

With great bravery and determination on the part of the crews, American bombers caused significant destruction, but more importantly accelerated the dispersal of the ball-bearing and aircraft industries. That action, according to Prof. Willi Messerschmitt, cost Germany 50 percent of its potential aircraft production.[21] The cost to Eighth Air Force made it impossible to repeat the attacks for 2 months, allowing Germany to repair much of the damage achieved at such great cost. The increasing flow of men and aircraft across the Atlantic would replace Eighth Air Force's losses in time, but could it continue to win such Pyrrhic victories and still defeat the Luftwaffe and destroy Germany's ability to wage war?[22]

Eighth Air Force did not return to deep penetration missions beyond fighter escort range until 6 September, when it attacked Stuttgart. Again losses were heavy—17 percent this time, forty-five more bombers. The weather then turned sour, to the temporary good fortune of the aircrews of Eighth Air Force who stayed in their Quonset huts. Missions continued, but depended on H_2S and H_2X radar for navigation and bombing. Bad weather kept losses low. But the skies cleared in early October and the bombers returned in force.

In one week Eighth Air Force launched four major attacks against targets deep in Germany beyond fighter escort. On the eighth the mission to Bremen cost Eaker 8 percent of the attacking force—thirty bombers. On the ninth the bombers went to Anklam/Marienburg, losing another 8 percent—twenty-eight more bombers. On the tenth the target was Münster, at the increased cost of nearly 13 percent—thirty heavy bombers. The climax came on 14 October with a return mission to Schweinfurt. Sixty bombers went down—a 26-percent loss rate.[23] Losses of 8 and even 13 percent were heavy, but acceptable; 26 percent was not. In seven days Eighth Air Force had lost 148 four-engine bombers, each with ten crewmen. The American daylight bombing campaign against Germany had reached a crisis point.

Eaker wrote Arnold on 15 October that Second Schweinfurt had been a success and that the Luftwaffe's successes were "pretty much as the last final struggles of a monster in his death throes." Arnold was not so sure. His initial reaction was one of succor: "the cornered wolf fights hardest." The next day his response was more sober: "Hope that losses are worth the results." In November he ordered Eaker to set up a committee to analyze the accomplishments of the Combined Bomber Offensive to date. Arnold and the Air Staff recognized the crisis for what it was.[24]

To be sure, the Luftwaffe was suffering also, though not as much as Eighth Air Force intelligence officers deduced. American claims for the week were absurd—702 enemy aircraft downed. The reported total was more than twice as many defensive fighters as the Luftwaffe actually had stationed in Germany. In the first three missions the Eighth claimed the downing of 503 German fighters, certainly enough to win air superiority. Yet when 229 B-17s flew their 14 October mission to Schweinfurt, the Americans reported attacks by hundreds of Luftwaffe fighters. Actually Schmid launched 567 sorties, including many second and third missions for individual pilots.

Especially did the American fliers make extreme claims. For them it was psychological compensation for the danger and rigor of their endeavors, but with much self-deception. If two dozen or more gunners on bombers riveted their fire on an interceptor slashing through their formation and it began to smoke and dive away or exploded, the marked tendency was for all to claim it as a different victim for each gunner. Often they claimed it whether it was seen to crash or not. Allowing for enthusiasm and tension in the heat of battle and some inaccuracy of observation, the sum total of claims was often ridiculous in the extreme. American fighter claims, the only ones to have been officially recognized by the U.S. Air Force (successor of the Army Air Forces), should have been more accurate. They were based on certain definite criteria, including gun camera film and the confirmation reports of witnesses.[25]

Claims were distorted, but less so, on the German side. ULTRA intercepts reported the Luftwaffe shooting down 139 bombers at Second Schweinfurt alone.[26] But whereas claims were warped, what was clear was that both sides were engaged in a battle of attrition. Eighth Air Force lost 148 bombers, the Luftwaffe lost between 80 and 125 defending aircraft, depending on the German source.[27] Germany was trying to maintain its industrial production. The Americans were trying to destroy it. In late 1943 German war production was in fact expanding. The arithmetic of attrition warfare was murderously clear—Eighth Air Force was losing.

One factor contributing to the German success on the Schweinfurt-Regensburg raids was a change in German tactics beginning in October 1943. According to Josef Schmid, "Headquarters of I Fighter Corps received the explicit orders from the Commander-in-Chief of the Luftwaffe [Göring] to firstly destroy the enemy four-motored bombers while avoiding combat with enemy fighters." The heavy bombers had always been the priority target for German fighters, but American fighters were also significant targets. Now the unescorted bombers were to be the only target. Schmid ordered his day fighters to leave stragglers from the combat boxes for the night fighters and concentrate on breaking up the boxes with the heavy use of 21-cm rockets. All attacks were to be made with group-size units, with one squadron from each group given the responsibility of screening American fighters from the attacking force, if American fighters were present. Schmid developed these tactics to take advantage of his force composition: 200–300 single-engine fighters, 60–80 twin-engine day fighters, and 100 twin-engine night fighters.

Though Göring's order to avoid combat with American fighters had the effect of increasing American bomber losses and reducing American fighter losses, another side-effect was what General der

Flieger Adolf Galland called *"jägerschreck"* or fear of fighters. He claimed the order worked against the natural aggressiveness and offensive spirit of fighter pilots, damaging morale and reducing efficiency. General der Flieger Josef Kammhuber supported the order, arguing that defense "has real value only when it affects the main attack being carried out by the bomber planes." Of Galland's argument, Kammhuber said a defensive commander must fight against "the nature of a fighter pilot to want to fight other fighter pilots." American Maj. Gen. O. A. Anderson was less charitable, pointing out that any fighter trying to avoid combat with another "invites disaster." In Anderson's opinion, Göring's message was a "suicidal order."[28] The problem for the Luftwaffe was that its aerial defense of the Reich was based on a series of tactics designed to operate in an environment free of enemy fighters. The Luftwaffe had no plan to keep its air space free of American fighters. To concentrate on bombers might make strategic sense, but to ignore the American fighters appearing over Germany in increasing numbers was tactical suicide.

Despite the order to avoid them, in the field German units continued to attack VIII Fighter Command fighters, though the intention was clearly to facilitate strikes against the bombers. The Eighth's mission narratives reported these attacks, identifying them as attempts to get the fighters to break their escort or to force the fighters to jettison their drop tanks early.[29]

The success of these tactics, despite the controversy, was undeniable. Schmid's command claimed the downing of 383 American aircraft by fighter action and 66 by antiaircraft artillery during the month of October—an overall American loss rate of 7 percent. German losses, according to Schmid, were 151 of the 4,551 fighters I Fighter Corps launched—a 3.3-percent loss rate. At the same time Schmid had reason for concern. Attrition was decimating his forward units. His First Fighter Division was down to group strength—about forty serviceable aircraft. Stationed in Holland, this division had to attack American formations escorted by P-47s. On the 10 October mission to Münster First Fighter Division attacked the P-47 escort to open the heavy bombers to attacks by the Second and Third Fighter Divisions, but lost twenty fighters in the process. Schmid's reaction was immediate: His units would no longer try to attack escorting fighters—the command to avoid combat with American fighters would have gone out to I Fighter Corps forces even if Göring had not ordered it. Schmid's fighters were to withhold attacks until the P-47s reached the limit of their endurance and turned for home. For the 14 October Schweinfurt mission this order had deadly implications for American bombers.[30]

According to the official American historians of the air war, "the fact was that the Eighth Air Force had for the time being lost air superiority over Germany . . . The Eighth Air Force made no more deep penetrations in clear weather into Germany for the rest of the year. That failure was, prior to December, the result of a command decision based on the lack of escort and the need for recuperating the bomber force." These historians overstated the case. As Eaker's biographer, James Parton, pointed out, Eighth Air Force had no air superiority to lose. What it had lost, at least temporarily, was its ability to compete in the battle for air superiority. Parton also asserted that no command decision was made to refrain from bombing Germany, but that bad weather caused the absence of such missions. He called the claim of lost air superiority "ivory-tower superficiality."[31] No one could deny, however, that Eighth Air Force had entered the fall crisis of the daylight bombing campaign.

The fall weather was bad and did interfere with operations, but there was more to the problems of the fall crisis. Eaker himself, despite Parton's defense, admitted that Eighth Air Force had lost its competitiveness versus the Luftwaffe. On 13 December he wrote Giles that "we are not justified in striking at them [the Germans] unless the conditions auger success. These deep penetrations and the impossibility of fighter escort will cost us 80 to 120 bombers. We will suffer this loss any time we penetrate in force to these targets." Eaker's targeting officer said later that "the severe casualties suffered in these successive raids into Germany, without fighter escort, convinced us all that such losses could no longer be sustained or the Eighth would shortly cease to exist as a fighting force." For him there was no question of "ivory-tower super-ficiality." "Operations beyond fighter cover were sharply cur-tailed." Arnold wrote after the war, "Could we keep it up? . . . To this day, I don't know." In any case, "weather obscured the argu-ment forever."[32]

Despite the use of drop tanks beginning with the 28 July mission to Emmerich, VIII Fighter Command escort had been ineffective for deep penetration missions. Because the P-47 was a poor climb-er, VIII Fighter Command told its pilots to "stay with the bombers" and "never go below 18,000 feet." A shortage of fighter groups and tactics requiring fighters to fly in close formation with the bomb-ers multiplied the ineffectiveness of the escort.[33]

The Luftwaffe was bruised, but still existed in sufficient power to prevent any cross-Channel invasion. The self-defending bomber had proved unequal to the task of gaining its own air superiority. One of Eaker's staff officers wrote that "it had been a most gallant effort, but many, too many, had paid with their lives in disproving the Air Corps pre-war theory that the Flying Fortress could defend itself, unaided, against enemy fighters." Historians of air power have clearly and bluntly evaluated Schweinfurt's importance. "The disaster at Schweinfurt ended the nonsense about unescorted bomber formations." "The Army Air Forces's peacetime theory failed in wartime practice."[34] Allied leaders looking beyond the recent travails of Eighth Air Force had even greater cause for con-cern about the air situation in the fall of 1943. When the Combined Chiefs of Staff met for the SEXTANT Conference in early December, Arnold announced that the American buildup in England had fall-en behind the rate of reinforcement planners had stated was neces-sary to achieve POINTBLANK objectives, by 30 percent in May, 43 percent in August, and 41 percent in October. Even more ominous were intelligence reports of a rapid expansion of German fighter strength on the Western Front and in Germany, up from 765 in

January to 1,750 in October (more than three times its actual strength), and of German fighter production from 640 to 875 for the same period (less than one half the actual production).[35]

Even Eighth Air Force appeared to lose confidence in its ability to win air superiority for OVERLORD. Recording its impressions a year later, the Eighth Air Force Operational Research Section concluded, "By the fall of 1943, growing enemy fighter power precluded bomber operations to targets deep in Central and Southern Germany until long-range fighters were available to provide full escort."[36] Despite the bravado of public statements, mission statistics continued to indicate Eighth Air Force bombers were doing worse, not better, in the struggle for air superiority.[37]

The Luftwaffe did not see the crisis it had caused in the American bombing effort. Generalleutnant Schmid only knew that American bombers kept coming and his forces continued to bleed. He constantly refined his tactics, hoping to reduce his losses and shoot down more American aircraft. At a high-level meeting in Berlin on 6 and 7 November, with Weise, Galland, and divisional commanders, Schmid decided to move all units back to East Holland and the Rhine area to escape American fighter escort and medium-bomber attacks. Thereby he began a retreat that would continue through the spring of 1944, moving the Luftwaffe farther and farther away from western France, which Allied forces were already planning to invade. Though Schmid argued he had insufficient aircraft, Weise ordered him to use a small number of light single-engine aircraft to attack the American escort force in order to open the heavy bombers for attack by heavy single- and twin-engine fighters. All the participants agreed to withdraw twin-engine fighters beyond Hannover, at the extreme P-47 range, because of their special vulnerability to American fighters. Schmid won permission to stop trying to interfere with every portion of each bombing raid in order to concentrate his forces on one specific point in the bomber stream. This desperate attempt to gain numerical superiority at the point of combat was a reflection of German intelligence indicating Eighth Air Force had three heavy bombers and 1.4 fighters to each German fighter.[38]

Schmid made other modifications to the German defense organization in response to continued losses. Especially hard for him to accept were continued heavy losses due to noncombat causes—the "plague" as Göring had once called it. For the last four months of 1943, the Luftwaffe in Germany and in the West lost 967 fighters to Allied action, but 1,052 to accidents and friendly fire.[39] On 11 and 12 December 1943 at a map exercise at I Fighter Corps headquarters near Zeist, Schmid ordered all antiaircraft units removed from the control of the nine surviving defense districts (*luftgauen*) and placed under the operational control of each fighter division in order to guarantee cooperation between the fighter and antiaircraft forces. He also assigned the fighter divisions control over the air-raid warning system. This profound restructuring of the Luftwaffe defense command made the fighter divisions responsible for collecting, collating, and analyzing all information on each enemy raid and managing the defenses deployed against each raid. The job of Air Command Center, soon to become Air Fleet Reich, was to assemble the air-raid-situation pictures produced by the fighter divisions and to assist in coordinating the efforts of the various German defense forces. Two weeks later Schmid disbanded the old fighter command centers (*jafü*) and assigned tactical control of fighters in flight to the divisional air-situation rooms. Because attacks by group formations of twenty to thirty aircraft were insufficient to overcome American defensive fire, he also told the new controllers to prepare for organizing attacks by wing formations of sixty to ninety aircraft.[40]

Despite these measures, attrition continued to take its toll. Especially damaging was the impact on the Luftwaffe's aces in the fall of 1943. The aces listed in Table 2 were in the van of a swelling number of the Luftwaffe's best that fell in the battle for air superiority during the closing months of 1943. Together these twelve pilots had claimed 1,160 Allied aircraft. The training establishment was not able to replace them.

Wilhelm Lemke led fifty-five aircraft attempting to intercept two American fighter groups over Holland on 4 December. Lemke, flying the lightly armed Bf 109, was attempting to force American

Table 2. Attrition of German Fighter Aces in West and Reich, Fall 1943

Ace	Victories (# in West)
Kurt Brändle	206 (29)
Erwin Clausen	180 (20)
Wilhelm Lemke	132 (14)
Werner Lucas	131 (6)
Heinrich Klöpper	106 (1)
Ernst Süss	94 (8)
Wilhelm Freuwörth	70 (8)
Hugo Dahmer	58 (3)
Johannes Seifert	57 (4)
Herbert Schramm	57 (46)
Heinz Grimm	42 (3)
Hans Philipp	27 (1 day/26 night)

Source: Obermaier.

P-47s to break off their escort of Eighth Air Force bomber formations. He died in the effort. Many German fighter pilots learned a fatal lesson over the next six months: combat experience and tactics learned on the Eastern Front were of only limited use against superbly trained and equipped American pilots on the Western Front.[41]

On the American side there were reasons for optimism and for anxiety. Losses had been heavy, but mission reports indicated the Germans were also suffering. Though American claims of German aircraft downed were grossly inflated (see Appendix), American leaders should have gained consolation in the attrition they were causing the Luftwaffe. Though American commanders were not fully aware of the extent of this damage, the available strength of the Luftwaffe's single-engine fighter force declined by 107 aircraft in the last 3 months of the year, despite the German production of 1,903 replacement aircraft. The twin-engine fighter force declined by 22, despite the production of 844 aircraft.[42] German victory was based on the superior ability of their relatively immobile heavy fighter-destroyers, which in the fall of 1943 had outranged bomber defensive fire. As Eaker had correctly pointed out, they were "duck soup for our fighters." If American fighters gained increased range, German twin-engine fighters would be terribly vulnerable. ULTRA revealed in October that the Luftwaffe had ordered replacement aircraft to go directly from factories to the fronts, indicating that it had consumed all of its reserves. It also had ordered cannibalization of existing aircraft to make up for spare-parts shortages.

Most revealing of the Luftwaffe's problems, however, was Göring's order in November for heavily armed assault squadrons (*sturmstaffel*) to make all-out attacks at close range "without regard to losses." He even suggested the possibility of ramming. In December the Luftwaffe decided to create special assault groups (*sturmgruppen*) to overwhelm American bomber formations. These, too, would be "duck soup" to fighters with protracted range.[43]

Still, by December Eighth Air Force was 3 months behind in completing its POINTBLANK mission. Intelligence sources concluded that German aircraft production was 645 aircraft per month at the end of the year. Actual production was 851. Portal, representing the Combined Chiefs of Staff, realized the obvious. The Allies had no choice but to send Eighth Air Force bombers back to Germany because these bombers and their accompanying fighters were the only force capable of defeating the Luftwaffe before OVERLORD.[44]

The key technology for solving the fall crisis was extended range for American fighters.[45] The great demand for the long-range P-38s in North Africa and the Pacific left VIII Fighter Command relying on P-47s with drop tanks. Because prime targets were deep in Germany and because of the Luftwaffe tactic of withholding attacks until the P-47s had reaching the limit of their endurance, these drop tanks in the fall and winter had a restricted impact. The Eighth had to await the arrival of newly formed groups flying long-range P-51 Mustangs and P-38 Lightnings from the United States. Tragically for the Americans, the first of these P-38 groups, the 55th Fighter Group, flew its first mission over Europe the day after Second Schweinfurt. The first P-51 group, the 354th, flew its first bomber escort mission on 5 December 1943. On that date Eighth Air Force could count on one P-38, one P-51, and seven P-47 groups. The 20th Fighter Group with P-38s began flying on 28 December and the 357th Fighter Group with P-51s on 11 February 1944. Though they were late in arriving and small in number, these few long-range units were all Eighth Air Force had in the winter of 1943/1944 to fight for air superiority over the Reich.

By June 1943 Barney Giles, confident that the Mustang would be the war-winner he was after, began taking steps to insure Eighth Air Force would get priority. He started the paperwork to convert P-47 groups in England to P-51Bs. He reassigned P-47s to replace P-40s in the Mediterranean instead of previously planned P-51s. For P-40s in the Pacific and the India-China theater, he changed plans to use a combination of P-47s and P-38s as replacements instead of P-51s. Fast action was necessary because Mustang production in the late spring of 1943 lagged 60 days behind schedule.[46] Everyone wanted the new, "hot" fighter, the P-51 Mustang. One veteran P-47 pilot expressed it this way: "The P-47 was garbage compared to the P-51 in bomber escort missions." He called it "a relief to get rid of the P-47s."[47]

Arnold, committed to getting all of these aircraft he could to Eighth Air Force, clashed repeatedly with the British over the Royal Air Force's contribution to gaining air superiority. According to the "Agreement on Air Supplies to the British in 1943 Made Under the Proceedings of the Lyttelton Mission," the Royal Air Force was to receive 600 P-51s in 1943, out of a total of 4,174 American aircraft tagged for delivery to the British. In return the British were to hand over 600 short-range Spitfires. Because P-51 production was behind schedule, this agreement made the fall crisis even more critical in Arnold's eyes.[48]

With this problem in mind, Arnold began a bitter, no-holds-barred correspondence with Sir Charles Portal, chief of the British Air Staff. In late September he wrote Portal asking that the British put all of their P-51 squadrons under Eighth Air Force or accept P-47s as replacements. Portal did not respond for 3 weeks and then in the negative, pointing out that the P-51s were needed to supply British reconnaissance squadrons and to replace Spitfires in fighter squadrons so that a Spitfire reserve could be built up for OVERLORD. Portal did, however, offer to loan Arnold four P-51 squadrons beginning in mid-January to use until the time of the time of the Normandy invasion.[49]

Arnold's response was somewhat less than diplomatic and did nothing to hide the anger and frustration he was feeling.

Overlord hangs directly on the success of our combined aerial offensive and I am sure that our failure to decisively cripple both sources of German air power and the German Air Force itself is causing you and me real concern . . . as presently employed it would appear that your thousands of fighters . . . are not making use of their full capabilities. Our transition from the defensive to the offensive should surely carry with it the application of your large fighter force offensively . . . Is it not true that we have a staggering air superiority over the German and we are not using it?

Arnold finished his letter claiming American losses over Regensburg would have been considerably less if Royal Air Force Spitfires had attacked German airfields.[50]

The next day, not waiting for a reply to his suggestions, Arnold once again wrote Portal, this time asking the Royal Air Force to assume total responsibility for meeting the commitments of aid to the Soviet Union. American aircraft production could then be used to reinforce Eighth and Ninth Air Forces, while Spitfires, relatively useless because of their lack of range, could fulfill promises made to the Soviets.[51]

Portal's reply on 24 October was diplomatic, but not without satire. He thanked Arnold for the "incisive, detached views which you have expressed." He also indicated that he had ordered the Royal Air Force's Fighter Command to begin attacking enemy aircraft on the ground and in the air in support of American bombers. The remainder of his four-page letter was a defense of British operations and a refutation of Arnold's charges.[52] Portal followed up this promise with a meeting of all concerned parties, where a "senior RAF officer" admitted that Arnold's criticism was justified and that the British Fighter Command would become more aggressive.[53]

A week later Arnold closed the subject with some satire of his own.

Your reaction to my suggestion re the Merlin P-51 was not on the scale or at the time I had hoped for, but it will in a small way, help in the alleviation of a situation which is, right at this minute, very critical.

Arnold notified Portal that he had cut off all shipments of P-38s and P-51s to all other theaters, at great sacrifice, in order to provide the necessary aircraft to Eighth Air Force. It was Arnold's way of saying the Army Air Forces would go it alone in the struggle for air superiority.[54]

In addition to technology, changes in tactics also added to the range of American fighters but brought on other problems. In September Eaker allowed the escort to be opened to 250 yards in order to permit weaving. Weaving, however, wasted fuel and reduced range.[55] In October, perhaps because of this waste but also because the fighters were ranging out seeking individual combat, Eaker told Kepner that "leaving the vicinity of the bomber formations to engage such hostilities should be avoided by individual pilots."[56] Under Eaker's direction, Kepner told his pilots that "it is not considered sound practice to attempt to engage enemy aircraft when they cease to be a direct menace to the bomber formation."[57] Fighters were to "leave your 'Big Friends' [only] for a damned good reason."[58] Now fighters flew so close that one observer noted that they were required "literally to fly formation with the bombers."[59] Although this saved fuel and increased range, such tactics allowed the Luftwaffe to assume the offensive in their defensive operations. German pilots could pick the time and place of their attacks. As the Germans had discovered in the Battle of Britain, close escort, sometimes remaining within 50 to 75 feet of the bomber formations, put fighters at an extreme disadvantage because they had to match their speed to the much slower bombers. But committed to strategic bombing, not air superiority, Eaker felt the fighters had no independent mission. He told his staff that "the major task of the fighter is still to protect and support our heavy bombers."[60]

The eventual solution was the relay or phased support system and the area support system, both first suggested to Eaker by Giles in August 1943.[61] In the former scheme, VIII Fighter Command assigned each fighter group a different segment of the bomber route. The groups would fly to their assigned areas at the most economical speeds, thereby gaining range, and accelerate to combat speeds after rendezvousing with the bombers at a preset time. In phased escort the fighters flew with the bombers to the limit of their endurance, relaying the bomber formations to the next awaiting group. In area support, the fighters patrolled a particular area along the bomber route. Bombers flew through each group's area in sequence. In both, short-range P-47s provided escort during the penetration and withdrawal phases of each mission and longer-range P-38s and P-51s support over the targets. Another advantage of both schemes was that they countered the German tactic of attacking American escort fighters early to force them to drop external fuel tanks.[62]

VIII Fighter Command flew the first mission of either scheme on 24 December 1943 to V-1 launching sites in France. The targets were all concentrated in a relatively small area and well within the range of American fighters, making general area support a logical tactic. Its potential was evident and Kepner ordered the first phased escort mission to Germany on 7 January 1944. Three P-47 groups handled penetration support, one P-51 and two P-38 groups provided escort over the target, and five P-47 groups gave withdrawal support. So successful was the tactic in extending the range of all fighters and in allowing fighters to maintain combat speeds without outrunning the bombers that Kepner dropped continuous close escort entirely. On 11 January mission reports indicated this type of escort had forced German twin-engine fighters to fire their

21-cm rockets ineffectively from extreme range. This observation alone justified the tactic.[63]

An extension of the area support and phased relay systems was the Free Lance tactic. One or two fighter groups flew independently along the bomber route, free to attack the Luftwaffe wherever it might be. These groups had no escort responsibilities, but were to attack German units as they formed up to launch large-scale attacks on American formations. The first experimental Free Lance mission occurred on 20 December 1943. It was an accident, however—a response to a particular situation. The bombers were 30 minutes late and the leader of the 55th Fighter Group received radio permission to launch a Free Lance mission. The other ten groups airborne that day flew close escort. Kepner did not commit VIII Fighter Command to Free Lancing because statistics still indicated that German fighters were most often found near the bombers.[64]

During this fall crisis in the Army Air Forces campaign against Germany, the two major objectives of Eighth Air Force merged into one. Though this convergence was less noticeable to some commanders than others, it nevertheless became another critical development at the end of 1943. In the POINTBLANK directive of May 1943 the Combined Chiefs of Staff had assigned Eighth Air Force the responsibility of weakening Germany sufficiently "to permit initiation of final combined operations on the Continent." This was the charge of the strategic bombing campaign so threatened by the events of October. Aware that the invasion would require air superiority, the Combined Chiefs had also assigned Eighth Air Force the responsibility for destroying the Luftwaffe. Air superiority was an "intermediate objective second to none in priority." By late 1943 the winning of air superiority would depend on bombers from the strategic bombing campaign being present over Germany to force the Luftwaffe to come up and fight. The continuation of the bombing campaign, however, would depend on winning at least a semblance of air superiority. This development brought Eaker, the bomber advocate, and others preparing for the cross-Channel invasion, into a confrontation that was responsible for arguably the most controversial leadership change of the entire American war effort.[65]

Ira Eaker and Henry Arnold had been long-time friends, collaborating on two books in the interwar era. Both were bomber men, dedicated to the Air Corps' doctrine of strategic bombing. Arnold had chosen Carl Spaatz to head Eighth Air Force in 1942, with Eaker as his bomber commander, but elevated Eaker to the top position when Spaatz left to lead American air forces in the invasion of North Africa. Eaker had the unenviable duty of building up the largest strategic air force the world had ever seen, while at the same time attacking the sources of German strength. The forces he had for most of his time as Eighth Air Force commander were insufficient to do the job. Perhaps it was inevitable that Arnold would lose some faith in Eaker's ability because of this insufficiency. Another factor bearing on Arnold's judgment of Eaker's performance was the fact that Arnold had never commanded so much as a group in combat and thus probably lacked the sympathy for the aircrews that such positions naturally encouraged in commanders. Nevertheless Arnold had good reason by the end of 1943 to consider replacing Eaker.

In his correspondence with Eaker in 1943 Arnold revealed a significant amount of dissatisfaction. In April Arnold complained that Eaker was not giving him the information he needed to justify Eighth Air Force's activities to the government, the military, and the public. Two months later Arnold renewed his complaint, sending Eaker a sample mission information form to insure Eaker got the message. Arnold criticized Eaker's command structure for having too many headquarters. The Air Staff expressed concern about the Eighth's imbalance between service and combat units. In June Arnold complained to Eaker about his unsatisfactory maintenance organization and his ineffective use of aircraft. "I am willing to do anything possible to build up your forces but you must play your part . . . you have to be tough to handle the situation." In July Arnold wrote to Eaker suggesting the retirement of some older officers who were failing in their jobs. Eaker, however, answered that all of his officers were doing an acceptable job.[66]

Eaker's response to these complaints was always the same— "Please rush replacement aircraft and combat crews as fast as you can."[67] All problems would be solved and missions would be accomplished when Eighth Air Force had sufficient aircraft and crews to do the job. A member of the "bomber will always get through" generation of air leaders from the 1930s, Eaker calculated that the magic number was 300. Three hundred B-17s or B-24s, in proper combat formation, could penetrate into Germany and destroy Germany's ability to wage war.[68]

Arnold did his best to satisfy Eaker's pleas. He directed that "practically all of the new units scheduled to be trained in the United States from now on are scheduled to go to the United Kingdom." He diverted all P-38s and P-51s to Eighth Air Force from their worldwide commitments after Second Schweinfurt. Despite Arnold's efforts, Eaker still had some justification in blaming his problems on insufficient forces. POINTBLANK had called for thirty-eight heavy bomber groups and ten fighter groups in England by 31 December 1943. On that date Eighth Air Force had only twenty-five heavy bomber groups and seven fighter groups, plus six fighter groups in Ninth Air Force. Still, Arnold felt Eaker should have done more with the force he had. He complained that 1,000 B-17s sent to Eaker should have allowed him to send more than 300 bombers on major missions. Arnold strived, in his own words, to "build a fire under General Eaker."[69]

One of the biggest causes behind Arnold's deteriorating confidence in Eaker was Eaker's apparent misunderstanding of the role of the escort fighter.[70] The latter's continuing support for Hunter as commander of VIII Fighter Command despite that unit's poor record in contributing to air superiority in 1943 stood in stark contrast to Arnold's decision to replace Hunter in late August. Eaker should have sensed Arnold's dissatisfaction. Hunter was Eaker's number 3 man. For Arnold to replace Hunter over Eaker's head, despite Eaker's attempt to save him, was a veiled reprimand.

Eaker's use of fighters in 1943 contradicted the mission Arnold and his assistant Barney Giles had in mind. When Arnold wanted to publicize the successes of fighter groups, Eaker resisted the idea, arguing that "we play down the destruction of enemy fighters as the secondary job, our primary job being to deliver our bombloads well aimed, on their targets."[71] That one statement, "we play down the destruction of enemy fighters," revealed Eaker's lack of understanding of air superiority in 1943. In June Eaker had called any study of the P-51, to become the finest escort fighter of the war, in the role of escort as "premature."[72] Both Arnold and Giles told Eaker that they felt fighter escort was the key to the bombing effort and to gaining air superiority. Many of their suggestions to him were "born of our great concern over the need for such an escort."[73] Eaker was a late convert to fighter escort; a conversion coming only after the bloodletting at Schweinfurt.[74] Giles, especially, pressed the issue with Eaker, encouraging him to find new and imaginative methods to destroy the Luftwaffe.[75]

Staff officers in Washington were not the only advocates of fighter escort. In May 1943 the commander of the Northwest African Strategic Air Force, Jimmy Doolittle, told Washington that long-range fighter escort had been "desirable in the past," but was "essential in the future." Brigadier General J. H. Atkinson, commanding the Fifth Bombardment Wing of Twelfth Air Force in North Africa, wrote in June that "the standard bomber, such as the B-17, cannot possibly cope with such a situation [deep penetration]." He saw only two solutions to the absence of long-range escort fighters. The United States could either invade continental Europe and set up forward fighter bases to provide escort deep into the Reich or it could abandon daylight bombing and join with the Royal Air Force in the night bombardment of the Ruhr valley. Atkinson was committed to strategic bombing, but believed the Army Air Forces had to have long-range escort to accomplish POINTBLANK.[76]

Eaker's misunderstanding of the importance of long-range fighter escort brought him a stiff reprimand in September. Eaker had placed a high priority on acquiring armor and self-sealing fuel tanks for troop carrier aircraft, to be controlled by Ninth Air Force. Arnold took the extraordinary step of replying to Eaker's list of priorities with a sternly worded message carrying the signature of Army Chief of Staff George Marshall. The cable stated that a program for improvements in troop carrier aircraft would delay the P-38 and P-51 range-extension program. Besides, Arnold reasoned, the improvements would be unnecessary because troop carriers could only operate after air superiority had been gained, at which time the improvements would not be needed.[77]

After Second Schweinfurt Arnold ordered that all P-38 and P-51 production go to Eighth Air Force for the next 3 months.[78] Considering the pressure of other theaters, it was a radical decision. Eaker was "greatly cheered" by the news, but almost simultaneously agreed with Maj. Gen. Lewis Brereton of the newly arrived Ninth Air Force that all incoming P-51s should go to the Ninth to simplify maintenance and repair. Ninth Air Force had the responsibility of preparing the close air support force for OVERLORD and Eaker had given over to it potentially the best escort fighter of the war. Seemingly only after Major General Kepner, Eaker's fighter director, protested did Eaker issue a clarifying directive of 31 December: "The primary tactical role of all U.S. Fighter units in U.K. until further notice will be support and protection of Heavy Bombers engaged in Pointblank."[79]

Eaker blamed his heavy losses in October on the British Ministry of Aircraft Production's failure to deliver the necessary number of drop tanks to allow P-47s to accompany his bombers to greater distances. He tactlessly wrote Chief of the British Air Staff Charles Portal and Minister of Aircraft Production Air Marshal Wilfrid Freeman and directly blamed the British for twenty of the heavy bombers Eighth Air Force had lost over Schweinfurt as a result of a lack of drop tanks.[80] The major responsibility for these delays in fact belonged to Eaker. He refused to accept early British protests that they lacked the industrial capacity to produce the needed tanks. As late as mid-June 1943 he had made drop tanks for fighters his fourth priority[81] and he did not place orders with British representatives for large numbers of tanks until July 1943.[82]

Committed to intensifying strikes against Germany, Arnold proposed to the Combined Chiefs of Staff at the QUADRANT Conference in August that the Army Air Forces begin operations against Germany from Italy. Arnold thought that the creation of a second strategic air force in Italy would ameliorate the problem of weather in operations from England. He told the Combined Chiefs that because German fighter strength continued to rise, more should be done to defeat the Luftwaffe. Arnold had by August determined that continuing to pour aircraft and crews into Eighth Air Force was not the solution to air superiority.[83] The first suggestion of the new air force and a new super command to direct all daylight strategic operations came from Assistant Chief of the Air Staff, Plans, Laurence Kuter in a memo to Arnold.[84] Arnold recommended to the Combined Chiefs of Staff at the SEXTANT Conference on 18 November that a single command, U.S. Strategic Air Forces in Europe, be created to coordinate the operations of Eighth Air Force in England and the new Fifteenth Air Force[85] in Italy. In part his purpose was to insure the Army Air Forces a position in Europe equal to Royal Air Force Bomber Command under its independent-minded commander, Sir Arthur Harris.[86] Despite initial opposition from the British and Eaker, though with the support of Spaatz, the Combined Chiefs approved the new organization on 4 December 1943. A shake-up in the leadership of the Army Air Forces in the European and Mediterranean theaters of operation seemed in the offing, because at Cairo and Teheran Arnold won the support of the Joint Chiefs of Staff and of Roosevelt for his new super command, with Spaatz to head it.[87]

Arnold's dissatisfaction with Eaker poured out at the SEXTANT Conference in late November and early December. He complained to the Allied Combined Chiefs that Eaker was using only 50 percent of his aircraft, while other theaters were using 60 to 70 percent. He used the example of Eaker's September effort, asserting that Eighth Air Force had 1,300 heavy bombers of which 800 were operational and available, with a 50-percent aircraft reserve and with two crews for each aircraft, and yet still only launched one mission of more than 600 bombers. Though Eaker may not have been privy to the content of these discussions, he certainly received word of a 3 December 1943 Combined Chiefs report that included the statement, "That General Eaker should be told to expand his operations to the extent possible with the aircraft and crews available." During the war the reports of the Combined Chiefs were models of generality. For Eaker to be singled out and referred to by name in such a report should have indicated to all, especially Eaker, that the Chiefs were seriously concerned with his performance.[88]

On 6 December Roosevelt announced his selection of Eisenhower as supreme commander for the invasion of France. Two days later, after gaining Eisenhower's approval, Arnold notified Spaatz that he would become the new overall American strategic air commander. Spaatz, for his part, expressed apprehension that his appointment would upset the command balance in the Mediterranean, because no senior American airman remained to balance the Allied command. Arnold then won Eisenhower's agreement to transfer Eaker to head the new Mediterranean Allied Air Forces in order to fill this void.[89] Over the next three days, Arnold, Eisenhower, and Spaatz met to work out the details of the new organizations. Spaatz would head U.S. Strategic Air Forces in Europe, created from Eaker's Eighth Air Force headquarters. Doolittle, at Spaatz's suggestion, would take over Eighth Air Force, created from Maj. Gen. Fred Anderson's VIII Bomber Command headquarters. Anderson would become Spaatz's chief of operations.[90]

Arnold notified Eaker by telegram of the decision on 18 December: "As a result of your long period of successful operations and the exceptional results of your endeavors as Commander of the Air Force in England you have been recommended for this position." Arnold's use of the passive voice, "you have been recommended," set the tone for much of the controversy that would surround the change in leadership. Arnold also sent his chief of staff, Maj. Gen.

Barney Giles, to tell Eaker confidentially of the change in command.[91]

Eaker objected vehemently, protesting to Arnold, European theater commander Lt. Gen. Jacob Devers, Portal, U.S. Ambassador John Winant, Eisenhower, and Spaatz. Arnold responded immediately and firmly that he would not change his mind. Spaatz had compounded the controversy, telling Arnold he would not go to England to head up U.S. Strategic Air Forces in Europe unless Eaker went to the Mediterranean. When Army Chief of Staff George Marshall questioned Arnold about the matter, Arnold was less than truthful when he suggested that the transfer was the idea of Eisenhower and Spaatz. At the same time Eisenhower replied to Eaker's objection, stating that the change of command was Arnold's idea.[92]

Part of this controversy surrounding the change in leadership was in the way in which it was done and by whom. Giles, as Arnold's chief assistant in a position to know, has been the only one of the major participants other than Eaker to state specifically the circumstances of the controversy. In a postwar interview Giles claimed that Arnold sent him personally to England to brief Spaatz and Eaker on the changes in command and that he did just that "at a closed session." He also stated that the decision was made "by General Arnold after consultation with General Eisenhower." Giles reported Eaker as being "very upset" over the decision, threatening "to take this up with the American people when it was all over."[93] There would be no Truman-MacArthur public controversy, however. More important matters, more important than personal feelings, were at hand. Spaatz assumed command of U.S. Strategic Air Forces in Europe on 1 January 1944 and Doolittle of Eighth Air Force on 6 January. Eaker headed for the Mediterranean.

For the men of Eighth Air Force in England, the general feeling about the change in command was one of uncertainty. One unit commander saw Eaker's transfer as a natural act. Eaker was "tough," "a man of very high standards," but he "needed a rest in the southern clime" because he had been at the head of Eighth Air Force too long. Richard Hughes, Eaker's assistant chief of staff in charge of the Operational Planning Section, saw the switch as coming none too soon.

General Eaker's personality and characteristics were very different from those of General Spaatz . . . General Eaker kept even the most minute administrative details in his own hands, and seemed to have very little time, or inclination, for discussing operational plans. For the ensuing year and a half the decision as to which targets our strategic bombers should attack fell squarely on my shoulders. With no sympathetic intellectual support, or understanding, from my Commanding General it was a difficult and heavy burden.

Eaker's greatest mission was the attack on Regensburg, yet Hughes identified Eaker as "completely disinterested" in the plan to destroy the center of German Messerschmitt production. Eaker became interested only after Secretary of War Henry Stimson visited England to investigate Eighth Air Force activities. When Eaker moved to the Mediterranean, he asked Hughes to accompany him as chief of intelligence. Hughes "thankfully, but respectfully, declined the offer." One co-pilot later expressed the attitude of most: "I didn't care. I was going to fly my twenty-five missions regardless."[94]

Spaatz and Doolittle had formed a successful air team in Africa—one that had confidence in Eisenhower and one in which Eisenhower had confidence. With OVERLORD pending, Eisenhower needed Spaatz and Doolittle in England because of their experience in providing air support for invasion forces and for ground operations. In the Mediterranean Arnold needed an air commander to begin strategic operations with sufficient stature to overcome British opposition to a unified air command. No American air officer had more experience than Eaker in building strategic air forces and more skill in dealing with the British. When these factors are combined with the above points of dispute between Eaker and Arnold, Arnold's decision to change the leadership in Europe loses much of its controversial air.

Arnold's memo to Giles on 5 January 1944 best summed up Arnold's dissatisfaction with Eaker.

A study of reports covering the heavy bomber effort of the Eighth Air Force during the past several months, forces me to conclude that aircraft and crews available in the United Kingdom are not utilized as fully and effectively as possible toward achievement of our aims in the European theater . . . There is a lack of firm endeavor to use the maximum number of aircraft and crews on every mission.[95]

At the head of the new leadership in England was Carl Spaatz, born in 1891 in Boyertown, Pennsylvania. He attended the U.S. Military Academy prior to the outbreak of World War I. Spaatz served in France, including 4 weeks of combat flying with the 13th Aero Squadron, downing three German aircraft. Between the world wars he gained experience in both bombardment and pursuit. During the Battle of Britain, as an observer, he predicted British victory and became convinced of the ability of the self-defending bomber to win the war. He was the first commander of Eighth Air Force before his transfer to North Africa. Promoted to lieutenant general in March 1943, he commanded Twelfth Air Force until Arnold appointed him to head the U.S. Strategic Air Forces in Europe beginning in January 1944. In 1944 his views on air power changed, reflecting the absolute necessity of the long-range fighter as escort and in a more or less independent strategic role to achieve air superiority.

Such a transformation was not inconsistent with his personality and career. According to one biographer, he was "taciturn," mental but not technical, self-confident, honest, loyal, and intuitive. He also loved to play poker and was not afraid to gamble, although he was not rash. Mary Gill recalled that "you didn't feel the personal touch with him." She remembered him as tall and thin, "somewhat cut and dry . . . [presenting] a stern appearance . . . more the professional officer." Spaatz was a subordinate officer's dream, distributing authority and responsibility to his staff, free of interference. He had no time for administrative problems; "General Spaatz's interest had always been intimately concerned with the conduct of operations." His finest asset was his broad experience. In England in 1944 this experience helped him to view the air war as the battle of attrition for air superiority that it had become.[96]

Major General Frederick Anderson was younger than the other leaders of the air superiority campaign, born in Kingston, New York, in 1905. He did not serve in World War I. After graduation from West Point in 1928 he entered the Air Corps. A heavy-bomber man from the beginning, influenced by assignment as director of bombardment at the Air Corps Tactical School in 1940, he arrived in England in February 1943, taking turns as the commander of Eighth Air Forces' Third and Fourth Bomb Wings. In these positions Anderson learned a great deal more about bomber operations than most other general officers in similar or higher positions. In March and April 1943 he scheduled himself to fly sixteen missions, only to have thirteen scrubbed because of weather and maintenance problems. In July Eaker selected him to command the VIII Bomber Command. Utterly confident in his ability and his command, Anderson told the Air Staff that American forces in England were "the greatest striking force the world has ever known . . . [that would] destroy the economic resources of Germany to such an extent that I personally believe no invasion of the Continent or Germany proper will ever have to take place."

Such bravado earned him the support and respect of Arnold and Spaatz because it revealed an absolute commitment to defeating Germany. When Chief of the Air Staff Maj. Gen. George Stratemeyer originally recommended Anderson to Eaker, he claimed "there is not a finer officer in the world." To Richard Hughes, the man charged with selecting targets for Eaker, Fred Anderson was a "truly great man," one who "completely understood" the problems of strategic bombing. Subordinates recognized his "exceptional" leadership—self-effacing, loyal, and single-minded in his devotion to completing his assigned job. So strong was this commitment that he could "continue ordering out children to their deaths" to achieve victory.

Mary Gill, who for a time served as Anderson's secretary, recalled Anderson as "ruggedly handsome," between 6'2" and 6'4" tall. He dictated correspondence "very rapidly," "spoke very distinctly," and was "very articulate." He seemed to Gill imperturbable, at least on the surface. When the heavy losses of Regensburg, First Schweinfurt, and the fall crisis became known, "it didn't seem to have any outward effect on him at all." He was a remorseless driver—"make it or break it" most clearly expressed his enthusiasm for the job. Anderson was not blindly dedicated to the self-defending bomber, however. In August 1943, as a result of his experiences during the Blitz Week attacks, he told Hunter that fighter escort was the key to victory. In December Arnold and Spaatz chose Anderson as deputy commander for operations for the U.S. Strategic Air Forces in Europe, in charge of the day-to-day employment of American strategic forces deployed against Germany.[97]

Taking over at VIII Bomber Command headquarters, now Eighth Air Force in the reorganization of the Army Air Forces command structure in Europe, was Maj. Gen. James "Jimmy" Doolittle. Born in Alameda, California, in 1896, he joined the Signal Corps in 1917. After World War I he pursued aeronautical engineering degrees, earning a doctorate from the Massachusetts Institute of Technology in 1925. He was especially noted for making the first successful outside loop-the-loop and for blind-flying experiments leading to modern flight instrumentation. Chafing under the conditions of the peacetime army, he resigned in 1930. One of the great aviation pioneers, he set a number of distance and speed records during the 1920s and 1930s. In the 1930s Doolittle spearheaded the development of 100-octane aviation gasoline in the United States. With the outbreak of war in Europe, he rejoined the Army. His recommendation to Arnold led to the Army Air Forces emphasis on bad-weather flying, which was one of the key factors behind the American victory in the European air war. Before assuming command of Eighth Air Force, he led the bombing raid on Japan that was to bear his name and commanded Twelfth Air Force and

Northwest African Strategic Air Force. He also was on the first Army Air Forces bombing raid on Rome. A great innovator, Doolittle had realized the importance of long-range fighter escort early in 1943.

He was also compassionate for his crews. Mary Gill rarely saw Doolittle's predecessor, Ira Eaker, but she was Doolittle's personal secretary from the time he took over the Eighth until well after the war. He was her favorite general. "Doolittle was so understanding," she declared. "He was so humane. He had a feeling for people." As her boss, "you never got the sharp orders you would get from other military men." As a senior military commander, "he could be just as stern and disciplinarian as he had to be, but you felt at times that he was forced into the disciplinarian situation, that he really felt sorry for the person he had to bawl out." During tense times such as the great battles for air superiority, he showed "no unnecessary strain," but was "serious." He was, however, "good at hiding his feelings."

Doolittle had to win his spurs with Eisenhower, Spaatz, and Arnold to overcome his status as a reservist. But determined and businesslike, yet flexible, he seemed the perfect choice to lead Eighth Air Force out of the fall crisis.[98]

Back in Washington, the key person besides Arnold was Maj. Gen. Barney M. Giles. During World War I he served in the 168th Observation Squadron and between the wars flew B-17s with the pioneering 2nd Bomb Group. In March 1943 Arnold named him assistant chief of the Air Staff, assigning him the responsibility of developing range for fighter escorts. He was the champion of drop tanks and for increased internal tankage in fighter aircraft. After the war he claimed this was his greatest contribution to American air power and to American victory in the war. Named chief of the Air Staff and deputy commander of the Army Air Forces in July 1943, he also contributed mightily to the tactics VIII Fighter Command developed to take advantage of long-range fighters. Giles pushed Arnold into transferring Hunter and recommended Kepner to replace him. He, along with Fred Anderson and Carl Spaatz, was one of the few to recognize the special importance of air superiority to the American war effort. Giles regularly filled the vacuum in the Army Air Forces leadership during Arnold's medical absences.[99]

Accompanying the introduction of this new leadership was a dramatic increase in the strength of the Army Air Forces in Europe.[100] October's twenty-one heavy-bomber groups and nine fighter groups became twenty-six and sixteen, respectively, by January. The latter included one long-range P-51 Mustang group and two long-range P-38 Lightning groups. In straight numbers this meant 1,304 operational heavy bombers and 1,405 bomber crews, backed by an additional 2,322 heavy bombers in the supply network. They had the support of 1,254 operational fighters manned by 1,140 pilots, backed by an additional 2,571 fighter aircraft in the supply network.[101] The spare aircraft allowed American units to absorb the punishment of attrition warfare.

By the new year, the U.S. Army Air Forces had the new leadership and necessary aircraft to begin the final drive for the air superiority necessary for OVERLORD. But these aspects of aerial warfare were the easy portion of the task. Battles would have to be fought and men would have to die to win that air superiority.

CHAPTER FIVE

TRANSITION TO AIR SUPERIORITY—BIG WEEK

By early 1944 the twin duties of the U.S. Strategic Air Forces in Europe and its two subordinate air forces, the Eighth and the Fifteenth, had become one—its job was to defeat the Luftwaffe in being and gain air superiority first and foremost while carrying out the selective destruction of German industrial power. One of Spaatz's first actions was to call a conference on 24 January to regularize and prioritize the relationship between two of the air forces assigned to complete these objectives: the American strategic air force in England, Eighth Air Force, and the American tactical air force in England responsible for close air support of invasion forces, Ninth Air Force. In part this was to solve the problem Eaker created when he ordered all P-51 groups assigned to Ninth Air Force. The new agreement called for all P-51s scheduled for shipment to England to replace the P-47s in most of VIII Fighter Command's groups, including the 4th, 352nd, 355th, 359th, and 361st. The freed P-47s would then be used to build up Ninth Air Force fighter groups in preparation for OVERLORD. Continuing in force was Eaker's order for Ninth units to support Eighth Air Force operations until both air forces came under Eisenhower's direct control in March for invasion preparation.[1]

In the meantime, the war went on. Giles pressured the field commanders, telling Spaatz that "General Arnold has not been satisfied with the efforts made to date."[2] Fred Anderson, as deputy commander for operations for the U.S. Strategic Air Forces in Europe, was determined to go on with the bombing, regardless of losses and the weather. Eighth Air Force, he told Spaatz, should not wait for the arrival of sufficient long-range fighter escorts. The Luftwaffe should not be given a respite. Anderson's decision and Spaatz's support for it symbolized the battle of attrition the air war had become.[3] In part it forced the Luftwaffe to continue bad-weather flying, for which it was remarkably unprepared. On 4 January I Fighter Corps lost twelve fighters to snow. An additional problem with weather showed up on the thirteenth. Heavy cloud-cover prevented the massing of fighters in wing strength. In the resulting action by small isolated groups, German defenses lost thirty fighters with an additional twenty-one damaged. In all, "approximately one-third of German aircraft losses was due to commitment under unfavorable weather conditions."[4]

The American mission of 11 January to Brunswick, Oschersleben, Halberstadt, and Osnabrück was, in the postwar words of I Fighter Corps commander Josef Schmid, "the last victory of the German Air Force over the American Air Forces." For the Americans, the mission was remarkable because of the performance of one fighter pilot, Maj. James Howard, whose exploits in a P-51 in defending single-handedly an entire bomber formation earned him a Congressional Medal of Honor.

We were under continual attack. We saw in front of us a swarm of German aircraft—just like bees. And they're going in this direction and here's a lone P-51 coming this way. And there was a great big cloud of black, fiery red-yellow-orange smoke and from this emerged fewer German aircraft and a single P-51. This was Howard. We saw him make persistent attacks on the Germans in front of us. And we marveled at this. It was a continual evaporative-type fighter attack in front of us. And we wondered and marveled at it. It was one man—where the hell are his buddies? I didn't see a single other aircraft of the United States Army Air Forces except that one P-51.

Despite Howard's heroics, I Fighter Corps claimed sixty bombers and five fighters downed that day and admitted to twenty-one fighters lost. Another German source put Luftwaffe losses at fifty-four for the same day. Eighth Air Force claimed two hundred fifty-nine German fighters downed and admitted to the loss of forty-four.[5]

Weather prevented further deep penetrations until the 30 January mission to Brunswick. On that day I Fighter Corps lost thirty aircraft because heavy clouds prevented massing. Schmid was learning that piecemeal attacks against heavily escorted American bomber formations were a losing proposition. Weather was causing more problems that just losses, however. On 24 January Doolittle launched his bombers, but recalled them because of worsening weather. Göring, who chose that day to be at the Air Fleet Reich headquarters in Berlin, saw reports of the initial bomber penetration and assumed the target was Berlin. He ordered the Luftwaffe to launch all available aircraft, including both the day and night fighters of I Fighter Corps, 7 Fighter Division in Austria, and all available aircraft from training schools. In all 821 fighters rose to attack the no-longer-existent bomber formations. Once Göring had determined that only Eighth Air Force fighters were left to attack, he ordered all German aircraft to land, in keeping with his own order to avoid combat with American fighters. The mission was notable because the difficulty of mounting the all-out effort convinced the Luftwaffe to put all fighters under the control of Air Fleet Reich, though the transfer was not completed until 31 March 1944. Another significant aspect of the German reaction on 24 January was the I Fighter Corps' ability to launch so many fighters under such poor weather conditions. Also noteworthy was Göring's telegram to Stumpff at Air Fleet Reich and Schmid at I Fighter Corps the next day, which demonstrated that the Luftwaffe commander could still see a little humor in the direction of the war. He wrote, "Yesterday's little maneuver may be considered a success except for the fact that April Fool's Day is still two months away."[6]

To further enhance I Fighter Command's performance, Schmid

called a meeting of his division commanders and Generalmajor Galland on 25 January. The conference produced three recommendations: German fighters must force combat with American fighters to make them drop their external tanks, the early warning system should pay more attention to Allied morning reconnaissance in order to predict the bombing target for the day, and wing commanders should work harder to achieve local numerical superiority "at a given time in a given place." The participants also predicted that American forces would increase their numbers and range, but that they would not be able to reach Berlin.[7]

Schmid's biggest problem was one over which he had no control. During January, despite a heavy loss of pilots, he received no pilot replacements or reinforcements. German industry was sending him all the aircraft he could use, but the number of men he had to fly them continued to decline. To conserve pilot strength, Göring continued his order that pilots avoid combat with American fighters. This tactic, however, unintentionally encouraged Doolittle to a critical command decision.[8]

Though some students of the air war have paid little attention to this change, in Doolittle's mind it was his "most important decision of the war."[9] It came early in January during an orientation visit to VIII Fighter Command headquarters. Kepner had been pressing Doolittle to allow VIII Fighter Command fighters to be more aggressive and to free them of their close-escort responsibility. In his own words, Doolittle saw a sign on Kepner's office wall: "The first duty of the Eighth Air Force fighters is to bring the bombers back alive." Asked about its origins, Kepner told Doolittle that the sign was a carry-over from Hunter's command. Doolittle then ordered him to replace the sign with another one: "The first duty of the Eighth Air Force fighters is to destroy German fighters." Doolittle was unleashing American fighters to begin truly offensive actions against the Luftwaffe in order to gain air superiority, not just to defend American bombers. "We'll still provide a reasonable fighter escort for the bombers, but the bulk of your fighters will go hunting for Jerries. Flush them out in the air and beat them up on the ground on the way home. Your first priority is to take the offensive."[10]

The irony here was that freeing the fighters represented a return to Hunter's tactics, where fighters would fight for air superiority, with bombers used mainly as bait to lure German fighters into combat. Doolittle was evidently reacting to Arnold's New Year's message to him: "Destroy the enemy air forces wherever you find them, in the air, on the ground and in the factories."[11] Doolittle formalized his decision to his commanders in a staff meeting on 21 January, telling them that "the fighter role of protecting the bombardment formation should not be minimized, but our fighter aircraft should be encouraged to meet the enemy and destroy him rather that be content to keep him away."[12]

According to Kepner, the decision to free the fighters was more evolutionary than anything else. He had wanted to send his fighters out to search the skies for several months—now he had the go-ahead. "If it meant getting out and scouring the skies, even by thinning down the escort, that would be okay with them [Spaatz and Doolittle]."[13] Eighth Fighter Command fighters as early as July 1943 had been encouraged to go on sweeps after escorting medium bombers to their targets in France, Belgium, and Holland. Freeing had been on Giles's mind since the long-range fighter began to come off the assembly lines in the summer of 1943. He described freeing in a letter to Eaker.[14]

The bombardment leader . . . will detach pursuit squadrons or even groups when the occasion arises to knock off enemy Pursuit or to attack anything that interferes with the bombardment formation. In this way not only will the bombers be protected but a large number of German Pursuit that come out to fight will be knocked down.

At the time Eaker was seemingly not impressed, besides not possessing long-range fighters to be freed on deep penetration. Doolittle's decision reflected the change that had taken place in the fall of 1943 in American strategy. Again in Doolittle's words, "German fighter production, which had long been one of our first priority targets, no longer really mattered . . . since the customer could no longer use the product for lack of fuel and trained replacement pilots."[15] Doolittle realized that Eighth Air Force's two POINTBLANK missions, air superiority and strategic bombing, had become one.[16]

When Doolittle freed the fighters, in the opinion of the Luftwaffe's General der Flieger Adolf Galland, the Luftwaffe lost the air war.[17] I Fighter Corps' commander Josef Schmid put the freeing decision together with Göring's order that German fighters avoid American fighters: "Knowing that they need not fear an attack by the German fighter aircraft, American fighters are able to move into range and attack the German fighters from above."[18]

The first mission in which Doolittle's decision reflected in the tactics of VIII Fighter Command was the 24 January mission to Frankfurt.[19] Kepner continued the phased escort tactic of continuous area coverage, assigning his groups areas to patrol. Twelve P-47 groups gave the bombers continuous protection on penetration and withdrawal, reinforced on withdrawal by Royal Air Force Spitfire squadrons. The three long-range fighter groups provided general target coverage. But Kepner further designated one squadron from each group the "bouncing" squadron. He gave these squadrons the freedom to attack and follow any Luftwaffe fighters penetrating within visual distance of the bomber stream. Once away from the bombers, the "bouncing squadron" had the "freedom of action of being able to roam about and smack down any Huns that may be forming up for future attacks well outside the usual range of our fighters' aggressive movements, which had hitherto been controlled by the necessity to remain with the bombers."[20]

Bad weather forced widely dispersed bomber formations and only fifty-eight bombers hit the required target. Nearly all of the "bouncing" squadrons had to fly close escort for the widely scattered bombers. Nevertheless, the 353rd Fighter Group's "bouncing" squadron claimed four enemy aircraft that day. The 356th Fighter Group's P-47s chased fifteen German fighters 65 miles from Brussels to Ypres before claiming six of them. One flight demonstrated an additional aspect of the freedom Doolittle had given them, following eight German fighters from 25,000 feet down to treetop level before downing three. In the fall of 1943 VIII Fighter Command policy prohibited fighters from going below 18,000 feet. Now "you had to explain why you didn't go down if there was a fight."

Air Fleet 3 bore the brunt of the assault, admitting to the loss of twenty-three fighters, many to weather. For once American claims of twenty German fighters downed was less than the actual number the Luftwaffe lost. Of the bombers and 678 fighters Eighth Air Force sent on the mission, it admitted to the loss of 2 bombers and 9 fighters.[21]

Initially German intelligence saw the change in tactics as orientation flights for new fighter groups away from the bomber stream. By the end of the month the true identity of the new American tactic was clear. The twin-engine, heavily armed destroyer fighters that had caused the fall crisis were now the "sitting ducks" Eaker had predicted. Slow and lacking in maneuverability, their strength had been hovering out of the range of bomber-.50-caliber defensive fire, slamming 20mm and 30mm cannon fire and 21-cm rockets into bomber formations. As such they were even more vulnerable than the bombers to fighter action, because at least the bombers had defensive weapons. The twin-engine fighter had little defense against American fighters. On the missions of 29 and 30 January to Frankfurt, Brunswick, and Hannover, the Luftwaffe lost 16 of these destroyer aircraft out of admitted total losses of 109. American victory claims were twice as high.[22]

Eighth Air Force was off on the race for air superiority and only looked back twice. Losses for Eighth Air Force seemed heavy for these two missions: an admitted forty-nine heavy bombers and nineteen fighters, though the bomber loss rate was only 3 percent. Freeing damaged the morale of bomber crews.

We were informally advised that the fighters were not going to stay close to us anymore. They are going to be with you, but if they see Germans they are going to leave you. That's when we started to feel the fighters are not for us, that we'd better damn well be prepared to defend ourselves. That gave you the feeling that we were expendable. They were going to go for the fighters, that we were bait. As individuals we were not told these decisions. We were not told the reasons for these decisions.

Kepner warned his pilots that they should be "bold," but without "recklessness," as most German fighters would be found "in the immediate vicinity of the bombers." Freeing to force heavier attrition on the Luftwaffe was to be encouraged, but not freeing just for the sake of freeing. And on 20 February, perhaps edgy with the launching of a major campaign to win air superiority imminent, Spaatz questioned the soundness of the change, but Doolittle stood by his decision, claiming it had actually reduced bomber losses and that it was logical considering the apparent German tactic of ignoring American escort to concentrate on the bombers. By late February freeing meant that "if there were no enemy aircraft attacking or in the vicinity after rendezvous with the bombers, approximately two-thirds of each fighter group were permitted to search well out on the flanks and above and below the bombers to engage and destroy any enemy aircraft encountered."[23]

Perhaps in no way could the dual impact of freeing and the advent of long-range escort have been clearer to the German high command than when Adolf Galland reported his experience with Mustangs in the early spring. Four P-51s, already 300 miles from home, chased him at top speed from the Rhine River to Brandenburg, near Berlin, a distance of 270 miles, at treetop level, with no bombers in sight. He escaped when he fired his guns into open air space. Galland hoped the resulting gun smoke would convince his pursuers that he had rear-firing guns. The subterfuge worked, but the revolutionary significance of what he had just experienced had been brought home. American fighter pilots had adopted an offensive spirit that would carry them through the remainder of the war. Instead of the defensive maxims of 1943, such as "Beware of the Hun in the sun," VIII Fighter Command now encouraged the aggression: "The only reason for failure to attack enemy aircraft is a fuel shortage."[24] Luther Richmond, a P-51 pilot in the 352nd Fighter Group, ordered his crew chief not to camouflage his aircraft, but to leave it shiny silver so Luftwaffe pilots could see it. "Everybody had trouble finding combat with the enemy—I was becoming a bit desperate to make contact."[25]

Another aspect of freeing was the expansion of the Free Lance tactic of employment begun in December 1943. Because of recent reinforcements, Kepner began releasing entire groups from escort duty in order to undertake wide-ranging sweeps up to 45 miles away from the bomber formations. The plan was to attack German fighters when they were most vulnerable—as they were forming for wing-size attacks. On 30 January the 352nd and 358th Fighter Groups flying Free Lance attacked German fighters forming up and claimed ten.[26] Though impressive in concept, the Free Lance tactic failed to deliver in combat largely because American fighters were flying blind. If contact occurred, it was usually by accident. The day before the 30 January success two Free Lance groups returned to base without a single claim.

The Allies developed two techniques to improve their ability to direct these units to their prey. Since the Battle of Britain, the British had been intercepting radio messages of the German Y-system used to control fighter aircraft from the ground and used by fighters to report their activities to ground control stations. The British Y-Service, named after the German designation, intercepted these transmissions, translated them, and passed the intercepts on to VIII Fighter Command. Controllers at the Eighth's three fighter wings would then vector Free Lance units to the same areas German controllers had ordered their fighters. Used first in October 1943, the procedure rarely worked in actual operations as well as it did in theory. The range was too great; Y-Service operations were limited to 150 miles initially. By February 1944 intercepts could be made no deeper than western Germany. In addition, fighter aircraft flew at combat speeds of greater than 6 miles per minute. By the time Free Lance groups arrived at their vectored positions, the enemy was usually nowhere to be seen.

Radar was also used to vector American fighters beginning on 31 December 1943. Known as Type 16 control, radar could reach no farther than Rotterdam. An additional problem with Type 16 was the inability of radar to distinguish between friendly and enemy aircraft. If a Type 16 vector was successful, as often as not the intercepted aircraft were Allied. Type 16's first success occurred on 14 January 1944 when controllers vectored the 4th and 354th Fighter Groups to a swarm of German fighters, resulting in eleven victories.[27]

Doolittle made two other critical decisions contributing to the battle for air superiority, both on 8 February. He ordered the conservation of his Eighth Air Force on noncritical operations "to avoid having the hammerhead force depleted between critical operations." Second, he ordered all qualified P-51 pilots to fly escort missions, regardless of all but the highest rank or responsibility. If insufficient aircraft were available for them, these pilots would borrow Mustangs from the Ninth Air Force. The need for these long-range escorts was so great that the 352nd Fighter Group flew P-51s in combat in late February after only two hours of orientation flying following its conversion from P-47s. "Crew chiefs had not yet received any tools for the aircraft [P-51s] and were unable even to remove a spark plug." The effort was all-out.[28]

Another command decision in the intense push to gain air superiority came from Arnold. On 11 February 1944 he wrote Doolittle and told him that the twenty-five missions bomber crews were required to fly before rotating back to the United States were insufficient. For the Army Air Forces to win the air war against Germany, they would have to do more. Arnold's idea was to eliminate any minimum number of missions and rely instead on the needs of Eighth Air Force to determine when bomber crews finished their tours. Doolittle responded by increasing the number of missions in a tour to thirty, but ignored Arnold's suggestion of open-ended tours of duty. Fighter pilots would only be eligible for rotation after 200 hours of combat flying, not automatic rotation after 200 hours as before.[29]

Despite the new tactics, additional aircraft, and extended tours, weather continued to delay any reckoning in the battle for air superiority. It was the single most important factor in the air war for the next month. On 3 February 609 bombers and 632 fighters flew to Wilhelmshaven, but the main challenge was weather, not German fighters. Even German claims for this and the next mission were relatively moderate. Eighth Air Force lost 4 bombers and 9 fighters, the I Fighter Corps 6. The next day 633 bombers went to Frankfurt with 637 fighters, but the Luftwaffe refused to do battle because of miserable weather. American losses were 20 bombers and 1 fighter, most to weather-related causes. The Luftwaffe in the West and in Germany lost only 6. On the next three missions of 8, 10, and 11 February, an average of only 183 heavy bombers made it to their targets because of weather. Nevertheless, losses for both sides were heavy, many to weather-related causes: an average of 16 American heavy bombers, 11 American fighters, and 10 I Fighter Corps's fighters. All German losses in the West and over the Reich, according to one German source, averaged 43 for those three days, the majority due to weather.[30]

Especially of concern to the commander of I Fighter Corps were the implications of the 10 February mission. American fighters had severely mauled Schmid's fighters over German territory, destroying an admitted thirty German planes. Such losses were acceptable only if they deterred American bombing efforts. The weather turned even worse for the next week, preventing any determination of how effective his expensive attacks had been against the American effort. Schmid complained that the Luftwaffe could no longer find American bombers without accompanying escort, that he was not receiving reinforcements, and that there still was little cooperation between his I Fighter Corps and the Seventh Fighter Division in southern Germany and Fighter Command Center Ostmark in Austria. One of his biggest problems, a continuing one, was his fighters' lack of range, which prevented any cooperation between units. Unknown to Schmid at the time, but soon crystal clear, the battle for air superiority was reaching a fevered pitch and the

Luftwaffe had done little since the summer of 1943 to prepare for it.[31]

Spaatz and his U.S. Strategic Air Forces in Europe were soon to test the effectiveness of Schmid's forces. American aircraft and crews were now available in substantial quantities, including over 678 operational fighters and 1,000 bombers on average during February for Eighth Air Force alone. Backing these up were an additional 1,000 bombers and 1,400 fighters in supply depots or undergoing maintenance. One new long-range fighter group arrived in January and three in February. New tactics had been developed to utilize them, and an incentive for quick action, the impending invasion of France, was ever present. Arnold provided the warning: OVERLORD would "not be possible unless the German Air Force is destroyed."[32] Behind the operational forces was an enormous supply and maintenance system under the direction of Maj. Gen. Hugh Knerr, one maintaining more than 190,000 different spare parts.[33] The turning point in the air war had arrived. Anderson's targeting officer expressed the question that was on everyone's minds:

Could we possibly determine whether or not we could gain air superiority before D-Day, and whether or not by the exercise of strategic air power on decisive Germany industrial target systems, we could appreciably shorten the length of time for which the Germans could resist. If we failed, this time, we would probably never have any more forces than we now had, with which to succeed, and it was essential to find out the answer quickly.[34]

These forces faced the Luftwaffe's I Fighter Corps, which had fewer aircraft (about 500 fighters) and tactics carried over from the fall of 1943, based on its successes against more or less escortless American bombers. Göring, Milch, and Galland had built this force from a position of desperation, augmenting its ranks with reconnaissance, test, ferry, and weather-probe pilots. Under Hitler's orders, the Luftwaffe also had reduced the recuperation period allowed wounded pilots.[35]

How now to force the Luftwaffe into ruinous attrition? Eaker's plan had been to destroy the Luftwaffe by bombing the factories that produced its planes. Spaatz's idea was to bomb the factories to destroy production and to bomb aircraft on the ground at airfields, and in so doing force Luftwaffe fighters to come up and defend the factories, where they could be shot down. When he took over in England, Spaatz inherited a plan designed to do just this.

The plan, codenamed ARGUMENT, was the brain child of the Combined Operational Planning Committee based in England and consisting of both Royal Air Force and Army Air Forces representatives, headed by Brig. Gen. O. A. Anderson. Its roots went back to March 1943. The stated goal of ARGUMENT was to "depreciate the German aircraft industry," in pursuit of the POINTBLANK intermediate objective of destroying the German single-engine fighter force. The Eighth Air Force staff had early in the planning concluded that such an effort would require 3,800 heavy bombers at a minimum.[36] Planning continued at a leisurely pace through 1943, taking a final, but flexible form by 4 November 1943. It called for an all-out Allied bombing assault on German single- and twin-engine fighter, synthetic rubber, and ball-bearing production. A shortage of heavy bombers forced planners to drop synthetic rubber from the list and reduce the emphasis on ball-bearing production. This led to a lowering of expectations, from the elimination of "Germany's capacity to wage war" to crippling "her war potential." If weather prevented attacks on the specific industries targeted in ARGUMENT, the bombers were to attack Berlin.[37]

So pressing was the need to force a dramatic reduction in the strength of the Luftwaffe that the intent was to proceed with ARGUMENT without long-range escort if such was not available.[38] United States Strategic Air Forces in Europe intelligence predicted the loss of 200 heavy bombers just to attack the Leipzig Messerschmitt complex. Spaatz and Anderson placed such importance on the effort that they were willing to pay such a price. They had the support of the Army Air Forces Board Project, which told Arnold that Eighth Air Force must intensify its efforts to destroy the Luftwaffe even if it meant "attriting [American] forces at a greater rate than replacements are available."[39] Arnold in Washington pleaded with Spaatz for action: "Can't we, some day, and not too far distant, send out a big number—*and I mean a big number*—of bombers to hit something in the nature of an aircraft factory and *lay it flat?*"[40]

The logic behind ARGUMENT was the attrition of the Luftwaffe by minimizing the "production-wastage differential." Attacking the factories would reduce production, but would mean nothing unless the Luftwaffe force in being also underwent wastage. Intelligence indicated that from April to June 1943 the Luftwaffe had a 530 "production-wastage differential" in its favor. From July to September the differential had turned in favor of the Allies, to a negative 395. Since October, however, the differential had turned back to Germany's advantage.[41] ARGUMENT was supposed to restore a favorable differential. Eaker tried to initiate the plan on the eighth, twelfth, fourteenth, fifteenth, sixteenth, seventeenth, and eighteenth of December 1943, but weather frustrated each attempt.[42]

The situation was worse than the Allies realized. Actual and planned German single-engine fighter production for the first 6 months of 1944 exceeded Allied intelligence estimates by 2½ and 3¼ times, respectively. Against a goal of 2,000 single-engine fighters by February 1944, actual German production did not reach the goal until June 1944, but was still ahead of Allied expectations. Unless Spaatz launched ARGUMENT, German production would continue to outpace losses, placing POINTBLANK and OVERLORD in jeopardy.[43]

The chief critics of the ARGUMENT plan were Eisenhower's tactical air chief, Air Chief Marshal Trafford Leigh-Mallory, and the Ninth Air Force commander, Maj. Gen. Lewis Brereton. Leigh-Mallory wished to commit Ninth Air Force and the Royal Air Force's Fighter Command to training for D-day, when it was anticipated that a great air battle would be fought over France to defeat the Luftwaffe. Brereton apparently supported Leigh-Mallory in this plan, but more clearly wanted to spend the next several months in

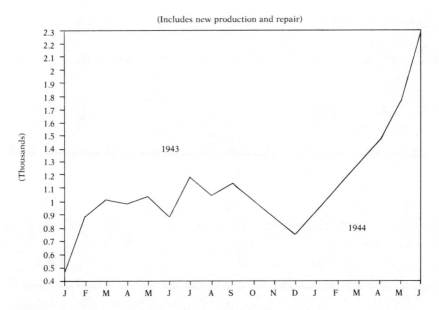

Figure 7. German Single-Engine Fighter Production
Source: Grabmann, "German Air Force Defense Operations," 1956, File K113.107-164, HRC.

training for his eventual role of supporting ground troops in the push across France to Germany. Spaatz and his deputy Fred Anderson countered that all forces should engage in the completion of POINTBLANK; the way to defeat the Luftwaffe was in a continuous battle of attrition right up to D-day. Spaatz won Eisenhower's temporary support, until the time his forces would come under Eisenhower's direct control, because Spaatz was involved in killing Germans and Leigh-Mallory and Brereton were not.[44]

By mid-February 1944 the Luftwaffe had built up its defensive fighter force, the I Fighter Corps, to its highest level yet in the war, including a daily average of 350 single-engine, 100 twin-engine, and 50 night fighters.[45] It was, however, only marginally larger than the force that had successfully challenged American bombing in the fall. The Army Air Forces, on the other hand, had expanded its forces and operations to a considerable degree, flying 5,694 sorties in October 43, but 17,038 sorties in February 1944.[46] The

Luftwaffe persevered with the same tactics that had brought it victory in the fall. The arrival of long-range escort fighters and the development of tactics for maximizing their use, however, had changed the nature of the American-German confrontation. By mid-February only two P-51 groups (IX Fighter Command's 354th, on loan to Eighth Air Force, and VIII Fighter Command's 357th) and two P-38 groups (the 20th and 55th) were operational in England. These long-range fighters were truly the "thin silver line" on which Spaatz and his men depended to reverse the fortunes of the air war in their favor.

February's weather continued abysmal. Day after day of solid overcast dimmed any hope of forcing heavy attrition on the Luftwaffe. The bombers were ready to go after Germany's aircraft industry—1,180 of them. Sleek, long-range P-51s, heavyset P-47s, and twin-boomed P-38s—676 of them—were set to begin the most intense series of missions of the air war with the Luftwaffe's Bf 109s and 110s and FW 190s. Then meteorologists made an unusual forecast for the depths of a European winter, based in part on ULTRA intercepts of SS weather reports issued at Krakow, Poland—about a week of more or less clear skies in late February. It was the most favorable period of weather in a thirty-year record of European weather. The stage was set for an all-out offensive against Germany's Luftwaffe—a "Big Week."[47]

By 20 February, when the spell of clear weather was to commence, the British-American Combined Chiefs of Staff, under American pressure, had narrowed POINTBLANK's priority objectives to fighter airframe and component production and ball-bearing manufacture.[48] POINTBLANK, the Combined Bomber Offensive, had become almost entirely a counterair offensive. Air superiority had come to occupy center stage. If German fighters were now unquestionably the weapon to be reduced, American fighters had become the lead actors. So important had the fighter role become that Spaatz authorized Kepner to break the chain of command through Doolittle and Ninth Air Force commander Lewis Brereton and deal directly with Maj. Gen. Elwood Quesada, commanding IX Fighter

Command, or even with individual Ninth Air Force wing commanders to be sure he got the fighters he needed to complete ARGU-
MENT.[49]

On 19 February 1944, Fred Anderson pressed Spaatz to unleash
ARGUMENT in view of the predicted spell of clear weather. Doolittle
repeatedly requested that Spaatz cancel the mission scheduled
for 20 February to kick off the Army Air Forces' part of the operation because he was reluctant to accept the projected losses. At a
7:30 P.M. meeting with Spaatz and Anderson, Doolittle and Ninth
Air Force commander Lewis Brereton complained that the bombers and fighters would experience wing and windshield icing
problems upon takeoff. Anderson left the meeting and hurried to
a nearby bomber base. He talked to a number of crew chiefs before calling Spaatz at 9:10 P.M. to convince him that the big show
should be launched the next day. Anderson told his boss that
using de-icing liquid on the wings and keeping the cockpit windows open would minimize the icing problem. Spaatz took 20
minutes to make one final weather check before returning the call
to his deputy for operations, at which time the U.S. Strategic Air
Forces in Europe commander gave the order to go, as scheduled.
Anderson notified Eighth Air Force and Ira Eaker in the Mediterranean that ARGUMENT was on and then sent for his toothbrush
so that he could stay by the telephone at operations. He wanted
to be ready to intervene again if necessary to prevent any weakening of Spaatz's resolve. Anderson's commitment to winning air
superiority had won out over Doolittle's caution. Spaatz would
later give all credit to Anderson for the results of that day's mission.[50]

Doolittle's hesitation was in keeping with a pattern he had established in the first month of his new command. He had already
earned a reprimand from Spaatz for what Spaatz saw as excessive
concern for his men and too little concern for completing his mission. At Anderson's request, Spaatz wrote Doolittle and told him to
stop using weather as an excuse for canceling missions. Spaatz
also told Doolittle that once the heavy bombers had crossed the

enemy coast, Doolittle should not recall them—only the air commander had that authority.[51] In Doolittle's own words, Spaatz had told him in January 1944, "It looks like you don't have the guts to command a large air force. If you haven't I'll get someone else who has."[52] The 9 February 1944 entry in Spaatz's diary revealed his opinion of Doolittle's caution: "Today is to go on record as completely wasted. Good weather at bases, good weather over target, and Doolittle sent *no* bombers."[53]

It began on the night of 19/20 February when 730 heavies of Royal Air Force Bomber Command hit Leipzig with their normal area bombing. The toll was 78 RAF bombers, a loss rate of nearly 11 percent, and 569 crewmen for the night's work—hardly a good beginning for an effort of this scale.

American fighter and bomber crews awoke early on the morning of 20 February to discover that the day's mission would be an all-out effort deep into Germany. Some groups would go to Leipzig, just 80 miles southwest of Berlin—the deepest penetration for Eighth Air Force since Regensburg in August 1943. As a B-17 pilot would recall years later, "The weather people had called the shot right; the weather was not a factor that morning."

At a B-24 base, such as Rackheath in Norfolk, the weather had been mostly bad since October. The officers and enlisted men of the 467th Bomb Group (Heavy) had suffered from "the wet North Sea cold that was as nothing we had experienced before. It cut through six blankets at night and lay about the coke stove [in the half-cylindrical metal Quonset or Nissen huts] like wolves about a dying doe." Some would be around when, in a few weeks, they could go "pubbing in the long, light, Spring evenings" and smell "the perfume of English hedgerows" and see "the woods blanketed in bluebells." All anticipation of spring had to be put aside on the night of 19/20 February as Rackheath and other Eighth and some Ninth Air Force bases began to come to life, like gears in a giant machine.

After the target . . . came from Eighth Air Force Headquarters . . . [the] Ordnance Section would start to haul the bombs from the revetted dump . . . and began loading the selected planes . . . Ordnance also installed the heavy, crudely-Mediaeval flak suits aboard the ships . . . The motor pool had to be ready to pick up the crews in the pre-dawn dark, take them to breakfast, to briefing, and out to the planes on the perimeter strip. The mess must break out the real eggs for the flyboys' breakfast.

It was somewhat the same at the fighter bases. A "mechanic who didn't give in to his sleepiness and extracted the tubercular carburetor for just one damn last treatment, might have won his part of the battle against a German mechanic who let his 109 go up with a dirty carburetor." A young Mustang pilot named Chuck Yeager would recall later that on "mission days you're up at five-thirty splashing icy water on your face because there is no hot." His memory of the early breakfasts was that they consisted of "a couple of cups of coffee . . . a piece of hard, dark bread spread thickly with peanut butter and orange marmalade." Important in the preparations, "You remember to pee . . . you'll be sitting in that cockpit for more than six hours and it gets so cold at high altitudes that the elimination tube usually freezes solid." Out on the strip his Mustang

always looks beautiful . . . the best American fighter in the war, equal to anything the Germans can put up against her . . . Her Packard-built Rolls-Royce-Merlin engine . . . provides terrific speed and maneuvering performance—a dogfighter's dream. Loaded with fuel and ammo, she's a tricky airplane to fly, and also vulnerable. Get a hit in your radiator and lose your coolant, and you're going down . . . You're alert now for engine-start . . . You always get butterflies before a mission."

From Eighth Air Force Headquarters WAC enlisted women operating the teletypes had sent the order for the first ARGUMENT mission down to the subordinate commands. Mary Gill, eventually made a warrant officer but still Doolittle's secretary, was thus in a position to socialize on both enlisted and commissioned levels, with a consequently better understanding of the WAC psyche generally. She remembered the headiness of those days. She and the other WACs of the U.S. Strategic Air Forces in Europe and its subordinate commands were aware of the struggle for air superiority. Some were bloodied in the Luftwaffe bombing campaign of early 1944, "The Little Blitz," on England, the hit-and-run raids, and the V-weapon offensive. They wore their Purple Hearts and, along with comrades male and female, the shoulder patches of the U.S. Strategic Air Forces in Europe, Eighth Air Force, and Ninth Air Force with great pride.[54]

The primary targets for Mission 226 were the aircraft industries in and around Leipzig, Gotha, and Brunswick, producing Bf 109s and 110s, Ju 88s and 188s, and FW 190s. If the weather over the primary targets prevented visual bombing, the bombers were to make the first Army Air Forces' strike on Berlin. Fifteenth Air Force was to launch an attack on Regensburg, but a combination of weather and the need to be ready to support ground forces at Anzio prevented its participation.

The high explosives and incendiaries dropped by the Royal Air Force on Leipzig the night before had not harmed the aircraft factories, but the effort to disrupt the vast British bomber stream had served to wear the flak crews out for the daylight battle to come. The Eighth's Third Division did not have escort as its six B-17 wings made a diversionary run to the north German targets of Tutow and Rostock (an airfield, an FW 190 factory, and various targets of opportunity) that served to draw away German interceptors from the main force by deceiving German controllers into thinking the target was Berlin. The First and Second Bomb Divisions, after crossing the Channel, had the benefit of 332 P-47s and 36 P-38s on penetration support, plus 16 Royal Air Force Mustang and Spitfire squadrons.

Over Brunswick some 250 B-24 Liberators pulled out of the bomber stream to attack targets in the Brunswick area, protected by 29 P-38s of VIII Fighter Command's 20th Fighter Group. The First Bomb Division's 330 B-17 Fortresses continued on to their Leipzig objectives. The 55th Fighter Group's 52 P-38s were to provide target support for these bombers, but they took off after a number of Bf 109s, in an apparent misinterpretation of the freeing policy. They never made contact with the bombers. When the B-17s reached the rendezvous, they met enemy instead of friendly fighters. P-51 Mustangs of the IX Fighter Command's 354th Fighter Group, also scheduled for target support, arrived early. Like cavalry to the rescue, the Mustangs drove the enemy off. There were yet some imperfections in the "Little Friend–Big Friend" relationship, but in this case the early arrival of the Mustangs was a welcome miscalculation.

Several minutes later these fighters on loan to the Eighth Air Force joined with a relatively new P-51 group, the 357th, Eighth Air Force's first Mustang group. This was the unit of Flight Officer Charles "Chuck" Yeager. Together the seventy-three fighters escorted the B-17s to their Leipzig targets—the Erla Maschinenwerke complex, which produced 32 percent of all Bf 109s built during the war. Few enemy fighters were in the area, however. Luftwaffe ground controllers had fallen for the northern diversion. By the time the Luftwaffe's forces had been turned around, many had reached the limit of their endurance. A few endeavored to attack American bombers during the latter's egress from Brunswick and Leipzig. Escorting fighters minimized their success.

American fighter pilots claimed to have downed many German aircraft this day, in their and the bombers' partly paper attrition of the Luftwaffe. Fourth Fighter Group Capt. Duane Beeson took pains to make sure his claim was validated. With his Thunderbolt group giving withdrawal support to several combat wings of B-17s and B-24s, Beeson and another P-47 pilot dove to engage two FW 190s circling like sharks below the bombers. In his encounter report, Beeson, a baby-faced ace, described the happening. "I closed in on the no. 2 who began to climb as his leader dived for the clouds. I opened fire at about 300 yards range, closing to 100 yards and got very good strikes around his fuselage and on his wings. As I overshot him he pulled straight up and jettisoned his cockpit hood, then bailed out." Other P-47s arrived and were witnesses. To be sure, however, Beeson "took a picture of the parachute with my cine-camera."[55]

VIII Fighter Command described German pilots as "inexperienced and unaggressive." Heinz Knoke, who had developed from a greenhorn in three years into a leading Luftwaffe ace, had little to say in his journal about the first day of Big Week. His squadron had "two long engagements with formations of Fortresses over North Germany and the North Sea . . . Bad shooting on my part caused me to miss a good opportunity of adding to my score."[56]

For their action on 20 February three members of Fortress crews won the Medal of Honor, an unprecedented total for a single mission of the Eighth Air Force. Two of these men were aboard the same plane, Flight Engineer S. Sgt. Archie Mathies and Navigator 1st Lt. Walter E. Truemper. With a dead copilot and unconscious pilot, the two combined to bring their aircraft back to its English base, a miracle in itself. Refusing to abandon the unconscious pilot, the other crew members having parachuted to safety, they tried for a second miracle, a landing. Mathies was in the pilot's seat as the aircraft approached the runway, "talked" down by a B-17 that had taken off to guide the other craft like a seeing-eye dog. Mathies made touchdown, but the plane bounced high. On descent the left wing tilted, caught in the ground, and sent the Fortress cartwheeling—violent impact, enveloping flames, three dead.

The other Medal of Honor episode involved, likewise, wounded crewmen whom their comrades refused to abandon. Their B-17 had a bombload that would not release over the target and was isolated as the rest of the formation surged upward as a result of the sudden lightening of their loads. German fighters swept in to attack the exposed Fortress. Controls were damaged, two crewmen were wounded, and the copilot took a cannon shell in the face. His slump on the control column sent the plane down in a spin. The good effect was that enemy fighters left what they thought was a doomed aircraft. The pilot, 1st Lt. William R. Lawley, Jr., splattered with blood, cut by glass about the face from the partially shattered windshield, managed to arrest the spin. Informed of two

North American A-6 Texans in formation. Nearly 20,000 of these advanced trainers produced during the war insured Americans received the most extensive
training of any fighter pilots in the world. (*Source:* USAF Historical Research
Center.)

Boeing's B-17 Flying Fortress. Its thirteen .50-caliber machine guns could fire over 5,800 half-inch bullets per minute—the Fall Crisis proved it not to be enough. (*Source:* National Air and Space Museum.)

Consolidated's B-24 Liberator. With three fewer .50-caliber machine guns and the inability to fly as high as the B-17, it was more vulnerable to Luftwaffe defenses. (*Source:* National Air and Space Museum.)

Republic's P-47 Thunderbolt. Superior numbers, eight .50-caliber machine guns, and unmatched diving ability and ruggedness made it the deadliest fighter the Luftwaffe faced during the battles for air superiority. It did not, however, have the legs to escort bombers on deep missions into Germany until later in the war. (*Source:* National Air and Space Museum.)

Lockheed's P-38 Lightning. Though not without shortcomings, it possessed the range to accompany bombers as far as Berlin in the key battles for air superiority. (*Source:* National Air and Space Museum.)

North American P-51 Mustang. Regardless of its other assets, its ability to fly to Berlin and beyond, either at treetop level or at 30,000 feet, made it the finest escort fighter of the war. (*Source:* National Air and Space Museum.)

First Lieutenant William R. Lawley, Jr. (*left*), is congratulated by Lieutenant General Carl Spaatz upon receipt of the Medal of Honor. Lawley brought home his damaged B-17, one engine afire and only one of the three remaining engines working, with seriously injured crewmen aboard from Leipzig on the first day of Big Week. (*Source:* William R. Lawley, Jr.)

Left to right, Eighth Air Force commander Jimmy Doolittle, 56th Fighter Group commander and fighter ace with 17.75 victories Hubert Zemke, and 56th Fighter Group ace with seven victories Robert Lamb. (*Source:* USAF Historical Research Center.)

Mary Gill, a pioneering member of the Women's Auxiliary Army Corps (WAAC), later Women's Army Corps (WAC), was the personal secretary to VIII Bomber Command's commanding general, Frederick Anderson, and later Eighth Air Force's commanding general, Jimmy Doolittle. (*Source:* Mary Gill Rice.)

Eighth Air Force had to make the air above Germany's cities sufficiently valuable to force the Luftwaffe to fight the battle for air superiority. The ball-bearing factories at Schweinfurt. (*Source:* National Air and Space Museum.)

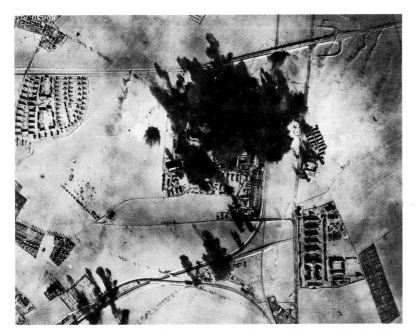

Leipzig's aircraft industry on fire after a Big Week attack. (*Source:* National Air and Space Museum.)

Attriting Luftwaffe strength at the source. Ju 188s in a Leipzig assembly building. (*Source:* National Air and Space Museum.)

A P-47 escort watches as a combat box formation of B-17s heads on into Germany beyond the range of the fighter—a test for the "self-defending bomber." (*Source:* National Air and Space Museum.)

The Fall Crisis—a formation of B-17s ringed by 21-cm air-to-air rocket bursts. (*Source:* National Air and Space Museum.)

"The first duty of the Eighth Air Force fighters is to bring the bombers back alive." P-47s stick close to B-17s. (*Source:* National Air and Space Museum.)

Escorting fighters practice "the weave" maneuver to maintain speed and yet stay close to the bombers. It was no solution to the range problem. (*Source:* National Air and Space Museum.)

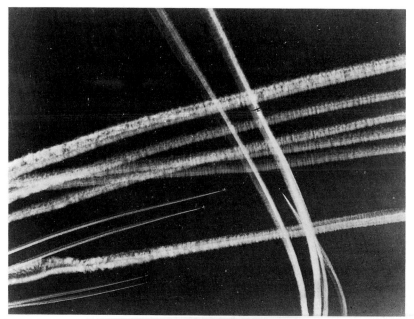

"The first duty of the Eighth Air Force fighters is to destroy German fighters."
Freed VIII Fighter Command fighters search for enemy aircraft. (*Source:* National Air and Space Museum.)

The bare essence of attrition warfare—gun camera photographs record hits on a Bf 109. (*Source:* National Air and Space Museum.)

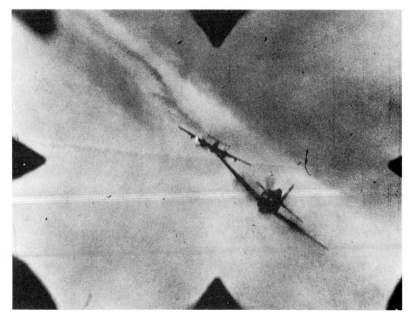

Against unescorted bombers the rocket-carrying Bf 110 was deadly. Against escorting fighters, it was an easy target. One fighter's gun camera records a P-47 registering hits on a Bf 110. (*Source:* National Air and Space Museum.)

A B-17 over Berlin. "Nervous? Hell yes! We were puckered!" (*Source:* National Air and Space Museum.)

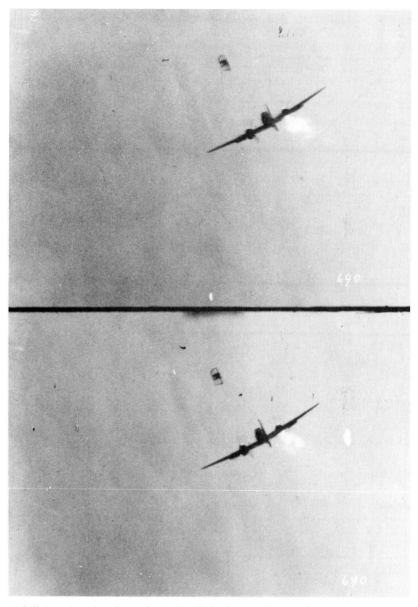

To kill American bombers, the Luftwaffe had to use large fighters with heavy cannons and rockets—sitting ducks for American fighters. An Me 410 crew prepares to bail out. (*Source:* National Air and Space Museum.)

"The flak bursts were so thick it seemed to me some of the shells must be colliding with each other." (*Source:* USAF Historical Research Center.)

Four American P-51 pilots from the 357th Fighter Group congratulate themselves after returning from the 6 March 1944 mission to Berlin. *Left to right*, Davis Perron (3 victories), Thomas Hayes (6.5 victories), G. V. Davis (0 victories), and Donald Bochkay (13.83 victories). (*Source:* USAF Historical Research Center.)

Kepner's "unorganized air guerrilla warfare." American fighters strafe parked He 177s. (*Source:* National Air and Space Museum.)

"When strafing 20 feet above the ground was 'too high.'" A *low*-level attack on parked Bf 110s deep in Germany. (*Source:* National Air and Space Museum.)

The costs of air superiority warfare. A B-17 falls victim to German antiaircraft artillery and American 100-octane gasoline. (*Source:* National Air and Space Museum.)

helpless crew members aboard, he made the decision to try to bring the crippled B-17 home. It was tedious, perilous, and, like the Mathies-Truemper flight, a classic journey. Lawley fought diminishing strength, passing out briefly on one occasion. The crew managed to drop the bombs at the French coast, and, with only one engine functioning as the English landscape rose to meet them, Lawley took his plane and crew in for a successful belly-landing at a Royal Air Force base.[57]

American losses that day were limited to twenty-one bombers and four fighters, though I Fighter Corps claimed twenty-seven bombers and eight fighters. The loss rate for bombers was only 2.8 percent, for fighters 0.5 percent—a far cry from the high losses of the fall crisis. The defense was especially ineffective because of the northern diversion, the division of the bomber formation into several small units, and the timely presence of long-range fighter escort. German fighter defense commander Schmid recorded that weather also prevented the efficient assembly of his forces, though American airmen reported no problems with weather this day. American forces claimed to have downed 126 German fighters, though I Fighter Corps reported losing 28 of the 362 fighters launched, with an additional 21 suffering 60 percent damage or more (7.7 percent). The Luftwaffe Quartermaster wrote off 58 fighters for the mission of 20 February.

Indirectly important for the winning of air superiority, the bombers caused serious damage: 65 percent of the floor space at Heiterblick and 83 percent at Möckau destroyed. The machine tools were saved and the plants returned to operation, but the Luftwaffe could not bear such damage to the factories that provided it with the sinews of war. It would have to speed up dispersal and to continue to launch all-out defensive efforts to stop such attacks.[58]

For Spaatz and Anderson, the lessons of the first day of Big Week were mutually clear. They felt they had touched a nerve, squashed it, and gotten away with considerably less cost than anyone had expected. This was the kind of war they wanted. As long as the weather held out, U.S. Strategic Air Forces in Europe would keep up the pressure. The next day gathering clouds over Germany promised to interfere with visual bombing, but Anderson again pushed hard for a mission to Germany. Eighth Air Force sent 762 bombers and 679 fighters to Brunswick and a number of airfields and aircraft storage parks on the twenty-first. Most of the bombers attacked various targets of opportunity because of heavy clouds over the primaries. As Anderson informed an interested Barney Giles by transatlantic telephone hook up, "The reason for the operation today was to shoot down enemy fighters as much as possible and we did not expect to be able to see many targets."[59]

Eaker, in the Mediterranean, canceled Fifteenth Air Force's participation in the Big Week mission planned for the twenty-first. Anderson, upon hearing of Eaker's decision, notified Spaatz. At Spaatz's direction, Anderson cabled Eaker, "There will be no let-up."[60]

Losses were relatively light because of the weather, including sixteen bombers and five fighters, compared to German claims of twenty bombers and seven fighters. Eighth Air Force bombers claimed nineteen Luftwaffe fighters and American fighters claimed thirty-three. According to I Fighter Corps records, the Luftwaffe launched 282 effective sorties, losing eleven, with fourteen suffering damage of 60 percent or more. Again, the Luftwaffe Quartermaster wrote off more fighters—thirty-two. Both sides continued their loose accounting of victories. The reduction in the number of defensive sorties launched compared to the previous day was due to a launch delayed by clouds, preventing second or third sorties for available aircraft.[61] Anderson grew more confident, telling Giles in Washington by telephone that U.S. Strategic Air Forces in Europe was in combat to the death and nothing would terminate that effort "until the Germans are knocked out." He knew the poor weather would cost the Army Air Forces additional lives, but that pressure had to be maintained on the Luftwaffe.[62]

As a result of the first two days of the Big Week operations,

Göring called an emergency meeting at Karin Hall of his top Reich defense commanders. He was troubled over the damage being done to German aircraft factories. Schmid again demanded the unification of all German fighter defenses. Despite the existence of Air Fleet Reich, I Fighter Corps still commanded the three fighter divisions covering northern and central Germany, II Fighter Corps the three fighter divisions in the West, the Seventh Fighter Division fighters in southern Germany and in Austria, and Air Fleet 4 fighter operations in Hungary. Within each defensive area, fighter forces were inadequate for American saturation raids without reinforcement from the other defensive commands. Each regional command wished to hold on to its fighters to the last minute, expecting a possible attack. By the time units were sent to reinforce other commands, American bombers were already on their way home. Air Fleet Reich had the authority to order reinforcements, but only with Göring's permission—a delay that prevented the timely use of all German forces against American aircraft. Göring accepted Schmid's argument and ordered all fighter defenses in southern Germany, Austria, and Hungary assigned to I Fighter Corps. The order, however, was not to be effective until 1 April 1944, too late for the threat at hand.

Schmid called his commanders together for a meeting at Stade the next day, after the meeting with Göring, to plan a strategy for dealing with the "tense and serious" situation. He correctly surmised that the current American attacks were in preparation for "air supremacy as a prelude to a large-scale invasion." Priority air operations would now be in defense of the aircraft industry. He reassigned divisional responsibilities because of heavy attrition to the units closest to American fighters. He ordered each fighter division to assign one group to attack the American fighter escort, a partial reversal of Göring's earlier policy of ignoring the escort. He assigned these groups to airfields in western Germany so they could divert the escort before the bomber formations reached their targets. Göring ordered an additional group from the Eastern Front to reinforce the First Fighter Division, which would then

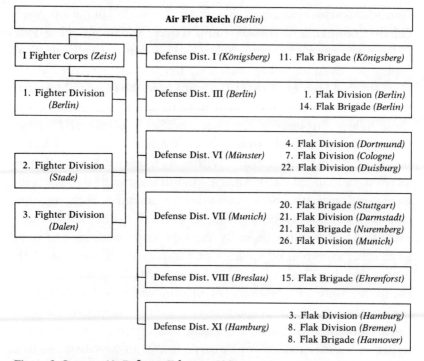

Figure 8. German Air Defense, February 1944
Source: Karlsruhe Collection, "Reichs-Luft-Vertg," 1956, File K113.312-1, vol. 1, HRC; and Generalleutnant Josef Schmid, "Luftwaffe Operations in the West, 1943–1945," vol. 5, "Command Structure of the Reich Air Defense Organization, 1 January 1943 to 9 May 1945," 1955, File K113.107-158–160, HRC.

launch wing-size attacks on American combat boxes. Other units retreated deeper into Germany because inadequate warning time had prevented them from attaining operating altitude without coming under attack from American fighters. And I Fighter Corps began taking greater advantage of available airfields to maximize second and third sorties.[63]

Any chance for the Luftwaffe to catch its breath was lost when Spaatz and Anderson ordered another all-out mission on 22 February. The skies were clear over Germany and over the Alps. Anderson cabled Eaker that Fifteenth Air Force must attack the Regensburg Messerschmitt complex, that weather was not an acceptable reason to cancel the mission. This was the first joint mission involving the Eighth and Fifteenth Air Forces—1,396 bombers and 965 fighters total were prepared to go. The targets were aircraft manufacturing centers at Bernberg, Aschersleben, Oschersleben, Halberstadt, Gotha, and Regensburg. Ball-bearing factories at Schweinfurt were also included in the list of primary targets. The weather closed in before the bomber stream reached the Reich, with clouds from 16,000 to 20,000 feet, and increasing numbers of Eighth Air Force bombers began to return to base without bombing their targets. Anderson was livid, especially because no one had bothered to call his headquarters to ask for permission to abort the mission. He tried to have the bombers fly beneath the clouds until they reached Germany, where they could find some clear weather, but the air commanders' recall was too advanced for two-thirds of the Eighth's forces. That left 255 bombers of the United Kingdom–based force pushing on, escorted by 659 widely scattered fighters. Fifteenth Air Force sent 183 bombers to Regensburg, but without long-range escort. With few such fighters, the Fifteenth was to rely on the planned larger Eighth Air Force formations attracting all German fighters away from the Fifteenth's largely self-defending bombers.[64]

Because of the weather, bomber formations were loose and losses were heavy. The German reaction was surprisingly strong, in many cases attacking Eighth Air Force bombers before the fighter escort caught up. According to German records, the I Fighter Corps launched 332 effective sorties, losing eleven, with an additional sixteen experiencing 60 percent or more damage. It claimed to have downed fifty-five bombers and ten fighters. The Luftwaffe Quartermaster again wrote off considerably more German fighters as a result of the battle of 22 February—fifty-two. Eighth Air Force admitted to losing 16 percent of its attacking bombers and Fifteenth Air Force 10 percent. American claims exceeded an unbelievable one hundred enemy aircraft downed.[65]

John Muirhead was a B-17 pilot with the Fifteenth Air Force and in probably the most literate and introspective memoir of the

Army Air Forces in Europe he described the mission to Regensburg
on the twenty-second.

We were seconds away from time to start our engines. It was now. A
flare burst in the center of the perimeter, an explosive puff that resolved
into a rising arc of green fire, soaring upward above us, then falling
back to earth . . . My hands moved through the ritual, doing the sacred
things that would bring *Laura* to life: master switch, on; generator and
batteries, on; throttles, idle cut off; fuel, full rich; fuel pumps, on; boos-
ters, on; carburator [*sic*] air, off; gyros, locked; . . . The engine spat
twice in protest as hot flame hit cold metal, but it caught and settled
down to a steady roar. Each engine, in turn, now joined the thunder of
thirty other planes, making a holocaust of the morning's quiet. Birds
flashed out of the grass in terror . . . It is routine that saves us, the details that must be served to whatever place we go: to a madness five
miles above a city in Germany or to a better purpose.

He discussed the temptation to return prematurely.

Three of our planes had turned back with mechanical troubles. We were
thirty-nine guns weaker. The tougher the mission, the more aborts; and
they would get away with it, claiming excessive engine temperature,
low oil pressures, oxygen system malfunctions . . . The crew chiefs back
at the base would check everything and find nothing to confirm the pilot's claim. There would be a half-hearted investigation.

He described the anticipation of a fighter attack.

There was not a blemish in the sky, yet we knew they were there. The
formation tightened. Dark hackles of guns raised from the gleaming
metal skins. My left wing tucked in about ten feet from the waist win-
dow of the flight leader. I could see the strange figure of his gunner
swaddled in his felt heated suit crouching over his weapon. Helmeted
and goggled with the dark mask covering the bottom of his face, he appeared grotesque, an inhuman creature watching for other demons. He
was firing . . . Bandits! Bandits! Christ, there's a million . . . I could hear
the top turret turning, then the short bursts of his fire joining the tail
guns and the ball turret . . . For an amazing moment, four MEs that
had pressed their attack through the lead squadron were framed in the

middle of the group. Every gun had them as they desperately rolled for a vertical dive toward earth. The last one didn't make it. He exploded in a geyser of flame that shot upward and made a white parasol of smoke.

And he described flak.

Crystal fragments of steel burned the air around us while we blundered through the greasy traces of brown and black smoke . . . a plane was falling out of the lead squadron. I watched for chutes. Suddenly she blew: a tremendous explosion of flame and debris leaped outward . . . *Laura* lurched upwards. Bombs away! Bombs away!

On the return trip the fighters harassed them "to make us pay for the rubble and corpses of Regensburg." Muirhead's Fortress was one of ten of his group that made it back to Italy.[66]

The effort of 22 February was not the kind of mission Anderson had in mind. Losses were heavy, but he attributed them to the small number of aircraft over Germany and the poor formations resulting from the weather. Doolittle called that night for permission to cancel the mission planned for the twenty-third because the weather forecast was unfavorable and he alleged his crews were worn out, "subsisting primarily on an alternate diet of benzedrine and sleeping pills." Anderson told him to "shut up" and to "carry out his orders." In the morning both England and Germany were locked in by bad weather and Anderson reluctantly agreed to a standdown. Hundreds of bombers and fighters sitting on the ground were not his idea of attrition warfare. "For us, this was the 'make or break' of the whole air war, and we were determined not to let a single 8th Air Force bomber sit on the ground as long as this fantastic freak of the weather lasted."[67]

Fifteenth Air Force did send 102 B-24s to Steyr, Austria, on 23 February, but with little success. The Fifteenth continued to show the effects of not having long-range escort in any quantity. Seventeen of the bombers failed to return; a loss rate of 17 percent. Bad weather forced the cancellation of all other missions.

Of special importance to the badly needed success of the planned mission for 24 February, ULTRA intercepts told Allied intelligence where German fighter forces in Holland would launch their attacks against American heavy bombers heading for Germany. As their first priority, Ninth Air Force light and medium bombers struck the airfields to suppress the fighter forces there, keeping Eighth Air Force losses on this day to less than they might have been.[68]

On the twenty-fourth the plan was to strike the great ball-bearing works at Schweinfurt, the Gotha aircraft industry, and aircraft assembly plants in northern Germany at Tutow, Posen, and Kreising. For at least one of the airmen that day, Clyde Bradley, the name Schweinfurt "scared the hell out of me. When they showed that target—Schweinfurt—I thought, 'Oh shit!' They'll be ready for us, because that is in the bowels of Germany." Some units were to make a feint over the North Sea as on the twentieth. Those bombers headed to the northern targets and to the northern feint left early to attract German fighters into the air and headed in the wrong direction. The weather in the north was bad, however, and the Luftwaffe did not take the diversion. The main force in clear weather struck behind this diversion, timed to arrive at its targets while German aircraft were refueling. The bombers of this force hit both Schweinfurt and Gotha. At Schweinfurt, despite the concerns of Clyde Bradley, "nothing happened. Flak, but no fighter attacks."[69] The Gotha attackers, however, suffered heavy losses despite escort by 767 fighters, including a record eighty-eight P-51s. Meanwhile the Fifteenth Air Force sent eighth-three bombers to the Steyr aircraft plant in Austria, with some P-38 long-range escort. The forces sent to Gotha and Steyr became the focus of German defensive attacks.

I Fighter Corps launched 336 effective sorties. Total American losses were sixty-six bombers (8 percent) and twelve fighters. Fifteenth Air Force bombers, forced to fly with only minimal fighter protection, lost 20 percent of its force. Claims for all American units totaled over 155 enemy aircraft, though the commander of the I Fighter Corps recorded the loss of only twenty-six, with twelve more suffering 60 percent damage or more.[70] Other German sources believed a total of sixty fighters were lost.[71]

Schmid's move to use single-engine night fighters to escort his twin-engine fighters caught the immediate attention of American fighter pilots. It was the Luftwaffe's admission that the heavy destroyer fighter responsible for the fall crisis had succumbed to the freed, long-range American fighter. The Army Air Forces shot down thirty-nine of these aircraft during the first three days of Big Week. The escort obviously helped, because only four went down on 24 February.

A Mustang pilot with a sense of humor, Col. Henry R. Spicer, Jr., claimed in an encounter report one of these four.

Lo and Behold, if there wasn't an ME-110 dashing across the horizon. He showed a little sense and tried to turn, so I was forced to resort to deflection shooting—opening up and spraying him up and down, round and across (I believe I was a little excited at this point). Fortunately the left engine blew up and burst into flames . . . the pilot dumped his canopy and started to get out. He was dressed in brown and had streaming yellow hair, the handsome devil.

Spicer saw no chutes, but reported that the aircraft "crashed into the center of the town of URFURT." He did not comment on the town's historical significance. Heinz Knoke, who had flown his Bf 109 on both 21 and 22 February, and on the latter shot down a B-17 that crashed "into a pasture . . . at the south end of my old hometown [Hamelin]," was up again on the twenty-fourth. He wrote in his journal, "The Squadron loses another six killed at noon today in a dog-fight with Thunderbolts, Lightnings and Mustangs covering another heavy bombing attack. Our little band grows smaller and smaller. Every man can work out for himself on the fingers of one hand when his own turn is due to come." It was a concise expression of the attrition factor that was the essence of ARGUMENT.[72]

The weather held on 25 February and again U.S. Strategic Air

Forces in Europe launched attacks on the German aircraft industry, this time at Regensburg, Augsburg, and Furth, and on the Stuttgart ball-bearing factory. First to strike at Regensburg were 149 Fifteenth Air Force bombers, escorted over the target by 85 P-38s. The Luftwaffe was waiting and shot down 39 bombers (26 percent) and 3 fighters. The Fifteenth's sacrifice, however, reduced German fighter reaction to Eighth Air Force's efforts, especially the bombers assigned to attack Regensburg in a follow-up strike. In addition, the 363rd Fighter Group, a new IX Fighter Command P-51 group flying its first mission with VIII Fighter Command, brought the long-range escort to 139 Mustangs. Of the 635 bombers attacking, 31 went down (4.9 percent). Against little resistance, 108 Eighth Air Force B-17s leveled what remained of the once great Messerschmitt factories at Regensburg.

Both bomber crews and fighter pilots reported that the Luftwaffe's response was notably unaggressive. I Fighter Corps launched only one hundred effective sorties, losing five, with one damaged, against American claims of fifty-nine downed. According to Josef Schmid, I Fighter Corps commander, the First and Second Fighter Divisions held their aircraft on the ground expecting a raid from the north, accounting for the small number of aircraft launched that day. Spaatz and Anderson preferred to see this ineffective reaction as a sign of German exhaustion. The Luftwaffe may in fact have withheld some of its force, but Schmid's explanation does not reveal why those forces that were launched were so apparently reluctant to press their attacks.

Knoke in part contradicted in his journal the American analysis of a lack of aggression on the twenty-fifth.

The bomber-alley lies about 6,000 feet below us—600 to 800 of the heavy bombers heading eastward. Along side them range the escort fighters. And now I am utterly absorbed in the excitement of the chase . . . We peel off for the attack. Messerschmitt after Messerschmitt follows [the squadron leader] . . . down. After them! The radio is a babel of sound, with everybody shouting at once . . . Thunderbolts are coming down after us. We are faster."

Knoke fired his cannon shells at a B-17's cabin, but he missed and his strikes on the wing failed to bring it down.

Then the Thunderbolts are upon us. It is a wild dog-fight . . . Everyone is milling around like mad, friend and foe alike. But the Yanks outnumber us by four or five to one . . . [a] Lightning passes me, going down in flames. There is a Messerschmitt on its tail.

An old principle had prevailed, for Knoke's wingman was in that Messerschmitt. At the end of the action, Knoke and his wingman returned to base. "The others have also been coming in to land. This is one day we all come back." Unaggressiveness or luck?[73]

Anderson pressed for another attack on 26 February, but he had pressed his luck too far. Bad weather set in for the next week. German and American units gained time for a breather.

By the end of Big Week, it was clear to I Fighter Corps' commander Schmid that the end was near. "In numbers as well as in technical performance, the daytime fighter units assigned to German air defense activity are inferior to the American fighter aircraft forces." He concluded that "in the long run our forces are fighting a hopeless battle."[74] Fritz Ungar, a pilot in the Luftwaffe's 54th Fighter Wing, dated the Army Air Forces' "air advantage" from the mission of 20 February 1944. Before Doolittle freed the American fighters, Ungar and his compatriots had been able to dive and spin away from American fighters. Since January, when German pilots performed this combat-proven maneuver, American fighters would follow them all the way to the ground. Ungar felt the factor that made the difference in the winning of air superiority during Big Week was the "numerical advantage."[75]

Bombing also took its toll. According to the official Speer assigned to head fighter production after Big Week, the bombings "created somewhat of a panic" in Germany.[76] The Big Week offensive of 19/20 through 25/26 February generated 3,823 American bomber sorties and 2,351 British bomber sorties to drop 18,291 tons of bombs on eighteen German airframe and two ball-bearing manufacturing centers. The British claimed 13 Luftwaffe fighters downed, American bombers claimed 391 fighters downed. American fighters claimed an additional 217 German aircraft. Depending on the German source, admitted losses for the week came to between 81 (Schmid's figure) and 282 (the Luftwaffe Quartermaster's figure).[77]

American losses were 227 bombers (5.9 percent), British losses 157 bombers (6.7 percent). In addition U.S. Strategic Air Forces in Europe launched 4,342 fighters, losing 42 (1 percent). More than 5,000 Allied aircrew either died or became prisoners-of-war. More revealing of the intensity of the conflict, however, 1,025 of the 3,823 American bombers credited with sorties against the enemy suffered damage. During the week, Eighth Air Force's operational bomber rate dropped from 75 percent to 54 percent and the fighter rate dropped from 72 percent to 65 percent.[78]

Statistics about losses, however, do not reveal the significance of Big Week. The "Little Friends" and their opponents in the skies over the Reich, the Luftwaffe day fighters, were critical to the battle of attrition ARGUMENT had become. Whereas the flood of new aircraft to VIII Fighter Command allowed it to end Big Week with 90 percent more P-51s than with which it began, the Luftwaffe lost over one-third of its authorized strength, including a considerable number of irreplaceable veteran pilots and air commanders.[79]

Who won the air battle of Big Week? American losses were heavier, but American industry replaced aircraft as losses occurred. The huge American training establishment replaced lost airmen. German industry was able to replace the Luftwaffe's lost aircraft, but the aircrew training establishment failed to replace the more than 100 pilots who lost their lives during Big Week.

The Big Week bombings were the most concentrated, intense effort of the entire war by either side to destroy one sector of a nation's economy and war production. Aircraft production at Augsburg stopped for two weeks. At Leipzig 160 new aircraft were damaged. Gotha's production was delayed for two weeks and seventy-four aircraft were damaged or destroyed. The Messerschmitt complex at Regensburg was completely destroyed and would not be rebuilt. Milch estimated lost production from the Big Week bombings of 350 at Leipzig, 150–200 at Regensburg, and 200 at Wiener-Neustadt.[80] Faced with the destruction of Germany's aircraft industry, Göring ordered the final dispersal of production. No single site was to produce more than 150 aircraft per month. The order saved the industry, but at the cost of losing the efficiencies of mass-production, delays in industry expansion, and the creation of transportation choke points vulnerable to Allied bombing.[81] Speer established a Fighter Plane Staff (*jägerstab*) under Dr. Karl Otto Saür to control fighter production, assigning it priority over all other areas of the German economy. Saür mobilized thousands of prisoners of war to build new dispersed factories and to repair damaged factories.[82]

One of the most important results of Big Week was an Allied decision to change the basic tactical planning for missions from one of evasion to one of challenge. In the words of Charles A. Foster, a member of the Combined Operational Planning Committee:

Up to Big Week, strong German fighter defences coupled with the restricted radius of action of our fighters and the absence of the long range B-17, made the tactic of evasion primary in the Committee's plans. Subsequent to the Big Week, the primary consideration in the Committee's plans was to seek out and challenge the German Fighter Forces, because the balance had changed to our favor as a result of the operations from 20th February through 25th.

In Foster's opinion, the key to this development was the arrival of the P-51, "which radically reduced the Committee's estimates of losses."[83]

The Combined Operational Planning Committee completed its evaluation of the Big Week operation with these words: "The scale of this offensive, the care with which it was planned, the precision with which it was executed, and the success which it achieved, should establish it for all time as a landmark in the history of aerial warfare."[84]

A U.S. Strategic Air Forces in Europe air intelligence summary evaluated Big Week in the context of air superiority. "We have put the German fighter command in a position from which they must either accept unopposed bombing by us for at least the next two months, or they must accept a scale of wastage in resistance to it which will cause continuous decline of their strength."[85]

Eighth Air Force had proved it could strike any target, anywhere in Germany, without excessive losses. There would be no more discussion of merging American strategic bomber forces with Harris's British force for night missions to area-bomb Germany's cities—the American loss rate during the day Big Week missions was 6 percent, compared to 6.6 percent for the British. Edmond Zellner, a pilot in VIII Fighter Command's 352nd Fighter Group, claimed that what he remembered most about Big Week was "seeing ten to twelve P-51s chasing the hell out of one German fighter and everyone trying to get a shot at him—we overwhelmed them."[86] Zellner wanted the world to know the loneliness that was the lot of the fighter pilot. "It sure was strange," with a thousand bombers and a thousand fighters milling around. "You got into a dogfight for a minute or two and you looked around and couldn't find another aircraft in the air." Despite the advanced weapons and tactics, the air war was still a struggle between men. Their training, their commitment, and their sense of duty should not be forgotten.

Despite the great victory in the air during Big Week and despite the achievements of the bombing effort, it was still evident that air superiority had not been achieved. When American bombers appeared over Germany, quantities of German fighters still rose to challenge them. Their performance might vary, but they remained a menace to OVERLORD. Further attrition was necessary.

CHAPTER SIX

BERLIN, THE STRATEGIC FIGHTER CAMPAIGN, AND CONTROL OF THE AIR

Berlin. The German capital had special meaning for both the Allies and the Germans. Although first attacked by the Royal Air Force in 1940, it had largely escaped a battering until powerful British bomber streams began to visit the city on an increasing number of nights beginning in November 1943. For Air Chief Marshal Arthur "Bomber" Harris ("Butcher" Harris to some of his crews), Berlin was "at the end of the road which . . . Harris had been traveling through the Ruhr, Hamburg, and Central Germany." He told the Americans that if they would join him in the effort against Berlin at night then the bombers would shatter the core of the Nazi state, making an invasion of the continent unnecessary. Eighth Air Force did not join the endeavor, but the great Lancasters and other British heavy bombers unleashed a torrent of high explosives and incendiaries in an effort to repeat the fire storm of Hamburg, generally without success. Subterranean hiding places and fire retardants limited damage while night fighters and flak batteries made the raiders pay a high price.[1] For the Germans, Berlin was the symbol of the thousand-year Reich. For the average American airman, Berlin was his worst nightmare: "Nervous? Hell yes! We were puckered."[2]

Harris felt that what the Americans were doing with their bombers was futile. Indeed, it had seemed so until Big Week. After that turning point in the air war, the Americans targeted Berlin for immediate attention. It was to be their first crack at "Big B," as the intelligence people and the crews called it. But the Americans wanted to bomb Berlin for a different reason. In fact Carl Spaatz's primary rationale for sending his bombers to Berlin was different from the one that had sent them out during Big Week. But that phase of POINTBLANK verified the Berlin rationale that had been forming in Spaatz's mind for several months.

Arnold had reiterated to Spaatz in January his belief that German fighters must be baited to attack and be destroyed in air battles. That same month U.S. Strategic Air Forces in Europe planners suggested that the heavy bombers strike a target so dear to the Germans that their fighters would swarm to defend it. They recommended Berlin. Spaatz had been thinking of Berlin as a target even before he took over the task of coordinating the American strategic daylight effort, perhaps inspired by a Soviet request that the Americans bomb the German capital. But ARGUMENT was foremost. Acknowledging that priority to Arnold on 23 January, he nonetheless made a pitch for Berlin, but in a somewhat strange way: "There is another type of operation under peculiar weather conditions when all Germany is fog-bound, during which time raids[3] might be made well beyond fighter cover on area targets, such as Berlin, to force the German fighters into the air under conditions which will result in heavy operational losses to their fighters." At first blush it would appear that Spaatz was still a devotee of the "self-defending bomber." When he identified such an operation as "beyond fighter cover," he had to mean bomber guns or weather would have to inflict the "heavy operational losses." However, in that same communication Spaatz disclosed why he would be willing to risk the bombers in such a manner. "I feel that you would become very impatient with me if this very large striking force spent most of its time on the ground or in training flights, waiting for the few days when visual bombing permits hitting our primary targets—the aircraft factories." To "confine our operations to that alone would not deplete the German Air Force at the necessary rate."[4]

Not only was Eaker's recent fate fresh in Spaatz's mind, he too had felt the sting of the impatient Arnold's lash. Spaatz could not afford the posture of appearing to wait around for clear days and enough fighters. Fred Anderson constantly reminded him of the imperative to act. Spaatz's letter of 23 January also revealed another change in his thinking. While official Army Air Forces policy was still to bomb in a precise way in European operations and not to single out civilians as targets or even admit that they were to be otherwise included in targeting, Spaatz used the term "area targets" with no specified industrial or other military-related ground objective. His purpose was to force up the German fighters so that they could become statistics in his planned strategy of "production-wastage differential." To bomb an "area target" implied bombing anything within the area. Arthur Harris understood that, and so undoubtedly did Spaatz. Their objectives were different—one to destroy the city, the other to lure up the enemy fighters—but area bombing was area bombing.[5]

There was a note of urgency in Spaatz's declaration that to "confine our operations" to bombing the enemy's aircraft manufacturing complex and only when the weather was clear was to fall behind schedule in achieving air superiority. Every day planning and events reminded him of how close OVERLORD was. He could see OVERLORD not long away beckoning like a shepherd who became clearer and clearer in the winter mist. Perhaps initially more than Spaatz, his deputy for operations, Maj. Gen. Fred Anderson, had extrapolated from the ARGUMENT experience the knowledge that the German day fighter forces had begun to suffer what could be an irreversible decline as a result of the battle of attrition American forces were waging. It was time to join the British Berlin campaign, but not in the way Harris wished. Anderson did not mind the "area" effects of bombing, as long as they were a concomitant of precision bombing. If American bombers get to Berlin, he told Eighth Air Force planner Brig. Gen. Orville A. Anderson, "there won't be a damn house left." But attrition was the thing. A few days after the last Big Week mission he wrote in his personal diary, "We've got to go to Berlin with three bomb divisions, then they'll come up."[6]

Anderson discarded Spaatz's notion that the heavy bomber could serve both as bait and hunter. Not only had Big Week demonstrated what the fighter with the longer reach could do, but long-range fighters continued to arrive in England. The re-equipment of many P-38 and P-47 groups with the long-range P-51 was underway by March. Problems with the Mustang's engine, including the coolant, and with balky guns made pilots reluctant to embrace it as the mount they could trust to carry them long distances to battle and the same distances back while often "hitting the deck" in perilous strafing runs.[7] Anderson had no doubts about what was needed. He told anyone who would listen that Eighth Air Force would have to go to the "big city" to attract the Luftwaffe into battle.[8] It was "a major German preoccupation to avoid wastage as it must be with us a major determination to provoke it."[9]

But more troublesome from Fred Anderson's position was an attitude that Jimmy Doolittle seemed to have adopted once again, as he had during Big Week—a McClellan-like reluctance to move, at least where Berlin was concerned. The excuse was the same— weather. Doolittle did not lack stamina, integrity, or grit. No one had more. He wanted to accompany the first mission to Berlin, having been on the first American raids on Tokyo and Rome, but General Eisenhower vetoed this idea on the grounds that Doolittle knew too much to risk falling into German hands. Perhaps Doolittle's hesitation had to do with his fear of what could happen to all those planes and men under his direct command. According to Doolittle's biographers, Spaatz, who could be the stern regular officer, changed his opinion of Doolittle's respect for the weather when on a tour of the Eighth's bases Doolittle and Spaatz had to land in severe weather, causing some tense moments.[10]

Doolittle, Spaatz, Louis Brereton, Ira Eaker in the Mediterranean, and Maj. Gen. Nathan F. Twining in Italy were on the verge of achieving or failing to achieve air superiority over Europe, with monumental consequences in either event. Twining's Fifteenth Air Force was still having teething troubles, as yet lacked long-range fighters, and would periodically have to give priority to the ground campaigns in Italy. So it was mainly up to the Eighth and the fighters on loan from Brereton's Ninth to go to Berlin and force the Luftwaffe to bleed.

Fred Anderson was determined that his forces make the trip to Berlin as soon as possible. Doolittle scrubbed a mission to Berlin for 2 March on the excuse that predicted weather would preclude it. Instead he sent the bombers to Frankfurt where the sky was relatively clear. Anderson was furious. He called Spaatz and complained, "I feel we missed the boat today." He was more pithy in his personal diary: "It doesn't matter if Berlin is overcast. That resulting air battle [over Berlin] would result in attrition, which makes it more important than any destruction on the ground and going to Frankfurt to find clear skies won't achieve the same result . . . We've got to stick at this god damn thing." Doolittle admitted to his commanders that his decision to keep the bombers from going to Berlin that day had upset U.S. Strategic Air Forces in Europe headquarters. He therefore told his subordinates not to send any optimistic reports about weather to the Pinetree headquarters without his personal approval.

Doolittle was not the only one to anger Fred Anderson on 2 March. Orville Anderson suggested that B-24s not be sent to Berlin because they could not fly high enough. Fred Anderson reminded the number two man at Eighth Air Force that Royal Air Force bombers flew over Berlin at the lower altitudes and insisted the Liberators should go too. The Eighth Air Force chief of operations argued, "God, they'll just get killed in them." Fred Anderson's response revealed more of his commitment to the task than mere callousness: "Well?"[11]

Out went the Liberators, Fortresses, and a swarm of protecting fighters on 3 March in what was supposed to be the first maximum daylight effort against the "Big B." The weather had been predicted

as marginal. The war diary of the Luftwaffe's I Fighter Corps described the result: "The majority of the bombers reversed their
course and headed back toward Great Britain, presumably turned
back by heavy cloud banks ahead." The official Eighth Air Force
report explained,

Steadily deteriorating weather conditions were encountered by the
bomber forces . . . Over the Jutland Peninsula cloud tops extended to
28,000 feet and, combined with dense persistent contrails, made formation flying virtually impossible. Consequently decision made by the
Combat Wing Leaders to abandon the operation at various points between the Jutland Coast and the Hamburg area.

The I Fighter Corps war diary gave somewhat the same rationale
for the inability of its interceptors to assemble in tight combat
formations with the result that only a few German fighter were
able to offer combat, and then only individually. The Americans
reported sighting about 200 enemy fighters in all, with 15 to 20
engaging the American escort and 30 to 35 attacking one combat
wing of the Third Bomb Division's B-17s. A formation of American
planes did manage to become the first to reach Berlin, but they
were fighters, P-38s, not bombers. The Germans reported the
clouds reaching only to about 21,000 feet, with clear visibility
above the clouds, good conditions for radar bombing.[12]

Had the bombing through clouds taken place, it would have not
constituted, officially, area bombing, for the bombers had as their
primary targets certain industries in and around Berlin. Somebody, but probably not the impatient Fred Anderson, must have
reminded Spaatz of official American policy in the interval since
his January advocacy of area bombing. After all, Berlin was one of
the most industrialized cities in the world. But Anderson wanted
Berlin for its air space, not for its industries. Radar bombing
through clouds was in reality area bombing, at least in part.[13]

For the 3 March mission the respective claims of losses inflicted
on the enemy and admissions of one's own losses were somewhat
unusual. The Germans claimed only nine bombers positively de-

stroyed and no fighters. The Americans admitted the loss of eleven bombers and seven fighters to enemy action, while claiming no enemy fighters by either Eighth Air Force fighters or bombers. The German fighters were generally unaggressive, most probably because the bombers had turned back without attacking.[14]

Jimmy Doolittle decided to cancel the Berlin show scheduled for 4 March, but Fred Anderson persuaded Spaatz to overrule the Eighth Air Force commander. Once again the forecast was for marginal weather, with possible snow flurries for takeoff. At takeoff time on the fourth, Doolittle's apprehensions seemed valid. The Second Bomb Division's B-24s remained on the ground because of snow and thick clouds. A Mustang crashed on takeoff, killing the pilot. Anderson's perseverance got 502 B-17s up and headed for Berlin nevertheless. Their assigned targets were the Erkner ball-bearing plant, an aircraft engine plant, and an electrical equipment manufacturer. The secondary target, if clouds obscured the primaries, was the Friedrichstrasse railroad facilities near the center of the city. The real target, however, was the German interceptors that were sure to challenge the American mission during all three phases of the operation: penetration, target, and withdrawal. The bombers entered into German air space around 10 A.M., protected by 338 fighters on penetration support, with 770 additional fighters waiting to pick up the escort over Berlin and on the return flight home. These were the hooks within the bomber bait, except in this case the hooks surrounded the bait.

I Fighter Corps scrambled 149 fighters, but again weather spoiled the showdown. Clouds and other bad conditions "combined to render impossible the effective employment of our daytime fighter units." American sources claimed the clouds reached 28,000 feet, whereas I Fighter Corps' meteorologists pictured the clouds reaching only between 13,000 and 16,000 feet. The bombers veered away from Berlin and attacked targets of opportunity such as airfields and marshalling yards wherever the weather was less formidable. However, as Eighth Air Force would later report, "a single combat wing . . . was able to surmount cloud difficulties and continue the mission." This persistent formation discovered the clouds began to thin as it approached Berlin.[15]

Finally B-17s appeared over Berlin. They bombed what they believed to be an industrial target in the southwestern section of the city, using radar guidance. Whether the bombers hit anything was no longer critical, because their mere presence over Berlin had achieved its objective. First Lieutenant Nicolas Megura of the 4th Fighter Group reported the results. "Fifteen (15) plus Bf 109s made a frontal attack on the bombers and were driven down with us giving chase—from 27,000 feet to 5,000 feet and up again along side the bombers." Berliners heard the passing drone of the bombers, the roar and whine of diving and climbing fighters, and the crump-crump of flak, which mission reports described as an "intense inaccurate barrage."

Allied reconnaissance could make no assessment of the damage because of clouds. I Fighter Corps recorded the "fairly heavy" damage to private property, industrial plants, and traffic installations at Bonn and Dusseldorf, but recorded no damage to Berlin. Perhaps the I Fighter Corps war diary refused to admit that American daylight bombers had finally gotten through to the German capital. There may have been no damage from the 69.3 tons of bombs these bombers dumped on Berlin, but the fierce if brief Luftwaffe challenge revealed that the bait and the place were well chosen for the struggle for air superiority. "At times," admitted the Eighth, "particularly near Berlin, it was not possible for the escort to cope entirely with the enemy aircraft."[16]

The claims for both sides were again surprisingly modest, even allowing for the poor weather. The Germans claimed seven bombers shot down, the Americans admitted to fifteen. The Germans recorded no fighters downed, while the Americans admitted to losing twenty-three. Eighth Air Force claimed eight Luftwaffe fighters downed by fighters and six by bombers. The Germans admitted to only four losses.[17]

Eleven of the lost American fighters came from the 363rd Group, a Mustang unit recently committed to battle. Eighth Air Force and

VIII Fighter Command authorities were unable to account for this shocking loss of one-third of the group's planes and pilots. VIII Fighter Command headquarters announced "reasons unknown." At debriefing, group returnees mentioned nothing about enemy fighters in the area where the planes disappeared, which was in the Rhineland region and not Berlin, where the Luftwaffe's reaction was the most aggressive. The 363rd pilots agreed that the weather was the worst they had yet encountered. Was it flak, malfunctioning engines, weather, or a combination? The 4th Fighter Group historian, 1st Lt. Grover C. Hall, Jr., asserted that his group's claim of three victories over Berlin would have been quite a bit higher if not for "considerable mechanical difficulties with the guns, glycol, etc." Yet this veteran group, the first to escort bombers over Berlin, lost at most three comrades in the area where the Luftwaffe reacted most strongly in the otherwise generally passive skies on 4 March.[18] There were too many missing faces at the 363rd Group's mess and in the Officer's Club that night. Such were the mysteries and tragedies of war.

Although not aborted, the mission of 4 March had not accomplished its major purpose. Weather had become for the Eighth, and, except for Fred Anderson, also its parent U.S. Strategic Air Forces in Europe, somewhat of a questionable excuse for action deferred. Weather seemed to be as much of a psychological as a physical barrier to Berlin. If one wing possessed the determination to reach Berlin, why had not the others? The Germans were now playing a waiting game, trying to avoid getting entangled in the wastage trap. They were obviously capable of sending up many fighters, but the lack of bad-weather training limited their reaction, while also providing a convenient excuse.

Doolittle, in going over reports predicting weather for 5 March, decided it was "no go" for Berlin. Increasingly concerned over the morale of his crews, and perhaps feeling a little guilty for the recent extension of tours, he wanted to give overnight passes to the First and Third Bomb Divisions (B-17s). In the dreary Quonset huts, even the Armed Services broadcasts of the Glenn Miller Army

Air Forces Band must have paled. Fred Anderson quickly came forward as a spoilsport, maintaining that all crews should be available for the possibility of a Berlin mission. "I feel," he told Spaatz, "the minutes are ticking away . . . Our time to do our job is getting critically short." Anderson personified the beckoning shepherd. Spaatz vetoed the passes.[19]

The Luftwaffe high command was still more concerned with the effects of the attacks on fighter production than the daylight threat to Berlin. In a meeting of 4 March, Feldmarschall Erhard Milch, the Luftwaffe's number two man, told the Fighter Production Planning Staff that "since July 3 [1943] the enemy has been striking systematically at our production," claiming "they have destroyed completely fifty of our aircraft factories. That is almost correct if one takes into consideration that some of the factories have been attacked repeatedly."[20] The Germans, with apparently no pipeline into Allied air planning, no equivalent of ULTRA, had no way of forecasting that the aircraft factories would not be the major target in the coming days of March. And, after all, the effort by daylight against Berlin was still most feeble.

The weather of 5 March did not appear to justify any effort against Berlin. I Fighter Corps reported only reconnaissance aircraft crisscrossing the capital in singles, doubles, and triples, but no interceptors were sent up to interfere. Eighth Air Force did send a force of B-24s into II Fighter Corps domain in southern France to strike airfields. There was some hostile reaction. Though considered a "milk run" compared to Berlin, for Flight Officer Charles "Chuck" E. Yeager, the mission was a reminder that the skies over all of continental Europe remained a dangerous place. A FW 190 attacked Yeager's P-51, which "began to snap and roll, heading for the ground." Yeager "just fell out of the cockpit when the plane turned upside down—my canopy was shot away."[21]

For 6 March the forecast by U.S. Strategic Air Forces in Europe meteorologists was not exactly a rosy one, but it predicted considerably improved conditions. The excuse of weather could not be used to cancel another mission to Berlin. "Early on the morning of

5 March the basic plan for the next day's operation, Mission 250, was complete and just before 6:56 P.M. the teletype machine at High Wycombe began clattering out initial operation orders" to the various operational commands that would participate in the mission. Group intelligence officers at each base "pulled back the curtain over the wall and there was the route to the target marked out in wool . . . There was a roar of consternation as the . . . red tape marking the route went on and on, finally to the biggest mass on the map which was Berlin." One can imagine the emotions of the assembled crews when one bomber group commander announced, "Yes, by damn, we're going back to Berlin and this time we're going to get it right . . . We're going to lead the first combat wing of the First Air Division of the Eighth Air Force."[22]

Into varying cloud thicknesses that were not very high or low, 730 heavy bombers began to take off around 10 o'clock in the morning and soon crowded the sky over the eastern part of England. They were followed by 803 Allied fighters. Their route was designed to take them north of the major flak concentrations at Osnabrück, Hannover, Brunswick, and Magdeburg and south of the one at Brandenburg, close to Berlin. Just past the Dutch coast German spotter aircraft began tailing them. The far-flung network of observers, radar, gun batteries, telephone systems, plotting boards and tables, radio communications, and controllers hummed with activity. The I Fighter Corps war diary recorded the details: "The bombers, with their large fighter escort . . . moved along lines Munster-Meppen, Goslar-Uelzen, Halle-Rathenau to attack Berlin from the west and south." Despite "widespread fog at all altitudes" limiting visibility to "one to two kilometers," the first interceptors took off from an eventual "total of 328 single and twin-engine fighter aircraft . . . committed that day."[23] It was the onset of a battle whose intensity would rank with any infantry assault or amphibious landing, any depth-charging, or any artillery barrage or armor engagement of the war.

Heinz Knoke flew his Bf 109 in the opening phases of this battle. As the bombers flew toward Berlin, he led his formation from their base at Wunstorf about mid-course of the land portion of the route to Berlin. As he later recorded in his memoir,

In the initial frontal assault I shoot down a Fortress just north of the airfield and leave a second one in flames . . . In the ensuing dogfight with the Thunderbolts my tail-plane was shot full of holes and my engine and left wing was badly hit also. It is all I can do to limp home to our field.

VIII Fighter Command described the early Luftwaffe challenge in the dry prose of its narrative of operations:

North of Drummer Lake 3 large boxes of S/E e/a [single-engine enemy aircraft] totalling about 100 came in at 8 oclock to bombers. [56th Thunderbolt] Group made 180° turn, combat ensued 25,000 to 5,000 feet. One half of e/a attacked from left of bombers, other passed in front of bombers and attacked from right. 4 bombers seen to go down vicinity combat. About 20 chutes seen.

Captain Richard Turner flew on 6 March. His 354th Mustang Group was in target support when he became separated from his wingman. After absent-mindedly but temporarily shutting off his engine when he failed to switch to internal tanks from dry drop tanks, he found himself pursued by four Bf 109s. In his memoir he described how he used flaps to maneuver two of the enemy craft to zoom far past him when the "Mustang almost hung in mid-air, full power keeping it from spinning." At a third overshooting Bf 109, Turner gave "a long hard burst of 50s from dead astern. He took a flash of hits about the cockpit and at the wing root, which exploded his ammo and snapped off his left wing. The canopy and the pilot followed in short order." The fourth Bf 109 had him at a height advantage and was preparing to make a diving pass when two other Mustangs arrived and the German pilot was "making tracks . . . I was almost overcome with relief."[24]

At their debriefing the pilots of the 354th reported the reality of aerial attrition warfare: "B-17 seen to explode . . . no chutes observed . . . pilots saw another B-17 blow up and one out of control."

The Third Bomb Division experienced the major onslaught of Luftwaffe fighters, both Bf 109s and FW 190s. The First and elements of the Third Bomb Divisions had drifted south of the planned route, apparently unnoticed by German controllers, and escaped the Luftwaffe's fury. One wing, the 13th, in the middle of the Third Division's formation, caught the full ferocity of the swarming interceptors, which overwhelmed VIII Fighter Command's escort. Such was the working of fate in war. One of this wing's groups, the 100th, with a reputation for being jinxed, quickly lost nine of its aircraft. Amid the shouts and screams of battle, nearly one hundred of its crewmen became statistics—killed in action (KIA) or missing in action (MIA). Those fortunate enough to parachute from danger faced imprisonment, if they escaped the rage of civilians or fanatical Nazis on the ground.

The Third Bomb Division suffered most of its losses on the way to the target area, but pressed on to its target—the Robert Bosch electrical equipment factory. After the early attack on the Third, the Luftwaffe shifted its attention to the First Bomb Division north of Magdeburg, using mainly twin-engine fighters. Like the Third, the First pressed on despite the attacks and made its run toward the ball-bearing complex at Erkner. Its losses were fewer, but the 457th Group lost twenty-nine dead and three B-17s, apparently the result of Luftwaffe rammings. The trailing Liberators of the Second Bomb Division, in some confirmation of Orville Anderson's apprehension about their height liability, lost more aircraft to flak than fighters as it headed for its primary target, a Daimler Benz factory producing engines for aircraft and ground vehicles.[25]

VIII Fighter Command pilots reported that the Germans "definitely seemed more aggressive than recently." Eighth Air Force, based on debriefing and encounter reports, concluded that enemy fighters "were aggressive and pressed attacks to close range," coming "in waves of 4, 8, and 12 aircraft and approaches were made simultaneously from all angles, although nose attacks were favored." Utilizing a tactic as old as World War I, the Germans made "extensive use . . . of the sun to cover approaches from above." The irony was reflected in the words of the Air Corps song: "Off we go into the wild blue yonder, climbing high into the sun / Down they dive zooming to meet our thunder . . . "[26]

The Luftwaffe, for the first time in weeks, made an all-out effort, including the deployment of both night fighter aircraft and twin-engine day destroyer aircraft. While certain types of twin-engine aircraft such as the Bf 110 were used both at night and during the day, those assigned night duty were fitted with radar apparatus, while those operating in the day were normally fitted for rockets. Twin-engine destroyers hovered beyond the bombers' defensive fire and loosed rockets with timed fuzes into the combat boxes, following up with 20mm cannon attacks on the resulting stragglers. The Bf 109s flew top cover for these slower, less nimble destroyers, freeing them to make their attacks without the interference of American fighters. The 20mm shells were of the incendiary type— the Americans described them as impacting with a "sparkler" effect—and they were responsible for causing many bombers, in a live performance of the Air Corps song's lyrics, to "go down in flame."

The German defenders of Berlin pulled out all the stops. Units from the Eastern Front were thrown into the battle without rest, refitting, or even a briefing as to what to expect. Günther Rall, Germany's third-ranking ace of the war, reported that upon arrival from the East he was told only to escort other German fighters attacking American bombers. VIII Fighter Command escort pilots claimed to have seen German aircraft dropping parachute bombs into the bomber formations, but with little apparent effect. At several sites the Germans tried to obscure potential targets with smoke screens. Pilots of the 354th Fighter Group noted smoke generators at Hannover and near Berlin saw a "large ring of white smoke going up to about 25,000 feet . . . believed to have been rocket trail." Others also reported ground-launched rockets. There were more incidents of German fighters ramming bombers, by accident or design. One such collision with a German fighter caused a B-17 to veer into a second Fortress and all three planes went down together. Stunned witnesses saw no chutes.[27]

Eighth Air Force evaluated the flak as being "intense and accurate" over Berlin and "moderate to intense and accurate" at various other places. Some bombers became "cold meat" for German fighters after antiaircraft artillery fire forced them to stagger out of formation. Others simply disintegrated when a flak burst exploded their bombs.

None of these defensive measures were new, but rarely if ever had they been used in such a lethal mixture. Despite the record number of protective fighters, those assigned target support were sometimes too few to do the job adequately, as reported by both American and German sources. Both sides boasted of their achievements this day. VIII Fighter Command claimed "enemy outsmarted and badly outfought by our fighters." I Fighter Corps claimed "a single formation from the Second Fighter Division managed to down forty-five enemy bombers." During the phased escort of the three bomb divisions the escort flew as close to the bombers as possible, but some free-ranging sweeps did take place, especially in withdrawal support. During this phase German intensity lessened. In the final analysis, VIII Fighter Command performed its mission—the main task was to destroy German fighters, only secondarily were they to protect the bombers, the bait.[28]

Eighth Air Force accounted for only 14 crew members killed and 38 wounded, but for 708 missing.[29] Time and time again, the surviving "Little Friend" escort fighter pilots and the "Big Friend" bomber crews told of how, after a Fortress or Liberator began to dive, spin in, or explode, the air was empty of parachutes or had too few. This day, 6 March 1944, was the most costly heavy bomber mission yet flown by Americans over Europe—sixty-nine bombers lost. Randall Jarrell's "Death of the Ball Turret Gunner" seemed grimly appropriate:

> From my mother's sleep I fell into the state
> And I hunched in its belly till my wet fur froze
> Six miles from earth, loosed from its dream of life
> I woke to black flak and the nightmare fighters
> When I died they washed me out of the turret with a hose.[30]

OVERLORD was too near with the prospects of what would happen if air superiority were not attained, whatever the cost. Though losses were high, as a percentage of the total aircraft involved (10.4 percent), the loss rate continued to decline.

Another change from the pessimism of the fall crisis was the confidence of top leadership. On 7 March Arnold sent Spaatz a "heartiest congratulations," expressing his delight over "the fact that you are forcing the enemy to expend his fighter aircraft." This justified the losses. Arnold assured Spaatz that "everything possible would be done here to replace your losses and maintain your Air Forces to full strength." This also justified the losses. Arnold was saying, "We now have the means," and was implying, "Keep it up, boy." Spaatz intended to keep it up and Fred Anderson would work to insure it. The same day the bombers reached Berlin in force Spaatz sent Arnold a plan for the "completion of the combined bomber offensive," made possible, Spaatz stated, by the Big Week battles and, by implication, what was happening in the Berlin battles. He did not use the term *air superiority*, but this is what he meant when he said that the circumstances were propitious for a "concerted effort against Oil, which would represent the most farreaching use of strategic air power that has been attempted in this war."[31] But that effort would await the completion of the battle for Berlin.

What were the accomplishments of the first big mission to Berlin? The bombing achieved mixed results. Field orders had identified multiple primary and secondary targets in the Berlin area, but weather conditions were "generally unfavorable to visual bombing." In such cases as this, the air commanders had a good deal of leeway, able to attack "any military objective positively identified as being in Germany." "In practice," summed up Jeffrey Ethell and Alfred Price, "this meant formation leaders bombed holes in the cloud and hit whatever part of the city happened to be underneath." On this day it meant scattering some 1,500 tons of bombs on the Berlin area.[32] The destruction included some railroad trackage, highways, a factory or two, and the residential

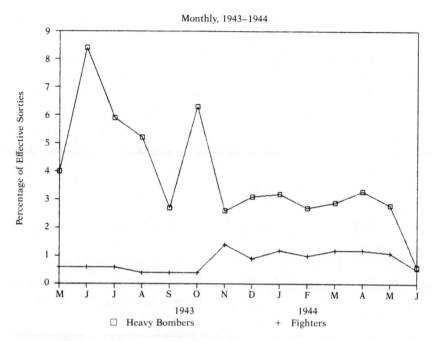

Figure 9. Eighth Air Force Loss Rates
Source: VIII Fighter Command, "Achtung Indianer," 24 July 1944, File 168.6005-54, Plate xxxviii, HRC.

areas of Steglitz and Zehlendorf. I Fighter Corps' commander Josef Schmid called the damage "comparatively slight." One of his pilots in contrast recalled that the city was "ablaze from end to end."[33] After the war historians and moralists could evaluate whether Eighth Air Force had attempted precision bombing or had succumbed to the expediency of area bombing. For now the only concern was that the bombers had done sufficient damage to force the Luftwaffe to defend the skies over Berlin and had bled in the process—the cruel and stark reality of air superiority warfare.

When Luftwaffe pilot Heinz Knoke returned from his third sortie of 6 March, his squadron commander requested that the squadron be given a rest, but the Second Fighter Division commander said no. Knoke stared at the pictures of dead veteran pilots around the walls of the ready room. Today's and past battles had taken their toll. The live veterans had dwindled to two. His recollection of that moment was more than just a bit of melancholia. It symbolized what the great air battles of the past several weeks were about. What had gone on beneath them was of little consequence to POINT-BLANK or OVERLORD. The 6 March bombing was only of tragic consequence to the 600-odd persons who had died or were injured in Berlin. For the survivors, "'the barrage from the air which mutilated, suffocated, burned, and destroyed, did not so much breed fear and a desire to bow before the storm, but rather a certain fatalistic cussedness, a dogged determination to survive.'"[34]

What effect did Mission 250 to Berlin have on the Luftwaffe's ability and strategy? The claims of both sides were at wide variance.

Eighth Air Force bombers claimed ninety-seven enemy aircraft destroyed, twenty-eight probably destroyed, and sixty damaged. Eighth Air Force fighters claimed eighty-two destroyed, eight probably destroyed, and thirty-three damaged. I Fighter Corps admitted to losing only eighteen of its fighters, with an additional thirty-nine suffering damage in excess of 60 percent. These admissions involved the loss of fourteen pilots, including Gerhard Loos and Hugo Frey, veteran aces with ninety-two and thirty-two victories respectively. Frey's loss was especially significant because he was one of the all-time heavy bomber killers, credited with the downing of twenty-six American four-engine bombers. Other German sources, including the Luftwaffe Quartermaster and Air Fleet Reich, reported the loss of sixty-two or sixty-three German fighters. A recent source, most valuable because it lists names and totals of personnel lost or missing, identified sixty-six Luftwaffe fighters destroyed or damaged beyond repair.[35]

German claims were also inflated. With the major burden for defending the Reich day and night, I Fighter Corps had very much an ego stake in this battle for which the Luftwaffe high command had chosen to ignore wastage and to commit a large percentage of its resources. Criticized by Göring, just as the U.S. Strategic Air Forces in Europe and Eighth Air Force before it had been criticized by Arnold, the fighter arm from crew to Schmid to Galland felt compelled to deliver. This was the root of I Fighter Corps' bloated claims: ninety-five bombers destroyed, ten probably brought down, and fifteen fighters "certainly brought down," against American admissions of sixty-nine bombers and eleven fighters lost. These losses indicated that Göring's mandate that the interceptors concentrate on the bombers was still being observed.[36]

What the Americans lost in terms of both aircraft and people was of much less import than what the Germans lost, especially with regard to people. The relatively small loss of American fighter pilots was much more significant than the 700-odd casualty figure for the bombers. The handful of American fighter losses was more than compensated by the swelling number of replacements. Air superiority would be determined between the American and German fighter pilots in large measure in the coming days. One indication of the growing plight of the Luftwaffe was the continued pullback of the fighter defense forces eastward, back into the Reich itself. The Allied Y-Service noted that as of 6 March Allied intercepts in England of radio transmissions between German aircraft and their ground controllers in the interior of the Reich was no longer possible because the transmissions were now out of range.[37] The most vital index to the bleeding of the Luftwaffe's defensive capability was the continued loss of experienced leaders such as Loos and Frey. Over the next three months, these losses would drain the life from the Luftwaffe. How could the Luftwaffe hope to win the air war when in three months it had lost the services of the twenty-eight aces listed in Table 3, together responsible for downing 2,118 enemy aircraft? Especially damaging was the loss of the aces and leaders with the greatest experience in shooting down American four-engine bombers: Anton Hackl with thirty-two heavy bombers, Hugo Frey with twenty-six, Egon Mayer with twenty-five, Ernst Börngen with twenty-four, Hans Heinrich König with twenty, Gerhard Sommer with fourteen, Karl Willius with eleven, and Walter Oesau with ten.

Most of the great American fighter commanders, and those who

Table 3.   Attrition of German Fighter Aces in West and Reich

Ace	Victories	Date Lost
Egon Mayer	102	2 March 1944
Anton Hackl	192	March 1944
Hugo Frey	32	6 March 1944
Gerhard Loos	92	6 March 1944
Rudolf Ehrenberger	49	8 March 1944
Egmont Prinz zur Lippe-Weissenfeld	51	12 March 1944
Emil Bitsch	108	15 March 1944
Heinrich Wohlers	29	15 March 1944
Johann-Hermann Meier	77	15 March 1944
Stefan Litjens	38	23 March 1944
Wolf-Dietrich Wilcke	162	23 March 1944
Detler Rohwer	38	29 March 1944
Hans Remmer	26	2 April 1944
Karl Willius	50	8 April 1944
Josef Zwernemann	126	8 April 1944
Otto Wessling	83	19 April 1944
Franz Schwaiger	67	24 April 1944
Emil Omert	70	24 April 1944
Kurt Ubben	110	27 April 1944
Leopold Münster	95	8 May 1944
Walter Oesau	123	11 May 1944
Gerhard Sommer	20	12 May 1944
Ernst Börngen	45	19 May 1944
Hans-Heinrich König	24	24 May 1944
Reinhold Hoffmann	66	24 May 1944
Horst Carganico	60	27 May 1944
Friedrich-Karl Müller	140	29 May 1944
Karl-Wolfgang Redlich	43	29 May 1944

Source: Obermaier.

were also role models as aces, such as the 4th Fighter Group's Col. Donald J. M. Blakeslee and the 56th Group's Col. Hubert "Hub" Zemke, would continue to lead down to OVERLORD. Under them subordinate commanders gained valuable experience.

After a stand-down on 7 March because of bad weather, Spaatz scheduled another Berlin operation for the next day. Field Order Number 488 identified the Erkner ball-bearing complex and the

Friedrichstrasse section of Berlin as the targets. Lieutenant Colonel Philip Ardery was to copilot a B-24 for 8 March. In his memoir he recalled:

We were up several hours before dawn. If the fellows ever felt like breaking into loud cheers upon having an important target announced in the briefing room, that morning they might have. But when the curtain was lifted from the big map, revealing the long route in, the target, and the long route out, there were no cheers.

Ardery, already knowing the target, watched the faces of the crews: "They became a shade more grave, but were otherwise unmoved."[38]

The 177 B-17s of the Third Bomb Division led the way, followed by 234 B-17s of the First Bomb Division and 207 B-24s of Ardery's Second Bomb Division. They were joined over Holland by the 294 fighters assigned penetration support. On that day it was literally "into the wild blue yonder," for the sky progressively cleared while the Germans waited.

There would be fewer German fighters to meet them, only 282, because, as Schmid's war diary later explained, "not all the aircraft put out of action by the operations on 6 March had been repaired." They would face 891 American fighters, supported by a dozen British fighter squadrons during withdrawal. The size of the American operation was testimony to the great buildup by March. The weather this day did not hinder American operations, but the I Fighter Corps claimed that "both ground and high altitude fogs . . . hindered the effective commitment of our fighter aircraft." Still it admitted the weather was "almost cloudless" over Berlin.

The route in was more direct than that of 6 March because "it was considered that the shorter distance involved would allow maximum fighter protection and that no indirect routings of feints would be likely to deceive an enemy who would be expecting the renewal of the attacks against Berlin objectives as soon as weather conditions permitted." The authors of the Eighth Air Force report for the 8 March mission were apparently unaware that Spaatz and

Fred Anderson wanted no feints. Once more the German defensive scheme was to strike hard against the incoming bomber stream at mid-route and then strike again with second sorties as the bombers turned northeast for their runs on Berlin. Once again, because it was in the lead, the Third Bomb Division took the initial lick. Thunderbolts of the 56th Group were riding herd in penetration support when "near Drummer Lake 3 bunches of about 20 S/E e/a each were seen approaching the Forts from the S.E. [southeast] and slightly below. Between this point and Steinhuder Lake a total of about 100 S/E e/a were engaged with our fighters and bombers."[39]

In its report to the Air Staff some three weeks later, Eighth Air Force analyzed the methods of the interceptors. "Achieving local superiority over escorting fighters by massing large numbers of single-engine aircraft east of Drummer Lake, the German Air Force directed the weight of their attacks against the two leading Combat Wings of [Third Bomb Division]." "After the first attacks by the German fighter formation," reported I Fighter Corps' commander Schmid, "heavy fighting developed over Magdeburg and Braunschweig [Brunswick]." The enemy, analyzed the Eighth, "made approaches from every angle, but the majority were from the nose or tail and level or above. Enemy pilots were described as skillful and persistent [making] effective use of the sun to cover approaches from above and at times simulated escorting fighter formations." They pulled other old tricks, employing "decoys . . . to distract attention from attacks developing in other directions. There were only a few reports of rocket fire and no attempts at aerial . . . bombing."[40]

For this and other deep penetration missions, Grover C. Hall, Jr., in his postwar classic account of the 4th Fighter Group, *1000 Destroyed*, summed up the spirit, audacity, and eccentricity of the American fighter pilot. He also paid tribute to the heavy bomber crews, the "Big Friends":

The Forts kept their dignity, the gunners just blazed away at the attacking fighters and though the pilot might close his eyes, he held it on the bomb run until he heard "bombs away." The fighter boys could always break off, climb, and dive. But the bombers had to keep wading through the death hail until the eggs were dropped. It was like being trapped in a submarine on the ocean floor.

Did the crews who had gone out on the third, fourth, sixth, and now the eighth of March realize they were essentially bait? One who did was Clyde Bradley, who piloted a B-17 over Berlin on several missions. He recollected that "they [American fighters] were going to go for the [German] fighters, that we were bait. As individuals we were not told these decisions." He remembered that during these early March missions "morale was declining."[41]

For the 8 March mission, German fighter pilots and crews went after the invaders with high morale, even the inexperienced ones. Heinz Knoke did not fly on the eighth, but Gerhard Kroll, seeing his first combat, did. A nineteen-year-old, he had come through the Luftwaffe training pipeline and had a stint as an instructor at a fighter ordnance school. He would later recall, "By the time I was allowed to participate, the war was practically lost, although we didn't know or believe it then." As the newest member he flew at the rear of the 9th Squadron, III Group, 54th Fighter Wing. He did not see the enemy until his formation of Bf 109s was "on top of the bombers." He confirmed that the "Little Friends" could not always protect their "Big Friends" or such was second in their consideration. "Lucky for us there was no escort fighters. Attack was made headon from above." After his group had dived through the bombers, his leader downing a B-17, they "climbed again for the second attack from the rear . . . I saw a straggler . . . it looked so good to me I left my squadron and turned on the B-17." Kroll was acting against standing orders, but the temptation was too much. His fighter "gained fast on the B-17 from behind and below . . . I pressed the buttons. Thick black smoke came from the right inboard engine" and the Fortress started down. "I believe I caught something from the tail gunner" and he had to make a hasty, clumsy exit from the cockpit in which his own smoke had begun to gather. At first "it was very quiet up there. I looked around at the green forests, the tiny roads and the little houses." Suddenly "a very strong wind made me sway back and forth and I became seasick . . . I kept my mouth shut when I was swinging forward and I would spit it out on the backward swing." He finally landed at an awkward angle and sprained an ankle.[42]

The trailing B-24s reached the outer rim of the city. Ardery recalled, "On in we went. Berlin seemed the biggest city in the world . . . the flak bursts were so thick it seemed to me some of the shells must be colliding with each other. A couple of bombers I could see were already heavily hit." In the confusion they could only bomb "the city, and one place was about as good as another." As they turned to leave, "the flak was all around us, and we could see the sheets of flame in the explosion of many shell bursts." Another pilot described the flak bursts as "fiery red, belching black and grey smoke." Ardery remembered the bombers reacting to the flak barrage "like canoes in a Lake Superior storm."[43]

As the bombers withdrew, escort fighters not only provided close support, but swept in search of enemy gaggles and picked up stragglers. One of VIII Fighter Command's most flamboyant aces, 4th Fighter Group's Capt. Don Gentile, and his wingman, 1st Lt. John T. Godfrey, were to become in a few weeks the most celebrated pair of fighter pilots in the Eighth Air Force, acknowledged even by Winston Churchill. But now, on 8 March, they were about out of ammunition. "There may have been one rump in the skies over Berlin that ached more than Gentile's. If so, it was Godfrey's. Both wanted to push the throttle back, streak home and get the harness off." But they saw a "limping, but majestic Fort," whose crew was "stomach-sick with dread" at the thought of the long journey home. Gentile contacted the bomber: "Mustang to Fort . . . Okay, we'll take you in," to which the bomber pilot responded, "Fort to Mustang . . . Thanks, little friend, thanks." Randall Jarrell, after reading of this type of interaction in a newspaper, gave it a poetic touch: "Then I heard the bomber call me in: 'Little Friend, Little Friend, I got engines on fire. Can you see me, Little Friend?' / 'I'm crossing right over you. Let's go home.'" The 4th Group's monthly history recorded laconically, "A B-17 marked 'JW-G' was met at 14,000 feet . . . and escorted to England."[44] It was not all a cold-blooded baiting of the hook.

A total of 468 bombers dropped over a thousand tons of high explosive and incendiary bombs on Berlin in the vicinity of the Erkner ball-bearing plant this day. Thirty others dropped around 100 tons near the "center of the city." I Fighter Corps reported "the attack on Berlin had left in its wake serious damage to both private properties and industrial plants in the eastern suburbs of the city." All of it, however, was secondary to the attrition of the Luftwaffe in the sky. The Germans claimed 50 bombers and 14 fighters destroyed. The Americans acknowledged the loss of 36 bombers and 17 fighters. American bomber and fighter claims totaled 150 enemy aircraft destroyed. The I Fighter Corps, with the responsibility of defending Berlin, recorded the loss of 21, with 20 more suffering more than 60 percent damage. The Luftwaffe Quartermaster, charged with replacing losses, recorded the loss of 55.[45]

Jimmy Doolittle worried both about his losses and his crews' morale. In contrast, Fred Anderson was elated with the battle reports. He chortled that Berlin radio had been "squealing like a stuck pig." He had not been happy about the 7 March stand-down, but was invigorated by the 8 March battle. Doolittle again tried to cancel the Berlin mission scheduled for the next day, arguing that his forces were worn out. Anderson insisted that the bombers had to go back to Berlin on the ninth and Spaatz agreed.[46] It did not seem as if one day would matter, but Anderson had noticed a crack in the German defenses. Why the drop-off in twin-engine fighters with their deadly rockets? Anderson saw it as a sure sign of the effect the Berlin missions were having on the Luftwaffe.

On 9 March out went the heavy bombers as before. The weather forecast was not good for the general Berlin area—6 to 8/10 overcast, but low enough to permit the use of radar bombing. The targets were three plants producing components for the Luftwaffe's only operational heavy bomber, the He 177. The weather turned out to be worse than expected, causing great confusion and delay in the conduct of the mission. The worn-out crews in American bombers and fighters braced for the expected first blow, but when it came it was almost a love tap in comparison. At 11:05 in the morning, some ten German single-engine fighters, flying high like the B-17s of the leading First Bomb Division, cruised out of range. Minutes later a few more distant twin-engine fighters fired a small number of rockets into the bomber boxes, doing little damage. The 56th Group, led by the great Thunderbolt ace, Lt. Col. Francis "Gabby" Gabreski, picked up the leading combat wings and led them uneventfully on.

Over the target area the veteran 354th Group was the first to pick up the Fortresses. Heavy flak began to splatter the clear blue sky above the clouds and the trails of ground rockets formed a few distinctive circles. But where were the German interceptors? Grover Hall, in the monthly history of the 4th Fighter Group, summed it up: "The group returned to Berlin, but found no one at home." Except for the intense flak, which claimed one bomber and one fighter over Berlin, the sky belonged to the Americans this day.[47]

Save for the early air-to-air rocket volley, there was no fighter opposition. An occasional Bf 109 or FW 190 tracked the stream and stayed out of range. The bombers claimed one enemy aircraft destroyed, the escort none. On withdrawal, in contrast to the last two missions, the bombers radioed the waiting withdrawal escort that they would be 15 minutes or more late, were as much as 50 miles off course, and were "happy." Eighth Air Force attributed the lack of reaction, the first to a major raid of the war, to the weather. For the Germans, Schmid claimed, "adverse weather conditions prevented the employment of aircraft."[48]

By all accounts, the weather was indeed bad, perhaps the worst of the March battles. Nevertheless, a few interceptors, including some single-engine types without radar, made it above the overcast. Twin-engine rocket-firing destroyer aircraft without radar had come up, too. On the previous days, in weather almost as bad, hundreds had appeared. Schmid complained constantly about the weather, but regularly launched his forces anyway. Training in instrument flying was one of the major deficiencies of the Luftwaffe, but it had not prevented the Luftwaffe from flying and fighting in bad weather before. But the most damning evidence that the Luftwaffe, at least temporarily, had for the first time since September 1940 lost its will was the absence of night fighters with a radar capability in the overcast or above it over Berlin. These aircraft could have challenged the bombers, whose work, according to I Fighter Corps, "was extremely effective and caused quite a bit of damage in the southern sectors of Berlin."[49]

The "bait" strategy of Spaatz, pushed by Anderson, and carried out by Kepner's now superb legion of fighters and by, if the commanding general was hesitant at times, Eighth Air Force's heavy bombers, had virtually accomplished what the crews and pilots of the Big Week battles had begun—the transfer of air superiority during daylight hours from the Luftwaffe to the U.S. Strategic Air Forces in Europe. ULTRA revealed that Germany had begun a policy of conserving its fighter pilots and of transferring bomber and transport pilots to fighter units "as a matter of emergency."[50] The Luftwaffe was not beaten, but it had revealed that it could not defend that most prestigious target—Berlin. Schmid, the one man in the Luftwaffe most responsible for the aerial defense of Berlin during these battles, admitted after the war that the month of March was crucial. "Thanks to the striking power and increased flight range of their fighter aircraft," he wrote, "the American forces captured air supremacy over almost the entire Reich and its territories. The only exception remained the German provinces in the east . . . and this meant the complete collapse of Germany's position as an air power."

The fact that there was "no systematic plan" apparent in American air operations, Schmid said, puzzled German commanders. The organized assaults upon the "German air armament plants, which were begun with such great success in February, was discontinued, and German observers could find no concentrated purpose in the American selection of . . . targets during March 1944." Unlike Big Week, the bombing aspect of the Berlin battle involved only the Eighth Air Force. The Germans could not understand this change from February either. But Schmid could draw several conclusions: American fighters outnumbered his day fighters by four to one and I Fighter Corps had lost 10 percent of its committed forces, while the Americans had lost only 1.8 percent of the fighters and bombers sent into combat.[51] Whether as a result of a loss of will or because of the wastage of attrition warfare, the Luftwaffe would be selective about where it would give battle in the future and how much it would commit to it.

On 11 March Doolittle sent a personal commendation to Kepner for the role of VIII Fighter Command "in a decisive air battle" that had taken place between 20 February and 9 March. Doolittle called ARGUMENT an "outstanding success." Of Berlin he said,

In the last seven days five missions have been directed against targets in the Berlin area . . . on 9 March, our penetration to Berlin was virtually unopposed by the Luftwaffe. The admission by German fighter controllers that they preferred to keep their aircraft on the ground even when Berlin was under attack, marks the turning point of the war in the air . . . the German fighters elected to stay on the ground, citing the solid overcast as an excuse for their failure to operate. There are indications, however, that in spite of inclement weather the German controllers could have sent up on that day a considerable number of fighters, for some, which did not engage, were able to come up through the overcast.

Given Doolittle's attempts to stall before some of the missions, these statements carried a certain irony. Still, he was essentially correct.

From this it must be assumed that the German fighter units are broken but not utterly crushed, and that the enemy has made a decision to conserve aircraft and pilots. We must expect that following a period of recuperation and regrouping, their fighters will again endeavor to resist our penetrations.

Doolittle's analysis of the condition of the Luftwaffe's daylight defensive ability was a bit exaggerated, but essentially accurate. He was not exactly a prophet in predicting that after a period of nursing its wounds the Luftwaffe would rise to contest the bombers again. It was an informed conjecture and he was being the cautious commander. The campaign against the Luftwaffe in the air and on the ground would have to continue.

Doolittle's sensitivity to the casualties of the recent air battles came across in the concluding paragraph of the commendation, something that was not obligatory in an official congratulation to a fellow but subordinate general officer: "While each individual loss is deeply regretted, the casualties suffered by the Eighth Air Force since February 20 have not been heavy when weighed against the results attained. Furthermore, it is sincerely hoped that the great majority of those who did not return from the recent missions will eventually be rehabilitated by one means or another."[52]

In an "eyes only" message to Arnold that same day, Spaatz coldbloodedly reiterated what the recent missions were about.

The operations during the past week had the major purpose of forcing the German fighter force into battle. Three attacks were made without any attempt at deception. Route followed on each attack being exactly the same . . . it is too early to gauge full effect of destruction of fighter production plus their heavy air wastage, we of course are all confident that the air battle is in our hands.

He did not mention casualties. For his part, Arnold told Spaatz that "the depletion of the GAF [German Air Force]" was the U.S. Strategic Air Forces in Europe's "sole purpose" and that Spaatz should do "everything possible" to complete that assignment.[53]

Hermann Göring was either whistling in Germany or quite self-deceived by the situation. According to Schmid, he was less worried in March about the course of the air war than he had been in February, seemingly because the attacks on the aircraft plants had lessened and because of what he considered the successful defense of Berlin on 6 and 8 March 1944. General Schmid did not record the Reichmarschall's reaction to the 9 March defense. General Galland knew better. He had flown in some of the action in March and was convinced that the great difficulties of coping with an American fighter force that outnumbered his own were not likely to be solved by reduced aircraft plant capacity and a critical and vulnerable fuel supply. The only possible solution was a fighter markedly superior to any the Americans had. It was at hand. In fact, two types were now available and, according to Schmid, Galland "did everything in his power to speed up production on the jet fighter, Me 262, and on the rocket-propelled Me 163."[54]

Galland was, of course, concerned about the effect of the weather on defensive operations. After he had fallen into Allied hands near the end of the war, he gave two accounts of the role of weather in hampering such operations that were apparently a bit contradictory. When asked by an American interrogator why the Luftwaffe did not hit the bombers with everything it had during deep penetration missions, he replied, "We always did, but our forces couldn't always take off on operations, sometimes on account of weather." During a British interrogation he claimed to the contrary that in spite of the frustration of flying in bad weather by the ordinary day fighter unit, the I Fighter Corps "continued to send up formations no matter how thick the cloud cover was."[55]

A German veteran of 6 March, ex-fighter pilot Sgt. Fritz Ungar, did not cite training as a decisive factor in the transfer of air superiority from the Germans to the Americans, which transfer he dated from 20 February. Instead, "the reason was the large amount of fighter planes that were employed at a time for a mission. The numerical advantage was too large for us, we couldn't counter such masses." Gerhard Kroll, on the other hand, underlined training as a leading cause of Luftwaffe failure: "The turnover of planes and pilots was very high in 1944 and 1945. Pilots . . . [did not] have enough training and therefore did not last long. My *total* flying hours I estimate at 1000." Kroll inadvertently contributed to the "plague" after recovering from his parachute jump on 8 March, when he crashed on takeoff while on an assignment to ferry a repaired Bf 109 back to his group, but he survived unscathed. Heinz Knoke made several revealing statements about the replacements his squadron was receiving in April. For the most part they were green as grass, but fine specimens. "I myself take them up for about 120 training hours. Two veteran combat pilots also give them instruction in blind flying." The only reason Knoke's squadron could devote so much time to this enriched but rare block of training for its newcomers was that it had at last been taken off operations to regroup. It was likely not a unique thing and may partially account for the Luftwaffe's continuing to have good morale and a stinger. That, and the same hope that Galland nursed; in April Knoke visited the Luftwaffe experimental field at Lechfeld, where he flew the Me 262. "One thousand of these are to be in operation by the end of the year. God help the Tommy and the Yank then!"

Late in April Knoke was surrounded by Thunderbolts. His plane caught fire and he went down for a crash landing, getting a P-47 on the way. He got clear of the blazing plane. Wounded in the head, he had a brief encounter with a tall American, pilot of the plane he shot down. At first there was tension between them, then gradually it melted and Knoke showed the American a picture of his wife and daughter. "There is not suggestion of hatred between us, nor any reason for it. We have too much in common. We are both pilots and we have both just narrowly escaped death." The American was fortunate, for he passed directly into military hands. Knoke was also fortunate, for an operation on his head wound would keep him out of action for months.[56]

Luther Richmond had little complaint about his training, but pointed to an almost Luftwaffe-like crisis. In their haste to switch to the long-range Mustang, some commanders sent their pilots on combat missions with just a few hours of flight indoctrination. "We had about two hours of flying time when we flew our first mission with the aircraft." The 4th Group, as part of the deal Blakeslee made to get P-51s ahead of schedule in March, flew off on the same thin thread of familiarity. Richmond did not mention teething problems that could have cost lives and loss of these prized of all fighters. Grover Hall did, but then was able to report after a few missions and mechanical readjustments that the Mustang had become the mount of choice.[57]

From the nature of post–6, 8, and 9 March Luftwaffe reaction to daylight heavy bomber missions through 29 March, certain behavior emerged. First, weather was not the overriding factor in whether there was a response, but it did have some effect on the degree of response. Second, the Germans had caught on that they were being "baited" by the missions to Berlin, with the Mecca of Nazism, Munich, being added to that strategy. Third, the reaction was intended to catch the Americans with their guard down and was therefore very selective. Fourth, although there was a gradual recovery by the Luftwaffe from the trauma of 6–9 March, it was not a vigorous or healthy force that would enable the Germans to reassert air superiority anytime soon.

There was no reaction, with weather as an excuse, to a raid on Münster on the eleventh. On 15 March a total of 165 interceptors rose, "despite low-hanging clouds, the danger of icing in the clouds, and scattered snow flurries" against bombers dispatched to Brunswick. "Enemy not very aggressive," reported VIII Fighter Command. They were perceived as much more aggressive on 16 March during a mission that saw twin strikes against Augsburg and Friedrichshaven, with the largest number of bombers, twenty-three, admitted lost since 8 March. Oddly, I Fighter Corps only claimed two bombers. On 18 March the largest combination bomber-escort formation, close to 2,000 aircraft, ever sent by the Eighth Air Force made the first daylight raid on Munich. It was an obvious "baiting" mission, but Luftwaffe reaction was moderate except over the target. The Americans made their customary extravagant claims. The Germans gave their by-now-lame excuse that weather prevented a stronger reaction, particularly along the route of the bombers. On one score, literally, it was as though the two sides briefly exchanged staffs: the Americans admitted the loss of more bombers, forty-three, and fighters, thirteen, than the Germans claimed—twenty-two and four respectively. The Fifteenth Air Force made the only heavy bomber operation on 19 March, hitting targets in southern Austria.

The next Eighth Air Force heavy bomber mission was a return to the "Big B" on 22 March and "adverse weather conditions precluded the commitment of aircraft by I Fighter Corps." However, the next day, when a smaller force divided to attack five targets mainly in western Germany, including Münster and Brunswick, the interceptors, heavy overcast notwithstanding, pounced on the lead element, which had arrived about a half hour early for rendezvous with the escort. The error cost twelve bombers. The other interceptors had less luck for, as Schmid took special note, "while engaged in assembly maneuvers, our fighters were engaged by the American fighters." Among the dead on the twenty-third was Col. Wolf-Dietrich Wilcke, commander of a single-engine wing, holder of one of the highest orders of the Iron Cross, and a 162-plane ace.

With a new phase of the air war, the pre-OVERLORD transportation campaign, beginning after 25 March, the regular strategic missions by heavy bombers slacked off for a time, but there were exceptions. On 29 March, in fairly severe weather conditions over the target, the Eighth's heavies went to Brunswick. I Fighter Corps sent up one of the largest number of interceptors, 258, since 8 March, in spite of "stormy weather" that made assembly difficult, but only a few made contact with the enemy. VIII Fighter Command commented: "Enemy definitely non-aggressive and dumb against all groups except one." Schmid recorded the largest number of German planes lost or unrepairable since 8 March—a total of thirty-three—and the largest number of dead, missing, or seriously wounded since 6 March—twenty-seven.[58]

On 21 March at a conference on supplies and procurement, several members of the Luftwaffe General Staff expressed thoughts that revealed the anxiety and frustration over the deteriorating air situation. General Karl Koller, chief of the Luftwaffe Operations Staff, stated that the fighter arm had to have a new heavy fighter, whether single or twin-engine, that had a time-in-air capacity of 4 hours. He claimed that "the somewhat meager results hitherto caused by weather conditions are due largely to the small time-in-air capabilities and difficult handling of" the relatively light standard single- and twin-engine fighters in inclement weather. Feldmarschall Milch replied that "a different solution of the problem will come anyhow through introduction of the jet-propelled fighter." Koller insisted that the light fighter would not suffice for the crucial time at hand. Milch got his back up: "We need large numbers. These requirements can only be met in the field of light aircraft." Koller was adamant about the need for a heavy fighter with more staying power. Milch fumbled around: "We must try to improve things through better training, through training in blind navigation." Koller remained feisty, arguing that "air armament must be given first priority within the entire armament program." Milch claimed he had been "preaching this for the past two years. Only the Führer can take the decision." Finally, Koller weighed in with a pronouncement redolent of Douhet: "In the constant interplay of attack and defense the only weapon that is strongest in attack is air power. The enemy is giving us evidence of this fact every day; in spite of our strong defense system we have not yet been able to repel their attack."[59]

At a meeting on 22 March, Jimmy Doolittle shared his own anxieties with his top-level commanders. In a mood swing from the optimism expressed in the commendation of Kepner of 11 March, Doolittle expressed his feeling that the struggle for air superiority had not yet been resolved, that it was still a case of who would fold first. He was worried about the depletion of the Eighth's resources in the recent battles. Still concerned about morale, he felt only a steady flow of replacement crews and aircraft, good food and quarters, and good flight formations could maintain morale. He urged commanders to look for signs of low morale such as excessive complaining, poor bombing, too many planes turning back shy of the target, too many planes landing in neutral countries, and refusal to go on a mission. He wanted to be advised when commanders felt the men were being pushed too hard.

Doolittle advised his subordinates to explain to the crews that there might be a lag between the attrition of German strength and the enemy's feebler performance. His commanders in turn suggested that more information about accomplishments be shared with the crews. They criticized certain press reports that suggested the Americans could now afford to expend bombers, which was especially damaging to morale. Doolittle also requested input that would help him in his on-going dialogue with General Arnold about a 30-day leave for combat crews before being returned for further overseas duty.[60] There were additional complaints at the meeting about such issues as the poor discipline of recently arriving aircrews. To have heard this complaint, Doolittle's anxieties about morale, and his annoyance that soon the Eighth would have to devote much of its effort in direct support of OVERLORD, an uninformed observer might have wondered who was indeed winning the air war at that point.[61]

Significant changes were pending in the pattern of the air war even as Doolittle spoke to his commanders. Carl Spaatz had sent to the Air Staff his plan for the completion of POINTBLANK, which had as its centerpiece a campaign against the enemy's oil refineries. Barney Giles approved of the plan, claiming it was within the boundaries of the last Combined Chiefs of Staff directive of 13 February 1944. But, cautioned Giles, the Air Staff was concerned lest General Eisenhower question aspects of the plan and if he did he would be backed up by the American Joint Chiefs. It proved not so much a questioning of the plan by Eisenhower as a Solomon-like decision on his part. The British Air Staff and various Royal Air Force brass wanted both the British and American strategic bombers diverted to strikes on the European, especially French, transportation system, with the objective of impairing Germany's ability to move reinforcements and supplies to contain and throw back the invasion.

On 25 March, with Eisenhower serving as judge, Spaatz presented his case that an oil campaign would weaken the enemy's ability to respond and would continue to cause attrition of the enemy's air forces. Air Chief Marshal Sir Arthur Tedder, Eisenhower's deputy for OVERLORD, argued the case for the transportation campaign. Present was Bomber Command's Arthur Harris, who was against the transportation plan because it would detract from his "city-busting," but who did not favor the "panacea" of an oil campaign either. There also, hoping to gain control of the strategic bombers to further the tactical aspect of OVERLORD, was the man who would command the tactical air forces, Air Chief Marshal Sir Trafford Leigh-Mallory. Eisenhower made the decision for the transportation plan, but Spaatz seemed both delighted and relieved that the bombers were denied to Leigh-Mallory.[62]

Despite Eisenhower's decision, Spaatz and the U.S. Strategic Air Forces in Europe were able to make several strikes against oil before OVERLORD. Because the oil campaign has been dissected in the official histories[63] and because the overwhelming majority of the effort against the oil targets came after the invasion, it will not be examined here. Instead, a late-blooming aspect of POINTBLANK more logically merits an examination.

United States Strategic Air Forces in Europe strategists developed several innovative tactics for coping with the carefully husbanded resources of the weakened Luftwaffe after the Big Week and Berlin battles and for dealing blows otherwise to the German economic and military infrastructure. One of these tactics was to place Y-Service operators aboard certain heavy bombers to accompany the strategic missions into the Reich. The operators would notify American fighters of the approach and often the direction of Luftwaffe interceptors. First tested operationally during Big Week, the first successful use of airborne Y-Service came in April. By May several Y-Service aircraft accompanied each bomb division.[64] The most devastating innovation, however, was the use of fighters in a role more or less independent of bomber escort and "freed" operations.

This role stemmed from several practices. Eighth Air Force fighters were used on occasion as dive bombers beginning in 1943. With roots going back at least to World War I, like the dive bombers, the fighter as marauding strafer had in Army Air Forces European operations begun to come into its own as a result of Doolittle's injunction to Kepner that his pilots "beat them up on the ground on the way home" from escort duties. As a consequence, American fighters began to strafe enemy aircraft in their lairs or spray them as they took off or landed. In addition, the .50-caliber tracers sought out trains, barges, motor transport, and barracks, among a widening selection of targets. By the time of the Berlin missions of early March, this type of activity, though still random and intermittent among the fighter groups, had become fairly common. Kepner described it thus: "On the way out from those deep penetration trips into Germany, we learned that frequently those boys would stumble against an airdrome with airplanes on the ground, press the trigger, go slashing along like a streak of greased lightning, and get out of there. This came to be a sort of unorganized air guerrilla warfare against the German's ground installations."[65] It was an apt phrase, for the sudden appearance of a fighter almost at treetop level with the muzzles in its wings winking like sparklers was as alarming as any guerrilla might have been who dashed from a forest to cast sticks of dynamite into the cab of a locomotive or out of a gully to cast a grenade under a parked aircraft. And it would become in time as risky.

It was the final product of the revolution in fighter-range technology begun the year before. For the civilians on the ground, the strategic bombing campaign was hell on earth. But the appearance of American fighters at treetop level deep inside Germany brought home to them just how close the Allies were coming to the German homeland, forcing them to endure the strafing that countless numbers of Europeans had undergone during the heyday of blitzkrieg warfare in the first three years of the war.

On 6 and 8 March pilots reported at debriefing that they had strafed and damaged or destroyed a number of parked aircraft, locomotives, a tanker just off the coast, several radar stations, barracks, antiaircraft gun positions, a flak tower guarding an airfield, and some barges. At least one German aircraft, perhaps a training aircraft, on making a landing approach was sent to a violent impact. Training flights in Germany became more and more hazardous, causing a further deterioration of the German training system. But a notation in the VIII Fighter Command narrative of operations for 8 March illustrated the danger to the strafer: "Lt. Henry fired his guns as he went down on the A/D [airdrome] and is believed to have hit a parked aircraft. His plane hit the ground and cartwheeling smashed into a hangar causing hangar to explode." It must have been an awesome sight to witness from ground level or above. On 9 March, giving some credence to the German claim that weather was too bad for its fighters to come up to intercept the bombers, American fighters did not go down to perform any low-level strafing.

The "unorganized air guerrilla warfare" continued for the remainder of March. On 29 March, when the weather was bad over the bombers' target of Brunswick, but unusually good elsewhere, most fighter formations went down to the deck in strafing forays after escort duties were over. The claims were, collectively, the largest to date and included seventeen locomotives destroyed and eighteen damaged, three whole trains destroyed and eight damaged, one oil dump destroyed, six factories, eight flak towers, eight barges, two radio towers, two signal towers, two hangers, one railroad station, one switching station, and one riverboat damaged.[66] This day's performance seems to have been the catalyst for a new phase of air guerrilla warfare.

On the eve of this new phase, General Kepner wrote to James H. "Dutch" Kindelberger, president of North American Aviation, the prime manufacturer of the P-51. His pilots, Kepner said, were still having a few problems with jamming guns, but he thanked Kindelberger for "the very fine work your Mustangs are doing. They are roaming around all of France and Germany like the proverbial Devil's Ghost." The Germans wondered what was transpiring, but seemed not to have been too alarmed even when on 30 March two Thunderbolt groups dive-bombed separate airfields in Holland. P-47 dive-bombing increased in the coming months because of its superior diving ability and the comparatively less vulnerability of its air-cooled engine to ground fire. Its pilots already knew it as the "Thunderbomber."

This, however, was not totally new and was not the wrinkle to air guerrilla warfare the Germans would come to dread. General Schmid made little reference to dive bombing or strafing in March, but that was quickly to change for the I Fighter Corps.[67]

Kepner later described the new phase. In the "unorganized" phase, he told interviewers while it was still fresh in mind, it "had come to a point where they were all doing it, and we decided we would organize this, specifying what they were going to do." The first "organized" mission came a few days later, preceded by some disagreement among planners. On 29 March Fred Anderson bucked back to Jimmy Doolittle a plan entitled "Destruction of German Fighters in Operational Units." "We're not yet ready for this," Anderson stated, for "in view of the trend of the GAF to move its operational bases further to the interior of Germany, it is believed that an attack of this nature will have the most fruitful results if carried out only after definitely establishing the ultimate location of German Air Force operational units."

By 5 April ULTRA sources had located the units and the first organized strafing mission went forward. "On the first mission . . . while 8AF bombers either stayed in England or struck V-weapon sites in France, 10 8FC groups struck 25 area targets, ranging from Strasbourg in the west to Berlin in the east." Weather hindered the mission and "only two groups, less than 100 P-51s out of 456 total aircraft assigned were able to carry out attacks. Nevertheless, results were staggering." The two groups, the 4th and 355th, for "the loss of nine aircraft, none as a result of air-to-air combat . . . claimed ten enemy aircraft destroyed in the air and 88 on the ground. The two groups also destroyed or damaged trucks, flak towers, hangers, gun emplacements, barracks, personnel, automobiles, boats, and several factories."[68]

General Arnold was ecstatic when the reports came in. On 7 April he wrote Spaatz through Eisenhower about the mission:

. . . outstanding. This successful counter air operation illustrates very efficient use of fighters and fighter bombers in the reduction of the German Air Force . . . Will continue to follow your fighter, fighter bomber, and dive bomber operations with interest . . . May I suggest consideration of an all out joint Tactical counter air force assault on the GAF using everything available except, possibly, the heavies?

Arnold suggested that such a combined operation would be valuable training for OVERLORD.[69]

Neither Eisenhower nor Spaatz accepted the advice, but on a more practical level, Barney Giles told Spaatz that the Air Staff was "keenly interested" in the results of this type of operation. Giles reported that British estimates for March "indicate . . . fighter strength of the G.A.F. has gone up 200. This is serious, unless we chop the Luftwaffe down to reasonable size in the next few weeks we are going to be on the spot." Perhaps this was preinvasion jitters, but true or not Giles urged "every possibility to bring the G.A.F. to action against our fighters or to destroy them on the ground. This will involve original and changing tactics and the problem is worthy of your best minds."[70]

One of the best minds had overseen a changing tactic. Doubtlessly with some exaggeration, as was the American tendency, Kepner later described it: "One day we got out here and shot down—in the air and on the ground, probably better than half of them on the ground—on the order of 150 aircraft. One group got about 50 on three fields down near Munich . . . another group went up to the west of Berlin and got 45 on two or three fields there." He was referring to a subsequent development, one that made it even more organized—the division of Germany into zones that Kepner assigned to one or more fighter groups. "They circled around the fields and counted the fires, of planes burning on the ground. Others were damaged; how many I don't know, but certainly it was enough to cripple the German Air Force . . . It just struck consternation into Germans."

I Fighter Corps commander Josef Schmid after the war evaluated the results of these strafing missions differently: "By this new

American practice of fighting the German Luftwaffe on the ground several hundred aircraft were destroyed and the same number of them was damaged. The striking power of the Luftwaffe, however, was only slightly impaired by these operations."

The Luftwaffe Quartermaster kept monthly records of the number of aircraft destroyed by strafing or bombing. These registers, including liaison and naval aircraft, listed the destruction or damage requiring replacement of 415 aircraft in April and 326 in May 1944, plus 185 and 168 damaged, respectively. Of the destroyed, 143 were single-engine fighters. Of the damaged, 71 were single-engine fighters. Schmid was in the best position to judge that his operations were "only slightly impaired," but this was attrition warfare. These numbers, added to losses from other causes, added up to air superiority.[71]

Generalmajor Walter Grabmann, while agreeing with Schmid that the attacks on the airfields did not cripple German air defenses, was, in historical perspective, quite somber about the effect of the strafing on the railroad transportation system.

In the 20–28 May period alone such attacks resulted in 500 locomotives damaged. The effects of these attacks, combined with attacks on traffic centers, were so serious that all German efforts to maintain the flow of traffic failed to prevent a backlog of 160 trains, loaded with vitally important military supplies and personnel.

The organized air guerrilla warfare had merged with Tedder and Eisenhower's transportation plan by late May. Kepner described how the merger came about. His pilots had always enjoyed

shooting up trains. When they hit a locomotive there is a big spurt up in the air—and that fascinates a fellow, you know. We weren't allowed to shoot anything up in France[72] then, but over Germany we got what we called a 'Choo-Choo mission.' I think we got 229 locomotives claimed destroyed and about the same number damaged. We know how that demoralized the transportation system in Germany. Immediately after that, approaching D-Day then, we got orders to go after the transportation for a short time in France.[73]

Strafing, the more it was employed, became an ever more danger-ous activity for a fighter pilot. Luther Richmond was one of its casualties. As his formation approached a German airfield on 15 April, several FW 190s attacked them. After maneuvering one en-emy aircraft into the ground, Richmond dove in pursuit of another, when "a Flak gun opened fire. The gun emplacement was squarely in my sights when I saw him so, rather than take evasive action, I held steady and squeezed off a rather long burst . . . I was hitting the gun emplacement when I took a hit in the wing root." He had to climb in order to bail out. Taken prisoner by the soldiers of the flak unit and incarcerated in a cell at the airfield, he was soon con-fronted with the eighteen-year-old gunner who had been the most instrumental of his crew in downing Richmond. An interpreter told Richmond that the gunner "says you were brave and you killed some of his comrades but he was brave too and he stayed with his gun and got you." The gunner was fortunate not to have joined his comrades. Richmond was fortunate to have survived and passed directly into regular military hands.

It was warfare fought up to 500 miles from friendly territory, at treetop level. The fighter pilots had no crews with whom to share the danger. Many soldiers have spoken of the sense of loneliness on the battlefield. Nowhere in the war was this more true than in these long-range strafing attacks on Germany. And these pilots paid a price for their audacity. "While prior to February 1944 no fighters were lost over enemy territory due to collisions with ground obstacles, over the next three months three percent, five percent, and two percent of all fighter losses were due to such causes." This was only the smallest part of it. "8FC told pilots that when strafing 20 feet above the ground was 'too high'. The loss of pilots to light anti-aircraft fire also increased dramatically as more pilots went to the deck: 13 percent of all losses to flak in February, 30 percent in March, 37 percent in April, and 44 percent in May."[74]

General Galland's primary concern was not air guerrilla warfare of either variety. In a Luftwaffe meeting of 21 April on supplies and procurement, he told those assembled with a deep note of pessimism, "The problem with which the Americans have brought our fighter forces face to face—I am referring intentionally only to the daylight fighter problem—is purely and simply the problem of air superiority . . . [and] the situation is very nearly one of absolute air supremacy."

In comparison to German training, Galland went on, American fliers were "exceptionally well trained and the technical performances of enemy aircraft so remarkable that we have to do something." He cited a figure of 1,000 Luftwaffe flight personnel losses in the past four months, including 400 pilots along with 200 aircraft in the last ten American raids. He called for increased production and vastly improved technology, but in the end he returned to the jet and rocket plane solution, especially the former, which could defeat the American bombers and "break enemy morale."[75]

Allowing for some exaggeration on Galland's part to stress his point, the undoubted rise in wastage, despite the measured response to daylight raids, resulted from a change in tactics by the Luftwaffe. Unable to attack American bombers through the growing number of VIII Fighter Command fighter escorts, Schmid and Galland organized the interceptors for mass attacks. By 21 April fifty to one hundred fighters had become the standard-sized assault formation. These formations would increase in size through the remainder of the spring, reaching a peak on 28 May when three hundred Luftwaffe fighters attacked two American combat wings. It was a tactic born of desperation. The 28 May swarming was in great part due to the bombers' major targets—synthetic oil plants. Even though the two wings suffered disproportionately high losses—twenty out of thirty-two admitted losses by the Americans and fifty-six claimed by the Germans from both fighter action and the growing accuracy of flak—the other bombers were more or less left free to inflict, as I Fighter Corps admitted, severe damage to the oil plants and other targets.

I Fighter Corps also admitted heavy German losses, a total of seventy-eight planes lost or heavily damaged and eighteen pilots killed or missing. Kepner described these mass attacks: the enemy "decided . . . that he would have to throw a big moving mass through the bombers . . . what we have chosen to call a 'flying wedge'." The American fighters's answer was to "put a barrage on them and let them fly through the barrage . . . He [the German] had some success in shooting down bombers for a few days [This essentially was a return to the close escort strategy] . . . until we finally arrived at the conclusion that we should never let him get started on that flying wedge." Schmid later described the result: "The American fighter attacks were . . . directed against the German single- and twin-engine fighter units while the latter were assembling or on their approach flight." The consequences of the rebirth of the "freeing" strategy were, according to Kepner's opposite number, "grave."[76]

The German crews and some of their leaders had been anticipating a miracle. On 28 May a teletyped message from Reichsmarschall Göring to Schmid, Galland, and Koller among other Luftwaffe brass, informed them that the Führer had directed that, for the time being, the Me 262 was to be used only as a high-speed bomber. Therefore it was removed from the jurisdiction of General Galland in his capacity as General of Fighters. The anticipated miracle would not have been ready for operational use as a defense fighter in May even had Hitler allowed it to be used as such. It was June before a suitable engine was available.[77] But Hitler's decree highlighted once again his irrational interference in military technology as well as strategy and tactics. Just as the failure of Luftwaffe training helped to bring about the loss of air superiority, the lost opportunity for technological recovery acted to insure that Germany would never reclaim air superiority. And the effect of Hitler's May decree could not have helped but accentuate the moat mentality of the now-besieged Luftwaffe.

In one respect the most significant American bomber or air guerrilla mission of the period January-May 1944 took place on 21 May. It was an organized air guerrilla mission codenamed CHATTANOOGA, likely based on the popular Glenn Miller tune, "Chattanooga Choo Choo," for its principal objective. Many a strafed locomotive sent a column of steam soaring into the sky that day. In addition, American fighter pilots claimed the most enemy aircraft destroyed on the ground to date, perhaps with some exaggeration. All this, however, was not the main importance of this mission. The key was "the intelligence brought back for OVERLORD planners. Every German aircraft seen on the ground was located east of Hamburg, some 500 miles from Normandy beaches—too far to interfere with Normandy landings on 6 June 1944."[78]

EPILOGUE

Both the Germans and the Allies prepared elaborate air plans for the coming invasion of France by the latter. Taking form in April 1944, the Allied plan had many facets, but the critical one was to blanket the beachhead area and its sea and land approaches with a quilt of fighters. The intention was to deny to the Luftwaffe this air space in its expected effort to strike at the invasion fleet and to make any landing untenable. So confident was General Eisenhower that his aerial component would quickly establish this air supremacy, this dominance beyond mere air superiority, he told invasion troops on 6 June, "If you see fighting aircraft over you, they will be ours."[1]

Closely related to this intended dominance were four other elements of the Allied plan: harassment of enemy ground forces in and adjacent to the landing area; securing of the flanks of that area by airborne troops; interdiction of the general landing area; and attacks on airfields within a 130-mile zone beyond that area. The plan also called for exploitation of the air superiority so recently won over the Reich by a continuation of missions against aircraft production and "mass attacks against sensitive . . . installations in Germany." Attrition was still the name of the game: "Any attacks which will inveigle the German Air Force into the air in defense will result in attrition to the enemy air force in being."[2]

The German plan was predicated on the rapid deployment westward to bases in France of day single-engine fighter units, the majority of which had been steadily pulled back into Germany between the fall of 1943 and May 1944. Once Allied forces were ashore, the air defense of the Reich would be left to only a relative handful of twin-engine destroyer aircraft and night single-engine fighter units. The high command believed that strategic missions against vital targets inside Germany would be suspended indefinitely or sharply curtailed when the invasion was launched. These reinforcements to France were to take over the main task of air support, fighter-bomber, and counterair operations. They would number about 600 aircraft. Air Fleet 3, within whose jurisdiction lay the most feasible cross-Channel landing sites, had only about 80 serviceable fighters among its 300-odd aircraft on the eve of the invasion. Arrayed across the Channel were some 7,000 aircraft, the Eighth Air Force alone possessing some 1,800 operational bombers and over 900 fighters.[3]

The German high command felt that the invasion must be hurled back in not over 10 days time or it would be counted a success. The code phrase to trigger the westward movement of the single-engine day fighters was "Threatening Danger West." Göring's order of the day for the invasion when it came was that it must be beaten back even if the Luftwaffe perished in the attempt.[4] The Luftwaffe was already breathing shallowly from the effects of Big Week, Berlin, and the strategic fighter campaign. The subsequent performance of the Luftwaffe on D-day must be measured against this condition.

When an opportune and required combination of conditions affecting tide, moonlight, and daylight was forecast for the night and early day of 5/6 June 1944, Eisenhower made one of history's most momentous command decisions—implement OVERLORD. Allied paratroops dropped in the moonlight, as the fleet bearing the beachhead forces came out of its harbors on the English side of the Channel. In the bare break of daylight, German defenders in pillboxes were stunned to see the great fleet looming out of the offshore mist. Combat engineers and naval specialists began to gap the beach obstacles and landing craft began to disgorge the assault troops into the surf. Up and down a 50-mile stretch of Normandy beaches and extending up one side of the Cotentin Peninsula the Allies returned to France. Naval guns pounded the pillboxes, gun positions, and troop positions while German artillery and small arms fire swept the beaches. It took prodigious effort and much heroism to scale the cliffs and begin to silence the fire from the defensive positions. Bodies littered the beach and bobbed in the surf. Smoke was dense and the din awesome. Everywhere the issue was in doubt—especially at American OMAHA beach—except in the sky.

As the drama was played out on the surface, the sky was full of airplanes. Practically all contained the three white stripes identifying them as Allied invasion aircraft. It could be described as almost Douhetian in that classical sense, except for the irony of the key role played by fighters. In the night a few German bombers had aimed their loads at the approaching invasion fleet with, as Galland would label them, "insignificant results." Only two of Air Fleet 3's fighters managed to penetrate the beachhead. Eisenhower's forecast was almost perfect.[5]

Then gradually, if unevenly, the assault troops, with some armor in support, began to move like a tide themselves, away from the beaches, up the cliffs, down certain roads, across certain fields, into certain battered villages, with the populace cheering them on. There had come against them no countertide of maneuvering greygreen or black-uniformed reinforcements. Feldmarschall Erwin Rommel's gamble to contain the invasion on the beaches was failing. A lodgement had been secured, well recognized by 7 June.

General Kepner, a few weeks later, described this near-command of the air:

On D-Day . . . we [British and American fighters] formed a screen across the English Channel to the east of the surface vessel traffic that went clear down around 50 miles south of the beachhead, across the [Cotentin Peninsula], and back across the Channel to the English coast—a half circle, and we maintained that thing from five minutes before first light on D-Day until 11 o'clock that day, solid . . .

Kepner incorrectly maintained that no German aircraft broke through to the beaches. Nevertheless, the "sanctuary" thus created allowed British and American heavy, medium, light, and fighter-bombers to perform their assignments in the beachhead area or beyond. It permitted airborne reinforcements to be brought in by glider. "Then," stated Kepner,

throughout the day after that we moved slightly south of the beach-head, to Paris and north of there, and looked for everything we could find. During D-Day we were chiefly interested in aircraft; then the next few days following . . . we were interested in every military vehicle, every staff car, every train that was carrying . . . oil and ammunitions.

Kepner seemed to relish the "pictures of ammunition trains blow-ing sky high, which show planes flying right through the explo-sions."[6]

General Galland in his memoir agreed with Kepner that from "the very first moment of the invasion the Allies had absolute air supremacy. Therefore the enemy, our own troops, and the popula-tion asked the obvious question, 'Where is the Luftwaffe?'" Increas-ingly German troops asked it in a bitter way.

Galland told his captors the answer at the end of the war and repeated it in his memoirs. That answer simply detailed the climax to one of the most egregiously bad strategies the Germans pursued in the war—the way it applied its air power. The German high command delayed the transfer of the fighter force to France be-cause for a time it believed the Normandy landing was a feint. Finally on 7 June the Luftwaffe took it upon its own authority to issue the triggering "Threatening Danger West." It was, however, not until the eighth that the transfer was fully underway. Almost immediately the carefully planned transfer process went haywire. Allied bombing had disabled many of the projected airfields and Air Fleet 3 had to scramble to prepare alternate landing fields. Most of these were close to Paris and poorly camouflaged, hence distance from the front and vulnerability were their chief features. Used to the guiding hand of a fighter controller in Germany, a number of pilots landed at the wrong bases. Others were not that fortunate, falling victim to roving Allied fighters. The advanced party of the air echelon arrived at its field by air, but the ground echelon had to travel by train over a ravaged network and were days, even weeks arriving. Spare parts, fuel, and other supplies most often had to make the same hazardous journey. Once the transferred units were able to fly missions, they were inept at the kind of low-level operations required over the widening bridge-head and were chewed up by the voracious Allied fighters. Within a week to 10 days after D-day ULTRA intercepts revealed that of the sixteen or so single-engine groups transferred to the west, most had returned to Germany in a depleted condition.[7]

The fiasco marked, essentially, a Luftwaffe switch to a defensive stance, whereby protection of supply routes and Wehrmacht units became the paramount and often futile assignment. There were not enough planes for operational purposes and the Allies maintained air superiority. A typical situation was that of 21 June, when the 21st Panzer Division complained to the headquarters of II Fighter Corps that it had lost 50 percent of its supplies while moving up. Where, it wanted to know, was the Luftwaffe? During the Allied breakout from the bridgehead in July, the victories at Caen, St. Lô, and Avranches, the wreckage of German tanks and other vehicles and artillery, along with corpses, was strewn along French roads like mounds of dumped garbage—evidence of Allied air superiority.

Galland and his staff made an effort to shore up fighter resistance by centralizing supply and reinforcement and adapting tactics. Allied fighters did not fly unscathed. Still, it was a losing proposition. In August Hitler ordered the fighter reserves in the Reich, built up to a respectable 800 in number, to be sent to France. It was a repeat of the earlier transfer except the results were even more negative in what Galland described in his memoir as an effort to "throw fighter wings into gaps like infantry regiments . . . [with] 80 per cent inexperienced pilots . . . they were doomed to be destroyed in the air or on the ground without achieving any operational effect." Galland employed some exaggeration for the losses, but with Paris already in Allied hands it was a foolish expenditure of resources that were badly needed in the air defense of the Reich itself.[8]

If the deteriorating situation in France from June into August were not bad enough, the air defense of the Reich and the oil resources in the Balkans were confronted from D-day on by an aerial pincers movement from the strategic bombers and their escort of the Eighth and Fifteenth Air Forces. While flying less than the previous quantity of missions at first because of OVERLORD commitments, the bombers struck more and more at the enemy's jugular, its fuel sources. Soon after D-day the oil campaign was underway. Yet, the full might of strategic air power was not leveled at fuel. Diversions (such as carpet bombing at St. Lô) and other strategic targets (aircraft and armored vehicle production, among others, as well as eventually another transportation campaign) detracted. And perhaps the fear, lingering from the fall crisis of 1943, that full concentration on any target system might bring unacceptable losses, encouraged planners to order strikes on many targets. Then, too, there was the fear of a resurgence of the German fighter arm, in part brought about by the revamping of that arm by Galland and by the appearance in the summer of 1944 as combat fighters of the rocket-powered Me 163 and the jet-powered Me 262. They were not really miracles, for they were literally too little and too late, but caused a lingering anxiety in, among others, the American commanders, Arnold, Spaatz, and Doolittle.[9]

By September 1944, Allied armies were at the gates of the Reich. The supreme Allied commander, General Eisenhower, cabled General Arnold on 3 September: "The basic conception underlying this campaign was that possession of an overpowering air force made feasible an invasion that would otherwise be completely impossible." Ike underlined the next sentence: *The air has done everything we asked.*" He then summarized air's achievements. It "has practically destroyed the German Air Force . . . it disrupted communications . . . it neutralized beach defenses . . . it has been vitally helpful in accomplishing certain breakthroughs by ground forces." And, "while all this was being done, the strategic forces have been committed to the greatest extent possible on strategic targets and have succeeded in preventing substantial rehabilitation of German industry and oil production."[10]

From the perspective of history certain other conclusions can be drawn from the American effort over Europe. By the time OVERLORD was sprung, strategic bombing had in and of itself accomplished nothing vital. The results of the first transportation campaign are yet controversial. The first tentative strikes of the oil campaign showed the potential of this target system, but then that potential had already been shown by earlier missions against Ploesti and other refineries. The missions against aircraft and related production had not yet produced the results claimed at the time. Area bombing had not destroyed morale, much less the infrastructure of the German state. In fact, area bombing seemed to have stiffened the German resolve to keep going.

The major contribution of strategic bombing by June 1944 was its role in bringing about the weakening of the Luftwaffe's fighter arm, particularly the day fighters, through attrition. Not many of the crews who flew in the B-17s and B-24s during ARGUMENT and over Berlin realized that their principal role was that of serving as bait to lure the enemy fighters up so that their "Little Friends" could (to use contemporary slang) "waste" the enemy. The American fighter pilots, in the final analysis, really did the primary job of wasting. No other specialists in the American armed forces were more deadly at a crucial time in the war, in spite of their tendency to exaggerate their claims. Of course, they had the advantage of overwhelming numbers. Their German opponents were no less brave, but were the victims of bad and even insane leadership. One of the most neglected subjects by historians of the air war over Europe has been training—but then the Luftwaffe neglected it also. The record clearly shows its bearing upon one side winning air superiority and the other yielding it in 1944.

The American fighter planes that played such a large part in the achievement of air superiority in 1944 have each had their postwar partisans among historians. In absolute terms the P-47 had the greatest impact during the battles of Big Week and Berlin, and the Thunderbolt proved with little doubt the finest Army Air Forces fighter-bomber over the long haul. In relative terms, however, although there were many more P-47s than P-51s, especially during Big Week, the P-51 was superior—even in the face of teething problems during much of this period while the P-47 had earlier gotten over its own. During Big Week and the Berlin battles of 3, 4, 6, 8, 9, and 22 March 1944, VIII Fighter Command launched 6,384 P-47 sorties in support of heavy bombers and 1,299 P-51 sorties. The Thunderbolts claimed 47 percent more enemy aircraft than the Mustangs for these battles, but it took P-47s 28 sorties to register a claim whereas P-51s averaged a claim every 8 sorties.[11]

In terms of unit battle honors for the period December 1943 through the strategic fighter campaign, Distinguished Unit Citations (DUCs) were awarded to seven American fighter groups based in England and controlled by U.S. Strategic Air Forces in Europe. Of the seven, five were bestowed upon groups flying P-51s at the time of the action cited (4th, 352d, 354th, 355th, and 357th). These actions ranged from general operations covering the period under consideration (354th) to specific missions such as the defense of bombers over Berlin in 6 March 1944 (357th) and the bombing and strafing of airfields on 5 April 1944 (355th). The only P-47 group to receive a DUC, the 56th, gained it for the claimed destruction of 98 enemy airplanes in the air and on the ground between 20 February and 9 March, compared to the 4th Group's (P-51) DUC for claims of 189 enemy aircraft in the air and on the ground between 5 March and 24 April. The 20th Group, flying P-38s, the least significant of the three fighter planes, also won a DUC for actions in connection with the strategic fighter campaign.[12]

It depended upon individual or unit experience with the three American fighter types as to which a Luftwaffe adversary ultimately thought superior or inferior to each other and to Luftwaffe fighters. After the war, however, two former senior Luftwaffe commanders gave an assessment of the three types. Besides chronic engine problems, the P-38 had the twin booms easily recognizable from a long distance, making it vulnerable to surprise attack. The "flying properties" of the P-47 were so "impaired" by full drop tanks that it had to release these when engaged by enemy fighters, a situation bringing into question its reliability as a long-range escort fighter. In spite of its early mechanical difficulties, "introduction . . . of the . . . Mustang from the beginning of 1944 on made it possible to provide effective escort protection over the target to be bombed."

General Kepner, in perhaps the best position to make a comparison of the Thunderbolts, Lightnings, and Mustangs in the 1944 battles for air superiority, had a somewhat shifting analysis before, during, and after these battles. In December 1943 he said in view of "pending developments in Germany" the P-51 was "distinctly the best fighter we can get over here." When air superiority had begun to pass to his side he declared, "If it can be said that the P-38 struck the Luftwaffe in its vitals and the P-51s are giving it the coup de grace, it was the Thunderbolt that broke its back." A short time after the battles were over, he pointed to the Thunderbolts as being the type that when attacked by enemy fighters "drop their tanks . . . [because] the tank cuts down on speed" making the plane "less maneuverable." He took note of the fact that the P-38's distinctive shape made it vulnerable. He also noted that the P-51 was such a smoothly operating plane that pilots with less combat experience than required of pilots flying Thunderbolts could "outfight either the ME-109 or the FW-190." Kepner summed up the teamwork of the three American fighters in his unique way: "We use the

Thunderbolt to crack the nut with; use the Mustang to go way out
again to roll the nut in—either crack it themselves or roll it in to
the Thunderbolt. We used the P-38 to see that he [the enemy] didn't
slip out when we were cracking him with" the P-47 and the P-51.[13]
Kepner was saying essentially that, as in the case with the Hurricane and the Spitfire in the Battle of Britain, all three fighters
contributed to the winning of air superiority in 1944.

The air battles of Big Week, Berlin, and the strategic fighter
campaign rank with Midway, the Battle of Britain, Stalingrad, the
Battle of the Atlantic, and El Alemain as of overriding importance
in the reversal of fortunes in World War II. Yet, Big Week, Berlin,
and the strategic fighter campaign collectively have not been given
their due by scholars and are hardly known as such by the public.
The occasion of OVERLORD has justly been celebrated and the
tombstones in the cemeteries overlooking the beaches have been
the focus of sober and appropriate international memorial services
attended by heads of state. No similar ceremonies have marked the
anniversaries of Big Week, Berlin, and the strategic fighter campaign, which made the invasion possible and whose veterans bore
the conflict no less bravely and whose dead should be no less hon-
ored. The problem, according to Dr. David MacIsaac, noted historian of the air war, is that there are no beaches, no battlefields
whose terrain features can still be pointed out or on whose waves
wreathes can be thrown. These battles took place across hundreds
of miles of ephemeral sky—their casualties, both men and machine, were scattered over half of Europe. Randall Jarrell expressed the problem in verse.[14]

> We died on the wrong page of the almanac,
> Scattered on mountains fifty miles away;
> Diving on haystacks, fighting with a friend
> We blazed up on the lines we never saw.
> We died like ants or pets or foreigners.

The battles for air superiority, and the men and women who fought
them, have earned their place in the history of World War II.

APPENDIX

COMPARISON OF AMERICAN BATTLE CLAIMS WITH GERMAN LOSSES

| Date | Eighth Air Force Claims | Luftwaffe Losses | | |
		Source 1	Source 2	Source 3
2 Oct 1943	20	9	10	12
4 Oct 1943	56	12	10	16
8 Oct 1943	179	23	28	20
9 Oct 1943	122	10	10	10
10 Oct 1943	202	12	26	25
14 Oct 1943	199	35	27	39
5 Nov 1943	45	17	16	18
13 Nov 1943	60	11	19	14
26 Nov 1943	60	26	22	37
29 Nov 1943	30	29	33	27
20 Dec 1943	40	14	10	27
22 Dec 1943	37	23	12	24
4 Jan 1944	12	12	12	—
5 Jan 1944	128	31	11	—
11 Jan 1944	259	48	21	45
30 Jan 1944	96	59	30	47
10 Feb 1944	98	49	30	46
11 Feb 1944	35	18	12	24

continued

Date	Eighth Air Force Claims	Luftwaffe Losses		
		Source 1	Source 2	Source 3
20 Feb 1944	126	54	28	58
21 Feb 1944	52	29	11	32
22 Feb 1944	93	42	11	52
24 Feb 1944	121	60	26	51
25 Feb 1944	49	44	5	41
3 Mar 1944	11	15	4	14
4 Mar 1944	15	20	4	18
6 Mar 1944	179	63	18	62
8 Mar 1944	150	47	21	55
9 Mar 1944	1	0	0	1
18 Mar 1944	84	25	12	36
23 Mar 1944	55	27	11	27
29 Mar 1944	65	33	12	34
8 Apr 1944	195	65	36	73
9 Apr 1944	84	28	13	21
11 Apr 1944	189	36	19	52
15 Apr 1944	58	12	11	23
19 Apr 1944	17	—	10	29
22 Apr 1944	60	—	17	19
24 Apr 1944	144	—	32	56
29 Apr 1944	95	—	11	30
8 May 1944	131	—	43	44
12 May 1944	66	—	34	70
13 May 1944	58	—	16	29
19 May 1944	77	—	42	60
24 May 1944	33	—	40	41
27 May 1944	44	—	16	31
28 May 1944	64	—	50	37
29 May 1944	117	—	152	51
30 May 1944	65	—	95	53
TOTAL	4,176	1,038	1,139	1,631

Sources: Column Two—Eighth Air Force Claims: VIII Bomber Command Narrative of Operations, 1943–1944, File 519.332, HRC; VIII Fighter Command Narrative of Operations, 1943–1944, File 168.6005-55, HRC; and Freeman, *Mighty Eighth War Diary*.

Column Three—Luftwaffe Losses Source 1: "Auswertung der Einsatzbereitsch der fliegenden Verb. vom 1 August 1943 bis November 1944," 28 June 1949, File K110.8-22, HRC. This source includes all fighters shot down in the West and over the Reich.

Column Four—Luftwaffe Losses Source 2: Generalleutnant Josef Schmid, "Day and Night Aerial Warfare over the Reich, 1943–1944," 1954, File K113.107-158–160, HRC. This source includes all fighters shot down in the area of I Fighter Corps (the Reich).

Column Five—Luftwaffe Losses Source 3: British translations of captured German documents: "German Air Force Losses in the West, 1 September 1943–31 December 1943," 1945, File K512.621 VII/148, HRC; " German Air Force Losses in the Area of Luftflotte Reich, 1 September 1943–31 December 1943," 1945, File K512.621 VII/149, HRC; "German Air Force Losses in the West, January-April 1944," 1945, File K512.621 VII/135, HRC; "German Air Force Losses in the Area of Luftlotte Reich, January-April 1944," 1945, File K512.621 VII/138, HRC; "German Air Force Losses in the West, May 1944," 1945, File K512.621 VII/133, HRC; and "German Air Force Losses in the Area of Luftlotte Reich, May 1944," 1945, File K512.621 VII/134, HRC. This source includes all fighters shot down in the West and over the Reich.

NOTES

Major sources and references cited frequently are listed with full publication data in the bibliography.

Introduction

1. P. D. L. Gover, "Air Supremacy—The Enduring Principle," in *War in the Third Dimension: Essays in Contemporary Air Power*, ed. R. A. Mason (London: Brassey's, 1986), p. 60; and Heflin, s.vv. "air superiority" and "command of the air."

2. United States Strategic Bombing Survey (hereafter USSBS), Report No. 2a, Chart No. 1; and Report No. 66, *The Strategic Air Operation of Very Heavy Bombardment in the War against Japan, Final Report* (Washington, D.C.: GPO, 1946), p. 5.

3. Studs Terkel, *The Good War* (New York: Pantheon, 1984), p. 209.

4. Overy, *Air War*, p. 158.

Chapter 1. The Challenge

1. Kennett, pp. 5–8.

2. Sterling Seagrave, et al., *Soldiers of Fortune* (Alexandria, Va.: Time-Life Books, 1981), pp. 25–26, claimed that the air-to-air exchange was in deadly earnest and a bullet from Rader's pistol hit the right wing of

Lamb's plane. Lamb, in a memoir, *The Incurable Filibuster* (New York: Farrar and Rinehart, 1934), pp. 90–95, maintained it was faked to appease one another's employers.

3. Kennett, pp. 36–37, has a description of air defenses in World War I. They included such things as smoke generators and dummy towns.

4. Ibid., pp. 17, 38.

5. Hallion, pp. 9–14, 44–46.

6. Ibid., pp. 55–56, 88–89, 142, 154–159, and 160–161; and Spick, pp. 12–35.

7. Hallion, p. 11.

8. Thompson, pp. 112–126; Hallion, p. 80; Callender, pp. 84, 87, and 97; and Cuneo, 2:376–377.

9. Douglas Robinson, *The Zeppelin in Combat* (London: Foulis, 1962), pp. 57–59, 96–97; C. G. Grey, *Bombers* (London: Faber and Faber, 1941), p. 31; Higham, p. 50; Stokesbury, pp. 87–89; Fredette, pp. 20–21; and Kennett, p. 50.

10. For a definition of air superiority, see Heflin, s.v. "air superiority."

11. W. A. Jacobs, "Operation OVERLORD," manuscript submitted to the Office of Air Force History for an anthology on air superiority, pp. 1–2.

12. B. H. Lidell Hart, *The Real War* (Boston: Little, Brown, 1964), p. 318.

13. The operational experience of the U.S. Army Air Service in World War I is covered in Hudson, and that of the U.S. Navy in Theodore Roscoe, *On the Seas and in the Skies* (New York: Hawthorne Books, 1970).

14. Mitchell to Chief of Staff, U.S. Expeditionary Forces, May 1917, in Maurer, ed., *U.S. Air Service in World War I*, 2:108, 110.

15. Churchill notes, 21 June 1917, in Maurer, ed., *U.S. Air Service in World War I*, 2:117; and "The Tactical Employment of Pursuit Aviation," prepared under Mitchell's direction, June 1918, in ibid., 2:213.

16. Few of the American veterans interviewed by the authors could remember any acquaintance with the ideas of the great prophets of air power. In an interview with Newton in 1988, Col. Starr Smith, USAF (ret.), pointed out that many younger crew members in World War II had only the few months of college training provided by the Army Air Forces and thus were even less likely to have heard of Giulio Douhet, Billy Mitchell, or Hugh Trenchard.

17. General Leon W. Johnson, an Eighth Air Force group and wing commander during World War II, said in a postwar interview that "we all had heard of Douhet, and we talked about Douhet." General Curtis E. LeMay, an Eighth Air Force group, wing, and air division commander during World War II, similarly stated, "I never saw a copy of Douhet's book. I had heard about him and that he generally favored the use of air power and

what it could do. We agreed with that. Of course, we had Billy Mitchell."
See Kohn and Harahan, *Strategic Air Warfare*, p. 28. Colonel Robert L.
Salzarulo, USAF (ret.), an Eighth Air Force B-24 pilot in 1944, recalled in
an interview with Newton in 1988 some acquaintance with the career of
Billy Mitchell when he was a civilian undergraduate at the University of
Indiana before he entered the army.

18. Atkinson; and Richard H. Kohn and Joseph P. Harahan, "Editors'
Introduction," in Douhet, pp. vii–ix. Douhet has as yet no biography.

19. Douhet, pp. 20–32, 55.

20. Ibid., p. 23.

21. Ibid., pp. 41–46.

22. Ibid., pp. 117–120, 298–348.

23. Mitchell's life and career are best told in Hurley. Edward Warner in
"Douhet, Mitchell, Seversky: Theories of Air Warfare," in *Makers of Modern
Strategy*, ed. Edward Meade Earle (Princeton: Princeton University Press,
1942), pp. 487–501, compares and contrasts the careers and techniques of
Mitchell and Douhet.

24. William Mitchell, "Notes on the Multi-Motored Bombardment
Group Day and Night," 1923, pp. 1–2, 13, 102–107, File 248.222-57, U.S.
Air Force Historical Research Center (hereafter HRC).

25. Sherry, pp. 29–30; and Hurley, pp. 111–135. Hurley felt that the
interaction of Trenchard and Douhet with Mitchell had definite influence
on the latter. See pp. 25–26, 31–32, 75–78, 114–115, 126–127.

26. Boyle, p. 299. Trenchard's life and career are best told in Boyle's
biography. His experiences with the Independent Force in 1918 are also
probed by Malcolm Smith in *British Air Strategy between the Wars* (Oxford,
England: Clarendon Press, 1984), pp. 55–57 and 67–69, especially for their
effect on air power policy after the war.

27. Boyle, pp. 576ff.

28. Smith, *British Air Strategy*, pp. 67–68; Harry H. Ransom, "Lord Trenchard, Architect of Air Power," *Air University Quarterly Review* 6 (Summer
1956): 66; and Boyle, pp. 576–577.

29. John Terraine, *A Time for Courage: The Royal Air Force in the European
War, 1939–1945* (New York: Macmillan, 1985), pp. 20–21; and Boyle, pp.
710–711.

30. Sherry, pp. 69–75, has a compelling argument that the American
public became increasingly if subconsciously less opposed to the possibility of using the bomber even against cities and their populations, as the
interwar period wore on.

31. Futrell, 1:39–52; and Greer, pp. 14–39.

32. Greer, pp. 20–25, 30, 48.

33. Futrell, 1:58; and Air Corps Tactical School, "The Air Force," 30 April 1930, File 248.101-1, pp. 44–45, HRC. This text examined the operations of Trenchard's Independent Force in 1918 to show, among other things, Trenchard's stressing the morale effect of bombing over the material (pp. 45, 88).

34. Finney, p. 31.

35. Hansell, *Air Plan*, pp. 4, 12–23; and idem, "Harold L. George: Apostle of Air Power," in Frisbee.

36. Finney, p. 32. Greer believed that "one factor" in the transition to day, precision bombing was "the general opposition to mass civilian bombing." See Greer, p. 57. Hansell, who was on the scene, agrees. See Hansell, *Strategic Air War*, pp. 13–14.

37. Wilson.

38. Hansell, *Strategic Air War*, pp. 12–14; idem, *Air Plan*, p. 18; and idem, "Harold L. George," pp. 77–78. While there seems little doubt that Wilson began the investigation leading to the adoption of the theory at the Tactical School, the French used a strategic bombing strategy in World War I incorporating the same idea if on a lesser scale. And in addition Sherman, p. 217, wrote, "The long range of the bomber should be utilized to the full, and every sensitive point and nerve center of the system put under full pressure, to paralyze the whole." See Kennett, pp. 28ff.

39. Hansell, *Air Plan*, pp. 12–20; and Finney, p. 33.

40. Byrd, pp. 51–52; Hansell, *Air Plan*, p. 22; and Chennault, p. 27.

41. Thomas H. Greer, "Other Training Programs," in Craven and Cate, 6:684; and "Bombing Development—Army Air Corps," 1937–1939, File 168.7012-23, HRC.

42. "The Air Force," 1934–1935, File 248.101-1, pp. 1–2, HRC; Greer, p. 115; Finney, pp. 33–34; Air Corps Tactical School, "Bombardment Aviation," 1937–1938, File 248.101-9, pp. 12–13, HRC; Capt. Ralph Snavely, "Bombardment with Pursuit Opposition," 1 March 1939, File 248.2208A-21, HRC; and Capt. Laurence Kuter, "The Power and the Effect of the Demolition Bomb," 1939, File 248.2208A-3, HRC.

43. Major R. P. Williams, "Orientation, Organization and Training of Bombardment Aviation," 15 May 1940, File 248.2209A-1, HRC; and Douhet, pp. 117–121.

44. "A Study of Proposed Air Corps Doctrine by the Air Corps Tactical School, Based on Information Furnished by the War Plans Division, General Staff, in Memorandum Dated December 21, 1934," File 248.211-65, Sec. I and II, HRC; and revised Regulation 440-15, War Department, "Employment of the Air Forces of the Army," 15 October 1935, File 248.211-65, HRC.

45. Bilstein, pp. 83, 88.

46. Ibid., pp. 83–88.

47. Maurer, *Aviation in the United States Army*, p. 289. Futrell, p. 79, suggested that MacArthur's "permissive attitude" as chief of staff caused the War Department to condone the experimentation with long-range bombers.

48. Maurer, *Aviation in the United States Army*, p. 354; and Dubuque and Gleckner, pp. 74–75.

49. Maurer, *Aviation in the United States Army*, p. 355; and Arnold, p. 149.

50. Dubuque and Gleckner, pp. 75–76; and Maurer, *Aviation in the United States Army*, p. 355.

51. Maurer, *Aviation in the United States Army*, pp. 388–391.

52. Ibid., pp. 212, 364–366.

53. Ibid., pp. 365, 375.

54. Alfred A. Goldberg, "Equipment and Services," in Craven and Cate, 6:179, 241; Arnold to Andrews, 14 November 1939, File 167.5-54, HRC; and Arnold to Delos Emmons, 14 November 1939, File 167.5-54, HRC.

55. First endorsement to memorandum of 14 November 1939, signed by C. S. Russell, 11 January 1940, File 167.5-54, HRC.

56. Goldberg, "Equipment and Services," p. 212.

57. Sherry, pp. 76–79.

58. See esp. Futrell, 1:77ff.

59. Hansell, *Strategic Air War*, pp. 25ff.

60. *Luftwaffen Dienstvorschrift* ("The Conduct of Aerial Warfare"), 1935 and 1940, translated in "Air Staff Post Hostilities Intelligence Requirements on the German Air Force," 1935–1945, File 519.601B-4, Sec. IVA 3, HRC; and Galland, "Defeat of the Luftwaffe," p. 23. File 519.601B, under various ttles, is a comprehensive and lengthy study of the Luftwaffe undertaken on the orders of the Army Air Forces Air Staff to determine if any Luftwaffe procedures, tactics, doctrine, or policies could be useful to the postwar U.S. Army Air Forces. It was based on captured German documents and German prisoner-of-war interrogation reports, many of which are included in the appendices of this enormous file.

61. Because close air support was its primary function, the Luftwaffe was always an auxiliary force. See interrogation of Generalmajor H. von Rhoden, in "Air Staff Post Hostilities Intelligence Requirements," Sec. IIIA 1 and 2. In his interrogation, von Rhoden quoted General von Richthofen's opinion of the relationship between the Luftwaffe and the German army: "The Air Force has become the Army's whore." Ironically, this controversy paralleled a similar dispute in the United States at the Air Corps Tactical School between bomber and pursuit (fighter) advocates. See Greer; and Hansell, "Harold L. George," pp. 73–97.

Director of the Technical Department of the Air Ministry Ernst Udet made one constructive change to Luftwaffe planning as a result of experiences in Spain, changing the ratio of bombers to fighters in production plans from 3:1 to 2:1. See Murray, p. 18.

62. "Air Staff Post Hostilities Intelligence Requirements," Sec. IIIA 1 and 2, and Sec. IVA 3. Kennett, pp. 78–80, contended that the German failure to build a fleet of long-range heavy bombers before World War II was due to two factors, and neither included the oft-cited death of heavy bomber advocate General Walther Wever in a crash in 1936. These factors were first that German production capacity would have been overtaxed by an effort to build both heavy bombers and aircraft for tactical purposes. The Luftwaffe opted for the latter because of the kind of blitzkrieg war the Germans were planning. Second, German planning initially focused on France as the enemy to be engaged and one that would not need to be bombed by heavies from long range. In 1938 the Germans added England and the Soviet Union to their list of possible targets, too late for a heavy bomber program to be effective when needed.

63. "Air Staff Post Hostilities Intelligence Requirements," Sec. IIIA 1 and 2.

64. Though Milch may have been the key figure in the Luftwaffe's transition to strategic defense in the West, until 1943 he was an advocate of offensive action. In 1938 he appointed Gen. Otto Rüdel (replaced in 1939 by Gen. Hans Stumpff) to be the Luftwaffe's first Chief of Air Defense.

65. Price, *Luftwaffe Handbook*, p. 97. For extensive biographies of the major German officials directing the Luftwaffe war effort, see both Nielsen and Suchenwirth. For brief biographical summaries, see Price, *Luftwaffe Handbook;* Cooper; Parrish; and card file biographies of major German officials, n.d., File K113.109, HRC. For a biography of Milch, see Irving.

66. "Air Staff Post Hostilities Intelligence Requirements," Sec. IVA 3.

67. Kennett, pp. 115–125; and Overy, *Air War,* pp. 40–46, have summarized the causes and results of the Battle of Britain. Neither credited Douhet's influence on the German doctrine or strategy, but both cited as key to that strategy defeat of the Royal Air Force in its lair as the precondition, acknowledged by the Germans, to conquest (but by invasion and not collapse of morale, as Douhet foresaw). Both scholars acknowledged morale as the key target of the Blitz. A participant in the Battle of Britain and later a major commander of German air defenses, Adolf Galland, noted the influence of Douhet with reference, particularly, to a lack of innovative development of German fighters before the war and how that contributed to the defeat of the Luftwaffe in the Battle of Britain. See Royal Air Force interrogation of Adolph Galland, "The Birth, Life, and Death of the German Day Fighter Arm," 1945, File 168.6005-82, HRC.

68. The first Royal Air Force bombing of Germany took place on 4 September 1939. Even in the early stage of air defenses, the Luftwaffe did not entirely depend on antiaircraft artillery. When British Wellington bombers, albeit in small numbers, attacked the German naval base at Wilhelmshaven on 14 and 18 December 1939, it was German fighters that so mauled the Wellingtons that the experience helped convert Bomber Command to night operations. The true Royal Air Force strategic bombing campaign did not begin until May 1940. See Kennett, pp. 111–113.

69. Weise had commanded I Flak Corps in the Battle of France. Under the pressure of British attacks, Göring in September 1940 brought Weise to Berlin to take over the defenses of Berlin as commander of Luftgau III. Several months later Göring added Luftgau IV (Dresden) to Weise's command, assigning him the title Leader of Air Defenses in Luftgauen III and IV. Later this headquarters became the Berlin and Central Industrial Region. See the British Air Ministry translations of captured German documents, "Luftflotten Kommando Reich," 28 May 1945, File 512.625L, HRC, and "Luftwaffe Area Commands Directly Responsible to Reich Air Ministry during Second World War," 1957, File K512.621 VII/165, HRC.

70. Ibid.; "Air Staff Post Hostilities Intelligence Requirements," Sec. IVB, vol. 1.

71. "Air Staff Post Hostilities Intelligence Requirements," Sec. IVB, vol. 3, Appendix VIIe. In all, Kammhuber came to control five fighter divisions: 1, 2, 3, and 7 in Germany, and 4 in France. For a time the Luftwaffe lacked sufficient officers of the general officer rank to command the fighter divisions. Initially its solution was to recall World War I generals to active duty, but because few had any experience with flying, younger flying officers of lesser rank replaced them by 1944. For elaboration of Army Air Forces operations in 1942 and the first months of 1943, see chapter 3 of this study.

72. Luftwaffe fighters in II Fighter Corps in France possessed a 3.5-to-1 kill ratio advantage over Allied aircraft during this period. See Cooper, p. 192.

73. "Air Staff Post Hostilities Intelligence Requirements," Sec. IVB, vol. 1.

74. Ibid., vols. 1 and 2. The Radio and Radar Listening Service never approached the level of the Allies' ULTRA network because its activities were generally tactical, but was similar to the Royal Air Force's Y-Service (see below).

75. For a map showing the locations of German radar stations, see "Air Staff Post Hostilities Intelligence Requirements," Sec. IVB, vol. 2, Appendix T.

76. Ibid., Sec. IC, Appendix XIII. In 1943, to expand the capabilities of visual observers, the Luftwaffe began equipping its fighter divisions with eight to ten twin-engine Ju 88 or Bf 110 shadowing aircraft (*fühlungshalter*). These aircraft would attach themselves to American bomber formations and transmit continuous data about their size, composition, speed, bearing, and location. The Luftwaffe eventually disbanded the shadowing force because of heavy losses to American fighter escorts and because the same information was available from other sources.

77. Interview with General der Jagdflieger Adolph Galland, in ibid., Sec. IVB, vol. 2, Appendix Vd.

78. The Luftwaffe employed two grid systems for identifying the location of enemy forces. The first was the bomber grid (*Gradnetz*), which divided Germany into 10° longitude by 10° latitude rectangles, designated by two digits (the first being the first digit of the longitude of the western boundary of the rectangle and the second being the first digit of the latitude of the northern boundary of the rectangle). The system then subdivided these grid boxes into one hundred smaller areas of 1° of longitude by 1° of latitude, designated in the same two-digit manner as above. The subdivision continued into eight, then nine, and finally four grid boxes, the smallest called reporting squares (*Melde Trapez*). The fighter grid (*Jäger Gradnetz*) followed the same technique, but the 10° by 10° box was divided into halves, which were in turn subdivided by four hundred, then nine, and finally nine reporting squares (*Melde Trapez*). See ibid., Sec. IVB, vol. 2, Appendix IVp.

79. German scientists in the meantime developed the Egon system of control, which used radar and VHF radio to direct fighters at a range greater than Benito. The Egon-equipped aircraft transmitted a signal tracked with Panorama radar using a precision-point indicator. Though less accurate than Benito, Egon permitted the control of four or five formations of fighters at a time. Accuracy was not essential because the system was only intended to vector fighters to within visual distance of day bomber formations. The Luftwaffe's decision in 1942 to adopt the Y-system, however, delayed the deployment of the Egon system until late in the war, after American air forces had already seized air superiority. The standard German aircraft radio until 1943 was the FuG 7a, with only one channel. In late 1942 and early 1943 the Luftwaffe replaced it with the FuG 16z, a VHF, line-of-sight set with five preset channels with a direction-finding loop. Channel 1 carried the higher headquarters running battle commentary. Channels 2 and 5 were for Egon and Benito ground control. Channels 3 and 4 were for navigation. See ibid., Sec. IVB, vol. 1, and vol. 1, Appendix Vd.

80. According to Luftwaffe commanders of the defensive system, the threat of such small, scattered attacks was their greatest fear. See the interrogations in ibid., Sec. IVB, vol. 1. In the spring of 1944, when Eighth Air Force sent its long-range fighters on low-level attacks in Germany, the defensive system broke down.

81. The system did not develop an IFF capability for the antiaircraft artillery, and losses because of friendly fire were therefore a constant problem.

Luftwaffe Fighter Losses to Friendly Fire over German Territory

DATE	LOSSES
Jan 43	24
Feb 43	18
Mar 43	12
Apr 43	11
May 43	23
Jun 43	12
Jul 43	29
Aug 43	35
Sep 43	21
Oct 43	10
Nov 43	14
Dec 43	20
Jan 44	2
Feb 44	17
Mar 44	5
Apr 44	9
May 44	14
Jun 44	8

Source: "Air Staff Post Hostilities Intelligence Requirements," Sec. IVi, vol. 2, Appendix III.

82. Futrell, 1:142; and "Air Staff Post Hostilities Intelligence Requirements," Sec. IIIA 1 and 2. Price, *Luftwaffe Handbook*, p. 65, gives 1.25 million as the size of the German flak arm at its height, but cites no source for his figure. The best German source on this subject is Koch.

83. By 1944 the Luftwaffe organized these batteries into "great batteries" (*grossbatterie*) of between eighteen and twenty-four guns. See U.S. Strategic Air Forces in Europe, "Flak Grossbatteries," April 1945, File 519.6461-1, HRC.

84. The supremacy of the 8.8-cm gun is shown by the number of shells each size of antiaircraft gun fired in 1944: 21.5 million 8.8-cm, 2.4 million 10.5-cm, and 0.9 million 12.8-cm. See "Air Staff Post Hostilities Intelligence Requirements," Sec. VII.

85. A postwar Army Air Forces study determined that of sixty-five important German targets studied, the average flak defense amounted to 61.5 heavy guns per target. See "The Causes of Bombing Error," 15 July 1947, File 143.504-3, HRC.

86. Price, *Luftwaffe Handbook*, pp. 79–81.

87. Arthur B. Ferguson, "The War against the Sub Pens," in Craven and Cate, 2:268–269.

The standard aiming radar the Luftwaffe used for most of the war was the Würzburg. The Würzburg A had inherent inaccuracies of ±500 ft. in range, ±1.75° in azimuth, and ±2° in elevation. An 8.8-cm shell created a killing-zone sphere with a radius of 30 feet (covering about 113,000 cubic feet). In theory, the Würzburg A could identify a bomber at 24,000 feet with no more accuracy than as being somewhere within a box with dimensions of roughly 1,000 by 1,700 by 4,000 feet (approximately 6 billion cubic feet). Such inaccuracy would require almost 59,000 evenly placed shells to destroy that bomber. These figures are based on "Air Staff Post Hostilities Intelligence Requirements," Sec. VII, although other sources provide different figures.

With visual aiming, 200 8.8-cm shells firing by barrage at a box 3,300 by 2,200 by 1,100 yards with perfect spacing would only cover 1/3,750th of the cubic space involved. See Walter Grabmann, "German Air Force Defense Operations," 1956, File K113.107-164, HRC.

The estimate of 4,000 shells to down one bomber is that of General der Flakartillerie a. D. von Renz, "The Development of German Antiaircraft Weapons and Equipment of All Types up to 1945," 1958, File K113.107-194, HRC.

88. A postwar Army Air Forces study calculated that American losses would have more than tripled and the B-24 would have been knocked out of the war had the Germans developed and deployed proximity-fuzed antiaircraft ammunition similar to that used by the United States. The average radius of bombing errors would have likewise tripled, reducing the overall effectiveness of the bombing campaign. See "Estimate of Effect on Eighth Air Force Operations if German Antiaircraft Defenses Had Used Proximity-Fuzed (VT) Ammunition," 15 February 1947, File 143.504-1, HRC.

89. A postwar Army Air Forces study determined that 39.7 percent of the radial bombing error of American bombers was due to nerves, reduced

Chapter 2. Training to Destroy

1. The best short history of German rearmament, including the air arm, is Whaley. Training between the world wars in the U.S. Army air arm is best summarized in Maurer, *Aviation in the United States Army*.

2. Werner Kreip and Rudolf Koester, "Technical Training within the German Luftwaffe," 1955, File K113.107-169, HRC; and Whaley, pp. 1–37. The Kreip and Koester document is one of a series of studies former Luftwaffe specialists and high-ranking officers wrote after the war under the sponsorship of first the U.S. Army and then the U.S. Air Force. The original German-language studies are deposited in the HRC, along with some English translations, collectively known as the Karlsruhe Collection (*Studiengruppe Karlsruhe*), after the place where the work was coordinated. Sections of the unpublished work cited above for this note and for notes 3, 5, 6, and 10 were largely based on the work of General der Flieger Helmuth Felmy.

3. Kreip and Koester, "Technical Training within the German Luftwaffe."

4. Ibid.; Whaley, pp. 25–26; Editors of *Flying* magazine, *America's Soaring Book* (New York: Scribners, 1974), pp. 16–20; and Don Dwiggins, *On Silent Wings: Adventures in Motorless Flight* (New York: Grosset and Dunlap, 1970), pp. 33–39.

5. Kreip and Koester, "Technical Training within the German Luftwaffe"; Whaley, pp. 33, 48–49, 102–104; and Tolliver and Constable, pp. 49–51. The student training program was to open in 1927, but political considerations both in Germany and in the Soviet Union delayed the opening until 1928, costing the future Luftwaffe an estimated sixty-five unit commanders. See "Technical Training within the German Luftwaffe."

6. Kreip and Koester, "Technical Training within the German Luftwaffe"; Whaley, p. 44; and Galland, *Die Ersten und die Letzen*, pp. 1–26. A subsection of "Technical Training within the German Luftwaffe" deals, among other things, with the conversion of the commercial flight school at Schleissheim into a fighter training base.

7. Candidates had to be male, U.S. citizens, unmarried, 20 to 27 years old, and high school graduates, with good builds and first-class health. See Maurer, *Aviation in the United States Army*, p. 54.

8. *Air Corps Newsletter*, 1 January 1936, File 168.69-1, p. 7, HRC; Maurer, *Aviation in the United States Army*, pp. 53–59, 83–84, 204–210, 213–216; and interview of S. Sgt. Charles D. Brown by Helen L. Gilbert, 28 October 1944, File 223.051, HRC. The Air Corps trained comparatively few men

from the enlisted ranks as pilots. Some reserve officers served as enlisted pilots on active duty and a few enlisted pilots served as flight instructors.

9. Maurer, *Aviation in the United States Army*, pp. 86–97.

10. Kreip and Koester, "Technical Training within the German Luftwaffe," based on the work of Felmy; and Whaley, p. 26.

11. Kreip and Koester, "Technical Training within the German Luftwaffe," based largely on the work of Felmy, Generalmajor Hans-Joachim Rath, a Major Weldin, and Generalmajor Otto Fruhner.

12. Ibid., based on the work of Felmy.

13. Ibid., based largely on the work of Massow. In contrast to Air Corps practice, but matching the Royal Air Force practice, Luftwaffe ordnance schools regularly turned out noncommissioned officer fighter pilots. The term *plundered* as referring to raids on the personnel of Luftwaffe training schools appears in several sections of "Technical Training within the German Luftwaffe."

14. Ibid., based largely on the work of Massow; and Galland, *First and the Last*, pp. viii, 16–17, 216. This is the English translation of *Die Ersten und die Letzen*, but the English version contains only a brief summary of Galland's background and training, which appears fully in the German version.

15. During the war Göring did away with psychological testing as being too time-consuming and otherwise a hindrance to recruitment.

16. Knoke, pp. 1–18, 21–37. In the Luftwaffe and U.S. Army Air Forces, the organizational hierarchy for operational units was echeloned downward from wing to group to squadron. In the Royal Air Force, in contrast, the hierarchy went from group to wing to squadron.

17. *Air Corps Newsletter*, 1 January 1936, pp. 17–18.

18. Maurer, *Aviation in the United States Army*, pp. 218, 348, 350–351.

19. Ibid., pp. 350–351; and *Air Corps Newsletter*, 15 February 1938, p. 15, and 1 March 1938, p. 7.

20. Beirne Lay served as a bomber pilot with the Eighth Air Force in World War II and later wrote a novel, *Twelve O'Clock High!* (New York: Arno, 1980), about that legendary organization, which he helped to script into one of the better motion pictures about the air war in Europe.

21. *Air Corps Newsletter*, 15 September 1937, p. 5.

22. Ibid., 15 February 1938, p. 11.

23. Ibid., 1 October 1937, pp. 18–19; and Maurer, *Aviation in the United States Army*, p. 437.

24. *Air Corps Newsletter*, 1 February 1940, p. 3.

25. Ibid., pp. 3–4.

26. Kreip and Koester, "Technical Training in the German Luftwaffe,"

based largely on the work of Feldmarschall Erhard Milch, Massow, and various others.

27. Ibid., based largely on the work of Felmy, Milch, Massow, and others.

28. Ibid., based largely on the work of Milch and others; and Alfred A. Goldberg, "AAF Aircraft of World War II," in Craven and Cate, 6:226–227.

29. Kreip and Koester, "Technical Training in the German Luftwaffe," based largely on the work of Milch and others.

30. Ibid., based largely on the work of Milch, Felmy, and others.

31. Ibid., based largely on the work of Milch and others.

32. Ibid.

33. Arthur R. Rooker, "Broadening the Base of Procurement," in Craven and Cate, 6:431–433; and Watry, p. 7.

34. Rooker, "Broadening the Base of Procurement," p. 431; and Arthur R. Rooker, "Procurement at Flood Tide," in Craven and Cate, 6:508–515. Because training at the core was only as effective as its instructors, however up-to-date the aircraft and training aids might be, the problems in securing and maintaining competent ground and flying instructors was of constant concern to the Army Air Forces. Civilian instructors were vulnerable to the draft, could be tempted away by the Navy, or could not get life insurance because of the hazards of flying. A central instructors' school partially alleviated the problem. It was expected that returning combat veterans would further improve things, but "the returned combat pilots we have seen so far have been 'burned out' on flying and are nervous and jittery in the air." See interview of Lt. Col. J. M. McAuliff, Central Flying Training Command, 29 September 1944, File 223.051, HRC.

35. Rooker, "Procurement at Flood Tide," pp. 495–497, 516–552; Arthur R. Rooker, "Basic Military Training and Classification of Personnel," and Thomas H. Greer, "Individual Training of Flying Personnel," in Craven and Cate, 6:545–564. The Army Air Forces also used a program begun in 1939 to train young people to fly called the Civilian Pilot Training Program (renamed War Training Service in 1942). The program's story is told in Strickland. The Army Air Forces also added several weeks of maintenance duty for cadets at various airfields to keep the pipeline full. See Greer, "Individual Training," pp. 564–566.

36. Rooker, "Basic Military Training," p. 263; McAuliff interview; Watry, pp. 96–97, 105–108, 144; Turner, pp. 8, 14–20; Yeager and Janos, pp. 11–14, 26; and "History of the AAF Flying Training Command and Its Predecessors," 1 January 1939–7 July 1943, File 221.01, vol. 1, pp. 855–856, HRC. Yeager was one of the rare noncommissioned officer fighter pilots who General Arnold had decided would be of value but who were soon given the new in-between rank of flight officer.

37. Greer, "Individual Training," pp. 589–595; Kohn and Harahan, *Strategic Air Warfare*, p. 35; and Greer, "Combat Crew and Unit Training," in Craven and Cate, 6:601–604.

38. Interview of Gen. Howell M. Estes, Jr., 27–30 August 1973, File K239.0512-686, HRC; "History, Eastern Flying Training Command," 7 July 1943–31 December 1944, File 222.01, pp. 467, 469, HRC; Kreip and Koester, "Technical Training within the German Luftwaffe"; and Generalleutnant Andreas Nielsen, supplemented and completed by Generalmajor Walter Grabmann, "Anglo-American Techniques of Strategic Warfare in the Air," 1957, File K113.107-183, HRC.

39. Kreip and Koester, "Technical Training within the German Luftwaffe"; History, Eastern Flying Training Command, pp. 508, 522–523; and Edmond Zellner to authors, 2 November 1988.

Chapter 3. Trial and Error—Early Operations

1. The mission by the 15th Bomb Squadron of 4 July 1942 against four Dutch airfields was the first under the control of the Eighth Air Force, but crews used borrowed Royal Air Force Bostons. The 31st Fighter Group flew the first Eighth Air Force fighter mission on 26 July 1942, using British Spitfires. The first Eighth Air Force heavy bomber mission was by the 97th Bomb Group on 17 August 1942 against the Rouen-Sotteville railroad marshalling yard in northwest France. For aircraft availability, see Alfred A. Goldberg, "Allocation and Distribution of Aircraft," in Craven and Cate, 6:423–424.

2. McFarland; Greer, pp. 82, 87–88, 56; and interview of William Kepner by Bruce C. Hopper and Charles A. Foster, 15 July 1944, VIII Fighter Command, File 524.0581, HRC. An Air Corps Board study in 1940 concluded that the defensive fire of the B-17 and B-24 was superior to all other aircraft in the world. See Air Corps Board Study No. 53, "Fire Power of Bombardment Formations," 3 January 1940, File 167.5-53, HRC.

3. The Air Corps Board studied the feasibility of building a multiengine fighter with 25 percent greater speed, a higher ceiling, and a better rate of climb than a bomber with the same range in 1935. The board's conclusion was that such a fighter would require more power and be larger than the bomber it would support (three engines to the bomber's two). Its performance would be "extremely unsatisfactory" and, in any case, the need for fighter support for bombers was "not as yet thoroughly demonstrated." Instead, the board recommended, the United States should concentrate on giving bombers better defensive weapons and developing better defensive

techniques. See Air Corps Board Study No. 2, "Multi-Engine Fighter Aircraft," 15 July 1935, File 167.5-2, HRC.

4. AWPD-1 and AWPD-42 plans, 1941 and 1942, Air Staff, Plans Division, Files 145.82-1 and 145.82-42, HRC; McFarland, pp. 189–190; and Hansell, *Air Plan*, pp. 92–97, 110, 106–107. AWPD-1 did suggest that the development of a long-range escort fighter would greatly enhance strategic bombardment, while still discounting its likelihood.

5. VIII Fighter Command created the 4th Fighter Group on 12 September 1942, equipping it with the three American-crewed Eagle squadrons (the 71st, 121st, and 133rd, renumbered the 334th, 335th, and 336th squadrons when transferred to American control) of the Royal Air Force on 29 September 1942. The transition to American control was handled with little difficulty, though the crews evidently did not miss British cooking. The 334th Fighter Squadron historian wrote, "Farewell to sprouts, cabbage, kipper and imitation sausage." Less kindly he also gave his recipe for cooking English mutton. "I find that if [English] lamb is cut and soaked in salt water overnight, the water makes an excellent cleanser for garbage cans. The lamb is then placed on a board, seasoned with salt and well heated in a warm oven. Then take the lamb, toss it in the nearest can, garbage GI 32-gallon, and serve the board." See Monthly Diary, February 1943, 334th Fighter Squadron History, File SQ-FI-334-HI, HRC.

6. Eaker to Arnold, 8 June 1943, File 168.491, vol. 1, HRC. The fear of Eaker and Arnold was that if their forces were going to remain in support of invasions and ground armies, they would never achieve an independent role. It was critical for the future of an independent air force that the strategic bombing offensive succeed.

7. Arnold and Eaker, *This Flying Game*, and idem, *Winged Warfare*.

8. "Biographical Study of USAF General Officers, 1917–1952," File 101-91, vol. 1, HRC; and Parton, pp. 17–127.

9. "Maj. Gen. Frank Hunter Dies; Commanded Force in Europe," *New York Times*, 27 June 1982, p. 32; Hunter personal records, File K141.2421, HRC; "Biographical Study of USAF General Officers"; and VIII Fighter Command, "To the Limit of Their Endurance," 1944, File 168.6005-62, HRC.

Brigadier General E. P. Curtis, chief of staff of the U.S. Strategic Air Forces in Europe, told an interviewer in 1944 that Hunter had served in the 103rd Squadron in World War I, not the 94th. See interview with Curtis, 23 August 1944, File 524.0581, vol. 3, HRC. Hunter also established somewhat of a reputation as a racial segregationist in the Army Air Forces. General Daniel "Chappy" James recalled an incident at Selfridge Field near Detroit, where Hunter ordered the restoration of segregated seating after airmen stationed at Selfridge had integrated the field theater. Hunter told the assembled black personnel of the field that the world was not willing to accept them socially and that if they did not stay in their place, he had other means to keep them in their place. See interview with James, 2 October 1973, File 168.7061-24, HRC.

10. The B-24 Liberator went through similar modifications, bringing its armament up to ten .50-caliber machine guns in the D model.

11. Eighth Air Force, "Eighth Air Force Tactical Developments," August 1942–May 1945, File 520.057-1, HRC.

12. "Fire Control in Heavy Bombers," n.d. (June 1943?), File 168.61-7, HRC.

13. "Eighth Air Force Tactical Developments."

14. Interview with Overacker by Brig. Gen. Laurence Kuter, 3 March 1943, File 145.95 (WP-III-A2), Great Britain #2, HRC; Eaker to Arnold, 16 April 1943, File Bomber Command to Great Britain #228, Box 48, H. H. Arnold Papers, Manuscript Division, Library of Congress; and Arthur B. Ferguson, "The Daylight Bombing Experiment," in Craven and Cate, 2:229.

15. AWPD-42, Part 5, Tab D.

16. This objective would be entitled the Combined Bomber Offensive in the spring of 1943.

17. Greer, p. 7.

18. VIII Fighter Command, "The Long Reach Deep Fighter Escort Tactics," 29 May 1944, File 168.61-4, HRC.

19. P-47s first flew an operational mission on 10 March 1943 in the service of the 4th Fighter Group, but radio problems would prevent its return to operations until 8 April 1943. See Arthur B. Ferguson, "Over Germany," in Craven and Cate, eds., 2:335.

20. "Joint American-British Directif on Day Bomber Operations Involving Fighter Cooperation," 8 September 1942, in James Lea Cate, "Plans, Policies, and Organization," in Craven and Cate, 1:608–609; Ferguson, "Daylight Bombing Experiment," p. 227; and "Eighth Air Force Tactical Developments."

21. Until April 1943, VIII Fighter Command held only administrative command over its units, which came under the planning and operational control of the Royal Air Force's Fighter Command.

22. VIII Fighter Command, "Intelligence Officer's Guide for VIII Fighter Command," 1942–1943, File 168.6005-60, HRC.

23. Squadron and Group Histories, 334th, 335th, and 336th Fighter Squadrons, 4th Fighter Group, September 1942 to March 1943, Files SQ-FI-334-HI, SQ-FI-335-HI, SQ-FI-336-HI, and GP-4-HI(FTR), HRC; and VIII Fighter Command, "Operations Fighter Tactical Doctrines," 20 March

1943, File 168.61-8, HRC. Evidence of this atmosphere is the bare statistics of low-level combat: not until February 1944 did VIII Fighter Command claim an enemy aircraft destroyed on the ground, losses to flak were insignificant, and no fighters were lost due to collisions with ground obstacles until the spring of 1944. See VIII Fighter Command, "Combat Statistics," 1943–1944, File 168.6005-57, HRC.

24. Eighth Air Force, "Lessons Learned about Aerial Warfare in the European Theater of Operations," 1943, File 168.61-7, HRC.

25. The first VIII Fighter Command escort mission of the war was of DB-7 Bostons on 6 September 1942 and of B-17s on 2 October 1942.

26. Freeman, *Mighty Eighth War Diary*, pp. 7–50.

27. Futrell, 1:141; Parton, pp. 236–237; and Eighth Air Force, "Reduction of Flak Risk," July 1944, File 520.525A, HRC. One German source indicates LeMay's prediction of 372 shells to down one heavy bomber was exceedingly pessimistic. Friedhelm Golücke, in *Schweinfurt und der Strategische Luftkrieg*, cited in Murray, p. 182, claims that the average number of shells needed to down one heavy bomber was much greater: 16,000 + 8.8-cm Flak 36 shells, 8,000 8.8-cm Flak 41 shells, 6,000 10.5-cm shells, and 3,000 12.8-cm shells.

28. "Eighth Air Force Tactical Developments"; Eighth Air Force, "Combat Wing Formations," 9 February 1944, File 168.61-7, HRC; Arthur B. Ferguson, "The War against the Sub Pens," and idem, "Over Germany," in Craven and Cate, 2:266, 332.

29. VIII Bomber Command, "The Case for Day Bombing," January 1943, File 524.547C, HRC; and Eighth Air Force, "Eighth Air Force History," 17 August 1942–1 May 1943, File 520.01, vol. 2, pt. 1, HRC.

30. Eaker to Stratemeyer, 2 January 1943, File 145.95 (WP-III-A2), HRC; and Eaker to Stratemeyer, 30 January 1943, File 168.491, vol. 1, HRC. By 3 January 1943, Eighth Air Force had claimed the destruction of 223 Luftwaffe fighters, with an additional 88 probables and 99 damaged. It was apparent to most, especially British intelligence, that such figures were vastly inflated. Under British pressure, but also pressure from American higher-ups, Eighth Air Force revised its claims downward to 89 destroyed, 140 probables, and 47 damaged. The unreliable nature of even these adjusted claims can be seen by comparing American claims to German loss records for air battles fought on 9 October 1942 (Lille) and 20 December 1942 (Romilly-sur-Seine). Eighth Air Force claims for the two battles, after adjustment, numbered 42 destroyed, 52 probables, and 22 damaged. Luftwaffe records admitted to the loss of 3 fighters on those two days, with one additional fighter damaged. See Ferguson, "Daylight Bombing Experiment," pp. 221–224.

31. "Eighth Air Force History," 17 August 1942–1 May 1943.

32. Combined Chiefs of Staff (hereafter CCS) 166/1/D, 21 January 1943, File 119.151-1, HRC.

33. Churchill, pp. 678–680.

34. "Report of the Committee of Operations Analysts," 8 March 1943, File 520.164, vol. 2, pt. 1, HRC; CCS 217, "Plan for Combined Bomber Offensive from the United Kingdom," 14 May 1943, File 119.04-6, HRC; CCS 309, "POINTBLANK," August 1943, Quadrant Conference, File 119.151-3, HRC; and Arnold to Eaker, 24 January 1943, File 168.61-10, HRC.

35. Eaker to Stratemeyer, 2 January 1943, File 168.491, vol. 1, HRC. Within a month, Eighth Air Force's strength would double in bombers, with the addition of six bomb groups (92nd, 351st, 379th, 94th, 95th, and 96th). VIII Fighter Command would not receive reinforcement until August 1943 (353rd Fighter Group).

36. "ULTRA: History of U.S. Strategic Air Force Europe vs. German Air Force," June 1945, pp. 44–45, Special Research History Number 13 (SRH-013), National Security Council, RG457, National Archives.

37. "The Birth, Life, and Death of the German Day Fighter Arm," 1945, File 168.6005-82, HRC; and "Fire Control in Heavy Bombers."

38. General Quartermaster, 6th Abteilung, "10-Tagliche Einsatzbereit-schaftsmeldung," in "Air Staff Post Hostilities Intelligence Requirements," File 519.601B-4, Sec. II, pt. 2.

39. "Birth, Life, and Death of the German Day Fighter Arm"; and Bullock, p. 419.

40. "Air Staff Post Hostilities Investigation of German Air Defenses," 1938–1945, File 519.601A-2, HRC.

41. Eaker to Giles, 28 May 1943, and Eaker to Echols, 17 June 1943, File 168.491, vol. 1, HRC.

42. Hunter to Eaker, 17 April 1943, File 145.95 (WP-111-A2), Book 2, HRC.

43. 4th Fighter Group History, March-August 1943, File GP-4-HI(FTR), HRC; 56th Fighter Group History, March-August 1943, File GP-56-HI(FTR), HRC; 334th Fighter Squadron History, October 1942–August 1943, File SQ-FI-334-HI, HRC; and 335th Fighter Squadron History, December 1942–August 1943, File SQ-FI-335-HI, HRC.

44. VIII Bomber Command memorandum, 3 May 1943, File 520.310, HRC; Freeman, *Mighty Eighth War Diary*, pp. 7–50; and McFarland, p. 190.

45. British Air Ministry, "The Rise and Fall of the German Air Force (1935–1945)," File 512.042-248, HRC.

46. "Report on Fighter Airplane Development in the United States," 22 October 1942, File 168.61-7, HRC; Army Air Forces Board, Report of 2 January 1943, No. 2407B, 19 August 1944, File 245.64B, HRC; and Eaker to Giles, 18 July 1943, File 168.491, vol. 1, HRC.

47. The Army Air Forces had determined the modification program would have seriously interrupted Vega's B-17 production line and therefore contracted with Douglas for the conversions.

48. AAF Materiel Center, "XB-40 and YB-40 Final Report," 16 October 1943, File 202.1-16, HRC; idem, "XB-40 Case Study," July 1944, File 202.1-16, HRC; idem, "XB-41 Case Study," April 1944, File 202.1-17, HRC; AAF Board, "Tactical Employment Trials of the YB-40 Airplane," 21 April 1943, File 245.64, HRC; and Eaker to Giles, 29 June 1943, File 168.491, vol. 1, HRC. Consolidated Aircraft of San Diego built the YB-41 battle-cruiser version of the B-24 with specifications similar to those of the YB-40 version of the B-17, with no better results.

49. Giles to Eaker, 30 July 1943, File 168.491, vol. 1, HRC. Difficulties with the original A-10 Bendix indirect gunsight caused further delays, until Giles ordered its replacement with the A-16 Bendix direct sight. See Eaker to Giles, 29 June 1943 and 18 July 1943, File 168.491, vol. 1, HRC.

50. The remaining XB-40s and XB-41s in the United States were stripped of their extra equipment and turned over to the Training Command.

51. Kelsey, pp. 66–69; "Air Corps Tactical School Study of Pursuit Aviation," 1931–1932, File 248.282-8, HRC; and Boylan, p. 46.

52. Benjamin Kelsey, Air Corps pursuit project officer, maintained that external tanks for fighters were a private venture at a time when official opinion opposed such devices, with the support of Burdette Wright of Curtiss-Wright and William Kepner of the Air Corps. See Kelsey, p. 67. The Air Corps also examined the possibility of extended range through air-to-air refueling and through the use of bombers to carry fighters into battle. See Air Corps Board Study No. 54, "Pursuit Training and Pursuit Plane and Tactical Development," 1939–1940, File 167.5-54, HRC.

53. Kelsey, p. 68, dates the meeting in January 1942. The Army Air Forces' "Case History of Fighter Airplane Range Extension Program," File 202.2-11, HRC, records the meeting as occurring on 20 February 1942.

54. Giles to MM&D, 28 June 1943, File 202.2-11, vol. 1, HRC; Lovett to Arnold, 18 June 1943, File 452.01B, HRC; and Boylan, pp. 90–91.

55. Goldberg, "AAF Aircraft of World War II," in Craven and Cate, 6:217.

56. Cate, "Plans, Policies, and Organization," in Craven and Cate, 1:604. Parton, p. 280, takes Craven and Cate to task, citing an interview with Eaker in 1959 where Eaker said he was surprised "that an historian would make such a statement." Such "surprise" does not, however, explain why the Army Air Forces, in its detailed plans for wartime aircraft production, did not include the need for a long-range fighter. That failure must remain the most serious shortcoming of Army Air Forces' war planning. Parton

incorrectly attributes this statement to Goldberg, "AAF Aircraft of World War II," p. 217. The statement in fact was Cate's, as correctly cited above.

57. Kelsey, p. 69.

58. Twenty-one years after the war, Giles told interviewers that he thought the development of the long-range fighter was the most important contribution of his military career. See interview with Giles, 1966, File K239.0512-779, p. 1, HRC.

59. Giles to Chidlaw, 9 September 1943, File 202.2-11, HRC; and Copp, pp. 421–424.

60. Boylan, pp. 119–129.

61. VIII Fighter Command, "To the Limit of Their Endurance."

62. "Plan for Combined Bomber Offensive."

63. VIII Bomber Command memorandum, 3 May 1943, File 520.310, HRC; Eighth Air Force, "An Evaluation of Defensive Measures Taken to Protect Heavy Bombers from Loss and Damage," November 1944, File 520.520A, HRC; and Army Air Forces interrogation of Galland, 5 May 1945, File 519.04-5, HRC.

64. "Eighth Air Force Tactical Developments"; and Eighth Air Force, "History of Eighth Air Force," 1942–1945, File 520.01, vol. 1, HRC.

65. Channel B was used for air-sea rescue communications and channel D for wing direction finding. See VIII Fighter Command, "Tactics and Technique of Long-Range Fighter Escort," 25 July 1944, File 520.549A, HRC. The terms "Little Friend" and "Big Friend" were apparently used first in the Eighth Air Force and confined to the European Theater of Operations.

66. "Eighth Air Force Tactical Developments."

67. Ibid.

68. CCS 217, 14 May 1943, File 119.04-6, HRC; and U.S. Strategic Air Forces in Europe, "Review of Bombing Results," April 1943–October 1944, File 519.552-1, HRC.

69. Anderson to Stratemeyer, 21 July 1943, File 168.491, vol. 1, HRC; and Anderson to Eaker, 30 July 1943, File 168.61-10, HRC.

70. Walter Grabmann, "German Air Force Defense Operations," File K113.107-164, HRC.

71. Major David G. Wright, ed., "Observations on Combat Flying Personnel," October 1945, File 141.281-7, HRC; Eighth Air Force, "Special Report on Effects of Prolonged Operations on Combat Crews," 1944, File 520.742-4, HRC; Eighth Air Force, "Statistical Survey of the Emotional Casualties of the 8AF Crews," 25 May 1945, File 520.7421, HRC; "Report of the General Board on 'Combat Fatigue,'" 1944–1945, File 502.101-91, HRC; and "Psychiatric Experiences of the Eighth Air Force," 1943, File 141.281-4, HRC. Of the seventy-four reclassifications, seven were given

honorable discharges, fifty-five other than honorable discharges, three reassigned, and eight awaiting action (at the time of the report). The remaining crewman resigned.

72. Mattie E. Treadwell, *The Women's Army Corps*, vol. 8 of *United States Army in World War II* (Washington, D.C.: Office of the Chief of Military History, 1954), pp. 289, 380–383; interview of Mrs. Mary Gill Rice by Newton and Eugene Huck, 11 February 1990; Eighth Air Force, "Utilization of WAC Personnel in the Eighth Air Force," 3 April 1943, File 519.766, HRC; and Eighth Air Force, draft of report on "WAC Personnel," 29 September 1944, File 519.766, HRC.

73. Memorandum, Kuter to Stratemeyer, 19 June 1943, File 145.95 (WP-III-A2), Book 2, HRC; and lecture, School of Applied Tactics, 27 March 1943, File 248.281-3, HRC.

74. Eaker to Spaatz, 9 October 1943, cited in Parton, p. 191; Anderson to Eaker, 8 August 1943, File 524.0581, vol. 3, HRC; Anderson to Kepner, 8 August 1943, File 524.02, HRC; Giles to Anderson, 30 August 1943, File 168.491, HRC; and Doolittle to Arnold, 22 May 1943, File 145.95 (WP-III-A2), HRC. Doolittle's commitment to escort was especially important because in 1944 Arnold would assign him responsibility for using fighter escorts to win air superiority in Europe.

75. Army Air Forces Advisory Council to Arnold, 12 June 1943, Box 39, Arnold Papers.

76. Arnold to Eaker, 26 June 1943, Box 39, Arnold Papers.

77. VIII Fighter Command, "Narrative of Operations," 15 August 1943 and 4, 22, and 27 September 1943, File 168.6005-55, HRC.

78. Speer, *Inside the Third Reich*, p. 290.

79. Eighth Air Force, "Minutes of Commanders' Meeting," 7 June 1943, File 520.141, HRC.

80. Hunter to Eaker, 17 April 1943, File 145.95 (WP-III-A2), Book 2, HRC; VIII Fighter Command, "Tactics and Technique of Long-Range Fighter Escort"; VIII Fighter Command, "Achtung Indianer," 1945, p. 165, File 524.0581, HRC; interview of Frank O'D. Hunter, 7 April 1981, File K239.0512-1270, HRC; and "History of Eighth Air Force," 1942–1945. Parton, p. 273, writing four decades later, claims the problem with Hunter was his insistence on close escort and that Eaker wanted to replace Hunter with Kepner. Documentary evidence, however, proves Parton wrong on both points.

Chapter 4. To the Brink—The Fall Crisis

1. "Biographical Study of USAF General Officers, 1917–1952," File 101-91, vol. 1, HRC. See also Paul F. Henry, "William E. Kepner: All the Way to Berlin," in Frisbee, pp. 151–176. Amazingly, Kepner is not listed in

Roger J. Spiller, ed., *Dictionary of American Military Biography* (Westport, Conn.: Greenwood Press, 1984); John Keegan, ed., *Who Was Who in World War II* (New York: Thomas Y. Crowell, 1978); David Mason, *Who's Who in World War II* (Boston: Little, Brown, 1978); or Parrish. In a postwar interview, Lt. Gen. Barney M. Giles, in 1943 chief of the Air Staff, stated that as a result of Kepner's performance in gaining range for American fighters, he decided "to take him [Kepner] out of there [Fourth Air Force] and send him to Europe and relieve Monk Hunter." See Giles interview, 1974, File K239.0512-814, HRC. Kepner's compassion for his men came through in the various letters he wrote to the kin of pilots who had been shot down. They are marked by a genuineness. See February-December 1944, File 168.6005-3, HRC. The kind side of this tough warrior's nature was also attested to in an interview by Newton and Eugene Huck of Mary Gill Rice on 11 February 1990.

2. Generalleutnant Josef Schmid, "Luftwaffe Operations in the West," 1943–1945, File K113.107-158–160, vol. 10, HRC. Schmid was the commanding general of the Luftwaffe's I Fighter Corps in Germany from 1943 to 1944.

3. This hodgepodge organization contained only two fully equipped fighter wings (26th and 1st) of four fighter groups each. The 101st, 104th, and 108th Fighter Wings were training and factory defense units. The 11th and 76th had three groups each. The 54th, 3rd, 27th, and 53rd controlled two or less groups—the remainder of Luftwaffe groups continued to operate on one of the other fronts.

4. Walter Grabmann, "German Air Force Defense Operations," 1956, File K113.107-164, HRC; and British Air Ministry translation of captured German documents, "Luftflotten Kommando Reich," 28 May 1945, File 512.625L, HRC, and "Luftwaffe Area Commands Directly Responsible to Reich Air Ministry during Second World War," 1957, File K512.621 VII/165, HRC.

5. Schmid commanded the Hermann Göring Division under Rommel in North Africa until May 1943. Göring rewarded Schmid with the command of the new I Fighter Corps for his Afrika Korps service on 15 September 1943, a position he held until 15 November 1944.

6. Berenbrok, pp. 461–462.

7. McFarland, pp. 190, 202; and Grabmann, "German Air Force Defense Operations."

8. Murray, p. 219, reveals that German new production and reconditioning production peaked in July 1943 at 1,263 aircraft and declined through the remainder of 1943, reaching a low in December of 687 aircraft.

9. "ULTRA: History of U.S. Strategic Air Force Europe vs. German Air Force," June 1945, pp. 60, 71, and 74, Special Research History Number 13

(SRH-013), National Security Council, RG457, National Archives; Webster and Frankland, 2:241; and Grabmann, "German Air Force Defense Operations."

10. The 76th Fighter Wing, for example, was a twin-engine fighter wing created in August 1943 mainly from former reconnaissance units.

11. Grabmann, "German Air Force Defense Operations"; and USSBS, Report No. 2a, Chart 2.

12. "ULTRA," p. 59.

13. "The Birth, Life, and Death of the German Day Fighter Arm," 1945, File 168.6005-82, HRC; and British Air Ministry, "The Rise and Fall of the German Air Force (1935–1945)," File 512.042-248, HRC.

14. Murray, pp. 217–218. Murray points out how Göring believed the destruction of German cities might work in Germany's favor because it would give the German people greater spirit and fanaticism.

15. Grabmann, "German Air Force Defense Operations"; and USSBS, Report No. 59, Figure 7.

16. Generalleutnant Josef Schmid, "Day and Night Aerial Warfare over the Reich, 15 September 1943–31 December 1943," 1954, File K113.107-158–160, vol. 1, HRC; and Grabmann, "German Air Force Defense Operations."

17. Schmid, "Day and Night Aerial Warfare over the Reich."

18. Ibid.; and General der Flieger Josef Kammhuber, "Problems in the Conduct of a Day and Night Defensive Air War," 1953, File K113.107-179, HRC.

19. Schmid, "Day and Night Aerial Warfare over the Reich."

20. "ULTRA," p. 106; and Grabmann, "German Air Force Defense Operations."

21. Interrogation of Prof. Willi Messerschmitt, 25 June 1945, File 519.607A-82, HRC; and USSBS, Report No. 4, pp. 7, 23.

22. Albert F. Simpson, "Conquest of Sicily," and idem, "POINTBLANK," in Craven and Cate, 2:483, 686–687; USSBS, Report No. 53, p. 29; and Copp, pp. 426–429.

23. An additional seventeen B-17s were damaged beyond repair, raising Second Schweinfurt's toll to 34 percent.

24. Eaker to Arnold, 15 October 1943 and 23 October 1943, File 145.95 (WP-111-A2), Book 2, HRC; Arnold to Eaker, 15 October 1943, Box 16, Folder 4, Ira C. Eaker Papers, Manuscript Division, Library of Congress; Arnold to Eaker, 16 October 1943, Box 48, Folder "Bomber Command to Great Britain #227," Arnold Papers; and Secretary of the Air Staff to Assistant Chief of the Air Staff, Plans, 13 November 1943, File 145.95 (WP-111-A2), Book 2, HRC.

25. Eighth Air Force, "Bomber Narrative of Operations," 6 March 1944,

File 519.332, HRC; VIII Fighter Command, "Narrative of Operations," 6 March 1944, " File 168.6005-55, HRC; Generalleutnant Josef Schmid, "The Struggle for Air Supremacy over the Reich, 1 January 1944–31 March 1944," 1954, File K113.107-158–160, vol. 2, HRC; and Office of Air Force History, *USAF Credits for the Destruction of Enemy Aircraft, World War II* (Maxwell AFB, Ala.: Office of Air Force History, 1978). One of the current authors, Newton, helped research this official listing of Army Air Forces fighter victory credits.

26. "ULTRA," p. 109.

27. USAF Historical Office memorandum, 28 June 1949, citing "Auswertung der Einsatzbereitsch der fliegenden Verb. vom 1 August 1943 bis November 1944," File K110.8-22, HRC, reports losses of twenty-three, ten, twelve, and thirty-five (eighty total) on 8, 9, 10, and 14 October. "Day and Night Aerial Warfare over the Reich" lists losses for the same dates of twenty-eight, ten, twenty-six, and twenty-seven (ninety-one total). British translations of German captured documents, "German Air Force Losses in the West, 1 September 1943–31 December 1943," 1945, File K512.621 VII/148, HRC, and "German Air Force Losses in the Area of Luftflotte Reich, 1 September 1943–31 December 1943," 1945, File K512.621 VII/149, HRC, include figures of twenty-seven, eighteen, thirty-two, and forty-eight (one hundred twenty-five total).

28. Schmid, "Day and Night Aerial Warfare over the Reich"; "Birth, Life, and Death of the German Day Fighter Arm"; "Problems in the Conduct of a Day and Night Defensive Air War"; and Boylan, p. 203. The "nature of a fighter pilot to want to fight other fighter pilots" was apparent on the many occasions when individual Luftwaffe groups ignored orders and attacked American fighter units. See, for example, "Fighter Narrative of Operations," 11 and 13 December 1943; 10, 11, 22, and 24 February 1944; 8 and 15 March 1944; and 25 May 1944.

29. "Fighter Narrative of Operations," 14 October, 3 November, 13 November, 29 November, 1 December, 11 December, and 13 December 1943.

30. Schmid, "Day and Night Aerial Warfare over the Reich."

31. Ferguson, "POINTBLANK," in Craven and Cate, 2:705–706; and Parton, pp. 327–328.

32. Eaker to Giles, 13 December 1943, File 523.301, HRC; memoirs of Richard D. Hughes, Eighth Air Operational Planning Section, 1955–1957, File 520.056-234, HRC; and Arnold, *Global Mission*, p. 495.

33. VIII Fighter Command, "To the Limit of Their Endurance," File 168.6005-62, p. 65, HRC.

34. Hughes memoirs; Murray, p. 213; and Werrell, "Strategic Bombing of Germany," p. 705.

35. CCS 403/1, 3 December 1943, File 119.151-4, HRC.

36. "Evaluation of Defensive Measures." This report was written by the Operational Research Section and signed by Eighth Air Force Commanding General James Doolittle.

37. Though overall loss rates declined because of the greater number of bombers launched, Eighth Air Force losses per combat event increased ominously. From a low of 5.8 heavy bombers lost per 100 cases of reported combat in the last quarter of 1942, by early 1944 this ratio of losses had doubled. See ibid.

38. Schmid, "Day and Night Aerial Warfare over the Reich."

39. "German Air Force Losses in the West;" and "German Air Force Losses in the Area of Luftflotte Reich."

40. Grabmann, "German Air Force Defense Operations."

41. Schmid, "Day and Night Aerial Warfare over the Reich"; and "ULTRA," p. 59.

42. "Uberblick uber den Rustungsstand der Luftwaffe (Chef TLR)," in "Air Staff Post Hostilities Intelligence Requirements on the German Air Force," 1935–1945, File 519.601B-4, Sec. II, pt. 2, HRC.

43. Eaker to Arnold, 15 October 1943, in memorandum from Secretary of the Air Staff to Assistant Chief of Air Staff, Plans, 23 October 1943, File 145.95 (WP-111-A2), Book 2, HRC; "ULTRA," pp. 103, 107, 112–114; and Grabmann, "German Air Force Defense Operations."

44. Webster and Frankland, 2:52; and Ferguson, "The Autumn Crisis," in Craven and Cate, 2:715. One voice spoke out against this conviction that Eighth Air Force had to gain air superiority prior to OVERLORD. Sir Trafford Leigh-Mallory, Eisenhower's tactical air chief, believed air superiority would be gained only on D-day, over the beaches. See Goldberg and Simpson, "Final Reorganization," in Craven and Cate, 2:738.

45. See chapter 3, pp. 102–106.

46. Weyland to Giles, 20 June 1943, File 145.95 (WP-111-A2), Book 2, HRC; and staff memorandum for Arnold, 4 May 1943, File 145.95 (WP-111-A2), Book 2, HRC.

47. Letter to authors from Edmond Zellner, of the 352nd Fighter Group, 2 November 1988.

48. "Agreement on Air Supplies to the British in 1943 Made Under the Proceedings of the Lyttelton Mission," n.d., File 145.95 (WP-111-A2), HRC; and "May Review of 1943 Allocations to U.K.," 4 May 1943, File 145.95 (WP-111-A2), HRC. American allocations to the British were governed by the Arnold-Evill-McCain-Patterson Agreement of 15 December 1942. The allocations and schedules were reviewed in May 1943.

49. Arnold to Portal, 25 September 1943, and Portal to Arnold, 14 October 1943, File 168.491, vol. 2, HRC.

280 NOTES TO PAGES 139–144

50. Arnold to Portal, 14 October 1943, File 168.491, vol. 2, HRC.

51. Arnold to Portal, 15 October 1943, File 145.95 (WP-111-A2), Book 2, HRC.

52. Portal to Arnold, 24 October 1943, File 168.491, vol. 2, HRC.

53. Eaker to Arnold, 22 October 1943, File 168.491, vol. 1, HRC.

54. Arnold to Portal, 31 October 1943, File 145.95 (WP-111-A2), Book 2, HRC.

55. "Fighter Narrative of Operations," 27 September 1943.

56. Eaker to Kepner, 17–18 October 1943, File 168.6005-69, HRC.

57. VIII Fighter Command Chief of Staff to Commanders of 65th, 66th, and 67th Fighter Wings, 17 October 1943, File 168.6005-69, HRC.

58. "Skywash," January 1944, File 524.01A, HRC.

59. Hansell, *Air Plan*, p. 126.

60. Eighth Air Force, "Minutes of General and Special Staff Meeting," 29 November 1943, File 520.141, HRC.

61. Giles to Eaker, 25 August 1943, File 168.491, vol. 1, HRC.

62. VIII Fighter Command, "The Long Reach Deep Fighter Escort Tactics," 29 May 1944, File 168.61-4, HRC.

63. "History of Eighth Air Force, 1942–1945," p. 214; "Long Reach Deep Fighter Escort Tactics"; and "Fighter Narrative of Operations," 24 December 1943, 7 January 1944, 11 January 1944, and 24 January 1944.

64. "Fighter Narrative of Operations," 20 December 1943; and "Tactical Commander's Report," 20 December 1943, 55th Fighter Group, File GP-55-HI(FTR), HRC.

65. CCS 217, 14 May 1943, File 119.04-6, HRC.

66. Arnold to Eaker, 10 April 1943 and 29 June 1943, File 168.491, vol. 2, HRC; Eaker to Deputy Chief of Air Staff Stratemeyer, 2 July 1943, File 168.491, vol. 1, HRC; Giles to Eaker, 26 August 1943, File 168.491, vol. 1, HRC; Arnold to Eaker, 15 June 1943, File 227, Box 48, Arnold Papers; Eaker to Arnold, 20 July 1943, File 168.491, vol. 1, HRC.

67. Eaker to Stratemeyer, 2 January 1943, and Eaker to Arnold, 15 February 1943, File 168.491, vol. 1, HRC.

68. Parton, p. 191.

69. Assistant Chief of Air Staff, Plans, to Deputy Chief of Air Staff, 14 August 1943, File 145.95 (WP-111-A2), Book 2, HRC; Arnold to Devers for Eaker, 29 October 1943, File 519.245-1, HRC; Arnold to Portal, 3 March 1943, File 145.95 (WP-111-A2), HRC; and U.S. Strategic Air Forces in Europe, "Statistical Summary of Operations," 1942–1945, File 519.308-9, HRC; Coffey, *HAP*, p. 314; and Arnold to Giles, 5 January 1944, File 168.491, vol. 5, HRC.

70. In a postwar interview, Giles told his interviewer that he thought

Arnold replaced Eaker and Hunter because they refused to support long-range fighters. Similarly, he felt Arnold appointed Kepner to replace Hunter because Kepner believed in long-range escort. See interview of Lt. Gen. Barney M. Giles, 1974, File K239.0512-814, pp. 98–99, HRC.

71. Eaker to Arnold, 20 July 1943, File 168.491, vol. 1, HRC.

72. Eighth Air Force, "Minutes of Eighth Air Force Commanders' Meeting," 7 June 1943, File 520.141-1, HRC.

73. Giles to Eaker, 30 July 1943, File 168.491, vol. 1, HRC.

74. Eaker's conversion to fighter escort was apparent on 31 October 1943, when the heavy bombers were recalled because the weather had closed in and kept the fighters grounded. See Cabell to Arnold, 2 November 1943, Box 48, File "Bomber Command to Great Britain #226," Arnold Papers. Also see Eaker to Giles, 2 November 1943, File 168.491, HRC. Eaker issued a memorandum to the commanders of VIII Fighter Command and the new Ninth Air Force on 31 October 1943 informing them that the primary role of all American fighters in the United Kingdom henceforth would be to support the heavy bombers in their POINTBLANK campaign. See Eaker to Kepner and Brereton, 31 October 1943, File 519.1612, HRC.

75. Giles to Eaker, 16 December 1943, File 168.491, vol. 1, HRC; and Giles to Eaker, 3 November 1943, File 168.491, vol. 1, HRC.

76. Doolittle to Arnold, 22 May 1943, File 145.95 (WP-111-A2), Book 2, HRC; and Atkinson to Commanding General Twelfth Bomber Command as enclosure to Deputy Chief of Air Staff, 19 June 1943, File 145.95 (WP-111-A2), Book 2, HRC.

77. Arnold/Marshall to Eaker, 21 September 1943, File 520.1622, HRC.

78. Arnold to Devers for Eaker, 29 October 1943, File 519.245-1, HRC.

79. "Minutes of General and Special Staff Meeting," 29 November 1943; Morrison, *Fortress without a Roof*, p. 165; Coffey, *HAP*, p. 316; Brereton, p. 216; Kepner to Giles, n.d. and 27 December 1943, cited in Ferguson, "Winter Bombing," in Craven and Cate, 3:11, 811; and Eaker to Commanders, Ninth Air Force and VIII Fighter Command, and Chief of Staff, Eighth Air Force, 31 October 1943, File 520.161-1, HRC.

80. See chapter 3, pp. 104–106; and Eaker to Portal, 14 October 1943, and Eaker to Arnold, 22 October 1943, File 168.491, vol. 2, HRC.

81. Murray, p. 168.

82. Hough to Hunter, 8 July 1943, in VIII Fighter Command, "Achtung Indianer," 1945, File 524.0581, p. 165, HRC.

83. Quadrant Conference, CCS 303, 9 August 1943, and 109th Meeting, 16 August 1943, File 119.151-3, HRC.

84. Kuter to Arnold, 30 August 1943, File 145.95 (WP-111-A2), Book 2, HRC.

85. Fifteenth Air Force officially began operations on 1 November 1943.

86. Arnold to Spaatz, n.d., File 168.491, vol. 2, HRC.

87. CCS 400, 18 November 1943, CCS 400/1, 26 November 1943, and CCS 400/2, 4 December 1943, File 119.151-4, HRC; Spaatz to Arnold, 4 September 1943, File 168.491, vol. 2, HRC; and Davis, "Bomber Baron," pp. 400–425.

88. SEXTANT Conference, CCS 403, 3 December 1943, and 134th Meeting, 4 December 1943, File 119.151-4, HRC.

89. Parton, pp. 335–336, has asserted that Spaatz recommended Eaker be moved to the Mediterranean, citing Spaatz's diary entry for 9 December. Spaatz's biographer, Davis ("Bomber Baron," pp. 409–410), agrees with Parton that Spaatz made such a recommendation on 9 December, but only after Arnold had already told Eisenhower the day before that Eaker should be transferred.

90. Davis, "Bomber Baron," pp. 400–410.

91. Giles interview, p. 97. Part of the controversy surrounding Eaker's transfer was Arnold's 7 July 1943 message to Eaker that "if there is anything serious you will be the first one to hear of it and it will come from me direct." Eaker's supporters believe Arnold then betrayed this promise to Eaker when Arnold transferred him without warning. The problem with this controversy is that Arnold did, on multiple occasions, complain to Eaker about his performance. See, for example, Arnold to Eaker, 7 July 1943, File 228, Box 49, Arnold Papers.

92. Davis, "Bomber Baron," pp. 414–419; Copp, pp. 446–452; and Parton, pp. 331–344.

93. Giles interview.

94. Oral interview of Gen. Hunter Harris, Jr., 1974 and 1979, File K239.0512-811, HRC; Hughes memoirs; and interview of Col. Clyde Bradley, USAF (ret.), by Newton, 5 and 7 April 1988.

95. Arnold to Giles, 5 January 1944, File 168.491, vol. 1, HRC.

96. Biography of Carl Spaatz, n.d., File 702.293, HRC; Davis, "Bomber Baron," pp. 40, 44–46, 62, 73; "Biographical Study of USAF General Officers," vol. 2; Rice interview; and Hughes memoirs.

97. "Biographical Study of USAF General Officers," vol. 1; Anderson to Stratemeyer, 21 July 1943, File 168.491, vol. 1, HRC; Stratemeyer to Eaker, 7 February 1943, File 168.491, vol. 1, HRC; Harris interview; Hughes memoirs; Rice interview; and Anderson to Hunter, 8 August 1943, in "VIII Fighter Command History," March 1944, File 524.02, HRC.

98. "Biographical Study of USAF General Officers," vol. 1; interview of

Lt. Gen. James Doolittle, 1971, File K239.0512-793, HRC; Charles K. Wilson, "James Harold Doolittle: American Aviator, Aeronautical Engineer, Aerospace Executive," Thesis, Air Command and Staff College, 1965; Doolittle to Giles, 19 September 1943, File 168.491, vol. 1, HRC; and Rice interview.

99. Biography of Lt. Gen. Barney M. Giles, n.d., File 702.293, HRC; and "Biographical Study of USAF General Officers," vol. 1.

100. Not only were fighters available in greater numbers, but small technological improvements in the fall of 1943 had made them more capable of winning air superiority. These included the development of the G-suit to prevent blacking out, water injection for the P-47 engine to permit greater manifold pressure, and the new K-14 gyro gun sight. See Eighth Air Force, "Eighth Air Force Tactical Developments," August 1942–May 1945, File 520.057-1, HRC.

101. "Statistical Summary of Operations."

Chapter 5. Transition to Air Superiority—Big Week

1. Brereton to Spaatz, 28 January 1944, File 519.1612, HRC.

2. Giles to Spaatz, 27 December 1943, File 168.491, vol. 2, HRC.

3. Rostow, p. 26.

4. Generalleutnant Josef Schmid, "The Struggle for Air Supremacy over the Reich, 1 January 1944–31 March 1944," 1954, File K113.107-158–160, vol. 2, HRC.

5. Ibid.; interview of Col. Clyde Bradley, USAF (ret.), by Newton, 5 and 7 April 1988; and British translation of captured German documents, "German Air Force Losses in the West, January-April 1944," 1945, File K512.621 VII/135, HRC, and "German Air Force Losses in the Area of Air Fleet Reich, January-April 1944," 1945, File K512.621 VII/138, HRC.

6. Schmid, "Struggle for Air Supremacy over the Reich."

7. Ibid.

8. Eighth Air Force, "History of Eighth Air Force," February 1944, File 520.01, vol. 1, pp. 16–17, HRC.

9. See, for example, Murray, p. 226. For Doolittle's evaluation, see Doolittle letter to authors, 28 October 1985. Colonel Hubert Zemke's 56th Fighter Group in December 1943 may have first tried out the "freeing" tactic and influenced the later widespread adoption of it.

10. Doolittle with Lay, p. xv; Paul F. Henry, "William E. Kepner: All the Way to Berlin," in Frisbee, p. 169; letter from James "Jimmy" Doolittle to McFarland, 28 October 1985; Boylan, pp. 168, 203; Eighth Air Force, "History of Eighth Air Force," February 1944, File 520.01, HRC; O. A. Ander-

son, "Development of U.S. Strategic Air Doctrine, ETO in World War II," lecture given to Air War College, 20 September 1951, in Futrell, 1:79; interview of Kepner by Bruce C. Hopper and Charles A. Foster, 15 July 1944, File 524.0581, HRC; Murray, p. 226; Morrison, *Fortress without a Roof*, p. 183; Copp, pp. 456–457; AAF Historical Office, "The War against the Luftwaffe: AAF Counter-Air Operations," April 1943–June 1944, File 101-110, p. 120, HRC; and Arthur B. Ferguson, "Big Week," in Craven and Cate, 3:48. Doolittle's biographers, Thomas and Jablonski, pp. 267–268, 271, give a slightly different version of this incident. For a sample of other alternate views of the freeing decision, see McFarland, p. 207, n. 23.

11. Arnold to Doolittle, 27 December 1943, File 168.491, vol. 5, HRC.

12. Eighth Air Force, "Minutes of Eighth Air Force Commanders' Meeting," 21 January 1944, File 520.141-1, HRC.

13. Kepner interview, 15 July 1944, Box 136, Subject File, Carl Spaatz Papers, Manuscript Division, Library of Congress.

14. VIII Fighter Command, "History of Eighth Fighter Command," 1943–1944, File 524.01A, HRC; and Giles to Eaker, 30 July 1943, File 168.491, vol. 1, HRC.

15. Doolittle with Lay, p. xv.

16. POINTBLANK continued to reflect the 1943 view that Eighth Air Force had two separate missions. The revision of 13 February 1944 made the bombing of Luftwaffe aircraft production the primary objective. See Eighth Air Force, "Policy File," 1942–1944, File 520.164, vol. 1, HRC.

17. Galland, *First and the Last*, pp. 273–280.

18. Schmid, "Struggle for Air Supremacy over the Reich."

19. On 20 December 1943 the 55th and 352nd Fighter Groups had "freed" themselves, three weeks before Doolittle gave his approval. The 55th undertook a sweep because the bombers were 30 minutes late in arriving and the 352nd sent its 486th Fighter Squadron after six to eight Bf 109s beyond the sight of the heavy bombers. Both incidents of freeing were unauthorized and contrary to established policy. See "Tactical Commander's Report," November 1943–February 1944, File GP-55-HI(FTR), HRC; and 352nd Fighter Group History, December 1943, File GP-352-HI(FTR), HRC.

20. "Fighter Narrative of Operations," 24 January 1944.

21. 356th Fighter Group History, January 1944, File GP-356-HI(FTR), HRC; "History of Eighth Air Force," 1942–1945, vol. 1, p. 212, HRC; "To the Limit of Their Endurance"; and "Auswertung der Einsatzbereitsch der fliegenden Verb. vom 1 August 1943 bis November 1944," File K110.8-22, HRC.

22. Ibid.; and "Fighter Narrative of Operations," 29 and 30 January

1944. Perhaps there is no better indicator of the momentous shift in air superiority warfare that Doolittle's decision represented than in the amount of .50-caliber ammunition being fired by fighters and bombers in the spring of 1944. Usage by heavy bombers declined 2 percent from February 1944 to March 1944, while usage by fighters increased 56 percent. See Eighth Air Force, "Statistical Analysis," August 1942–May 1945, File 520.308-5, HRC.

23. Bradley interview; Kepner to All Units, 14 February 1944, File 524.03, HRC; "History of Eighth Air Force," 1942–1945, vol. 1, pp. 16–17; and Spaatz to Arnold, 10 April 1944, File 519.161-4, HRC.

24. "The Birth, Life, and Death of the German Day Fighter Arm," 1945, File 168.6005-82, HRC; and VIII Fighter Command, "The Long Reach Deep Fighter Escort Tactics," 29 May 1944, File 168.61-4, HRC.

25. Letter to authors from Maj. Gen. Luther H. Richmond, USAF (ret.), 12 November 1988.

26. "History of Eighth Air Force," 1942–1945, vol. 1, p. 212; and "Fighter Narrative of Operations," 30 January 1944.

27. Eighth Air Force memorandum, 8 April 1944, File 520.6251-1, HRC; Combined Strategic Planning Committee memorandum, 8 March 1944, File 508.645-1, HRC; "History of Eighth Fighter Command," 1 August 1942–30 April 1945, File 524.01B, HRC; Eighth Air Force, "Y-Service Report," 1944, File 520.6251-1, HRC; and Clayton.

28. "Minutes of Eighth Air Force Commanders' Meeting," 8 February 1944; and letter to authors from Richmond.

29. Arnold to Doolittle, 11 February 1944, File 519.245-1, HRC; and Doolittle to Arnold, 4 March 1944, File 168.6007-2, HRC. In a postwar interview Doolittle claimed responsibility for the decision to extend tours, but Arnold's letter reveals clearly that the order had originated with Arnold. See Doolittle with Lay, p. xvi; or Thomas and Jablonski, p. 266.

30. "Fighter Narrative of Operations," 3, 4, 8, 10, and 11 February 1944; "Bomber Narrative of Operations," 3, 4, 8, 10, and 11 February 1944; Schmid, "Struggle for Air Supremacy over the Reich"; and "Auswertung der Einsatzbereitsch der fliegenden."

31. Schmid, "Struggle for Air Supremacy over the Reich."

32. Arnold to Doolittle, 27 December 1943, File 168.491, vol. 5, HRC.

33. "Material behind the 'Big Week,'" 25 April 1944, "Operations: The Big Week" Folder, Subject File, Box 169, Spaatz Papers.

34. Memoirs of Richard D. Hughes, 1955–1957, File 520.056-234, HRC.

35. Hinsley et al., 3:317.

36. Eaker to Eighth Air Force Staff, 18 March 1943, and reply memorandum, 23 March 1943, File 520.4231C, HRC.

37. ARGUMENT Plan, n.d., Box 135, ARGUMENT folder, Subject File, Spaatz Papers; Plans for ARGUMENT, 2–29 November 1943, File 508.401, HRC; Plans for ARGUMENT, December 1943, File 529.4231B, HRC; ARGUMENT target list, November 1943, File 520.4231B, HRC; and Planning Memos, February-March 1943, File 520.4231C, HRC.

38. Spaatz had grown so desperate to intensify efforts against Germany that in a 17 February 1944 meeting with Prof. Solly Zuckerman and Maj. Gen. Frederick Anderson, Spaatz proposed sending the bombers all over Germany to look for any visual openings in the clouds to attack small German towns. He felt the effect of hitting associated railroad facilities as well as destroying these small towns would be an important contribution to the air campaign. See 17 February 1944 entry of Spaatz's diary, February 1944 personal file, Box 14, Spaatz Papers.

39. Arnold to Spaatz, 27 December 1943, Subject File, Box 14, Spaatz Papers.

40. Arnold to Spaatz, 24 January 1944, January 1944 Folder, Spaatz Diaries, Box 146, Spaatz Papers.

41. Acting Assistant Chief of Staff, Intelligence, to Eaker, 9 December 1943, January 1944 Folder, Spaatz Diaries, Box 17, Spaatz Papers.

42. Eaker memorandum, n.d. (November 1943?), File 168.491, vol. 1, HRC.

43. USSBS, Report No. 4, p. 74, and Exhibit 2; Webster and Frankland, 2:54; and "Destruction of the German Air Force and Plan for Intensive Counter Air Force Action," 1944, File 519.3174-4, HRC.

44. Davis, "Bomber Baron," pp. 477–480.

45. Schmid, "Struggle for Air Supremacy over the Reich."

46. "Statistical Analysis."

47. Hinsley, 3:318–319.

48. Memorandum, 13 February 1944, Eighth Air Force, "Policy File," File 520.164, vol. 1, HRC.

49. Conference memorandum, 19 February 1944, February Folder, Subject File, Box 14, Spaatz Papers.

50. Interview of Col. C. G. Williamson, 14 June 1944, Subject File, Big Week Folder, Box 136, Spaatz Papers.

51. Spaatz to Doolittle, 24 and 28 January 1944, File 519.1612, HRC.

52. Doolittle with Lay, p. xv.

53. Diary entry for 9 February 1944, Spaatz personal file for February 1944, Box 14, Spaatz Papers.

54. Authors' interview of Col. William R. Lawley, Jr., USAF (ret.), 21 March, 5 April, and 8 May 1985. The description from the base at Rackheath is from Healy, pp. 42, 87–88. The material dealing with the fighter

mechanic is from Hall, p. 106. The material about premission activities on a fighter base is from Yeager and Janos, pp. 47–49. The material on the WAC is from an interview of Mary Gill Rice by Newton and Eugene Huck, 11 February 1990; and Mattie E. Treadwell, *The Women's Army Corps*, vol. 8 of *United States Army in World War II* (Washington, D.C.: Office of the Chief of Military History, 1954), pp. 381, 385.

55. Encounter report of Capt. Duane W. Beeson, 20 February 1944, File SQ-FI-334 (HI), HRC.

56. Knoke, p. 141.

57. "Fighter Narrative of Operations," 20 February 1944; Infield, pp. 107–116; and Lawley interview.

58. "Material behind the 'Big Week'"; "Fighter Narrative of Operations," 20 February 1944; "The War against the Luftwaffe: AAF Counter-Air Operations, April 1943–June 1944," August 1945, Army Air Forces Historical Office, File 101-110, pp. 116–142, HRC; United States, National Archives, Record Group 243, Records of the U.S. Strategic Bombing Survey, European War G-2 Target Intelligence File, Box 59, No. 2.b.(111), Tactical Mission Report #226, 20 February 1944, No. 7, Erla Maschinenwerke GmbH, Heiterblick, and No. 8, Erla Maschinenwerke GmbH, Mockau; "Bomber Narrative of Operations," 20 February 1944; Schmid, "Struggle for Air Supremacy over the Reich"; and U.S. Strategic Air Forces in Europe, "Mission Planning and Enemy Reaction File," 20 February 1944, File 519.601A-2, HRC.

59. Record of telephone conference between Giles and Anderson, 21 February 1944, Boxes 33 and 100, Spaatz Papers.

60. Anderson to Eaker, 21 February 1944, Spaatz Subject File, Box 3, Spaatz Papers.

61. Schmid, "Struggle for Air Supremacy over the Reich"; "Bomber Narrative of Operations," 21 February 1944; "Fighter Narrative of Operations," 21 February 1944; "The War against the Luftwaffe," pp. 128–129; and "Mission Planning and Enemy Reaction File," 21 February 1944.

62. Anderson to Giles, transcript of telephone conversation, 21 February 1944, Spaatz Diary, Box 100, Spaatz Papers.

63. Schmid, "Struggle for Air Supremacy over the Reich"; and Walter Grabmann, "German Air Force Defense Operations," 1956, File K113.107-164, HRC.

64. Telephone conversations between F. Anderson and O. Anderson, 22 February 1944, Boxes 33 and 100, Spaatz Papers.

65. Schmid, "Struggle for Air Supremacy over the Reich"; Fifteenth Air Force, "Fifteenth Air Force History," November 1943–May 1945, File 670.01-1, vol. 2, HRC; Fifteenth Air Force, "Fifteenth Air Force Mission

Folder," 22 February 1944, File 670.332, HRC; "Bomber Narrative of Operations," 22 February 1944; "Fighter Narrative of Operations," 22 February 1944; "The War against the Luftwaffe," pp. 129–133; and "Mission Planning and Enemy Reaction File," 21 February 1944.

66. Muirhead, pp. 47–48, 50–51, 53, 56–57, 60.

67. Hughes memoirs.

68. Hinsley et al., 3:321.

69. Bradley interview.

70. Schmid, "Struggle for Air Supremacy over the Reich"; "Fifteenth Air Force History"; "Fifteenth Air Force Mission Folder, 24 February 1944; "Bomber Narrative of Operations," 24 February 1944; "Fighter Narrative of Operations," 24 February 1944; "The War against the Luftwaffe," pp. 133–136; and "Mission Planning and Enemy Reaction File," 21 February 1944.

71. "Auswertung der Einsatzbereitsch der fliegenden"; "German Air Force Losses in the West"; and "German Air Force Losses in the Area of Luftflotte Reich, 1 September 1943–31 December 1943," 1945, File K512.621 VII/149, HRC.

72. "Fighter Narrative of Operations," 24 February 1944; encounter report of Col. Henry R. Spicer, Jr., 24 February 1944, GP-357-HI(FTR), HRC; and Knoke, pp. 141–143.

73. Schmid, "Struggle for Air Supremacy over the Reich"; "Fifteenth Air Force History"; "Fifteenth Air Force Mission Folder," 25 February 1944; "Bomber Narrative of Operations," 25 February 1944; "Fighter Narrative of Operations," 25 February 1944; "The War against the Luftwaffe," pp. 137–139; "Mission Planning and Enemy Reaction File," 21 February 1944; and Knoke, pp. 143–146.

74. Schmid, "Struggle for Air Supremacy over the Reich."

75. Fritz Ungar, letter to authors, 18 October 1988.

76. Interrogation No. 22 of Dr. Karl Saur, 18 May 1945, File 137.315-22, HRC.

77. Schmid, "Day and Night Aerial Warfare over the Reich"; "Auswertung der Einsatzbereitsch der fliegenden"; "German Air Force Losses in the West"; and "German Air Force Losses in the Area of Luftflotte Reich."

78. Spaatz to Arnold, n.d. (late February 1944), February 1944 Personal File, Box 14, Spaatz Diaries; and "Material behind the 'Big Week.'"

79. USSBS, Report No. 59, Table V-5 and pp. 61–66; Rust, p. 32; "The War against the Luftwaffe," pp. 140–142; Arthur B. Ferguson, "Big Week," in Craven and Cate, 3:43–46; "The Contribution of Air Power to the Defeat of Germany," 1945, File 519.601C, vol. 4, based on "Basic Returns of the German Quartermaster Staff," HRC; and Murray, p. 229.

80. Grabmann, "German Air Force Defense Operations." Feldmarschall Milch in February ordered the large number of new aircraft stored at the factories to be dispersed. Big Week caught these aircraft on the ground before Milch's order could be carried out.

81. USSBS, Report No. 11, pt. A, p. 21.

82. Speer, *Infiltrations*, pp. 235–237.

83. Comments by Charles A. Foster, attached to interview of E. J. Corbally, 23 June 1944, Subject File, Folder "Interview E. J. Corbally 6/17/44," Box 135, Spaatz Papers.

84. Ibid.

85. "Air Intelligence Summary," No. 17, 5 March 1944, "Operations: The Big Week" Folder, Box 169, Subject File, Spaatz Papers.

86. Letter to authors from Edmond Zellner, of the 352nd Fighter Group, 2 November 1988.

Chapter 6. Berlin, the Strategic Fighter Campaign, and Control of the Air

1. Webster and Frankland, 2:32–34; Generalleutnant Josef Schmid, "Day and Night Aerial Warfare over the Reich, 15 September 1943–31 December 1943," 1954, File K113.107-158–160, HRC; Beck, pp. 89–90; and Kennett, pp. 130, 154.

2. Interview of Col. Clyde Bradley, USAF (ret.), by Newton, 5 and 7 April 1988.

3. It is ironic but human that Spaatz, in a letter to Arnold of 10 January 1944, decried the use of the term *raid* to describe the missions of the American heavy bombers: "Ever since July 1, the Eighth Air Force has had a campaign on to restrict the use of the word 'raid' . . . " See Spaatz to Arnold, 10 January 1944, File 168.491, vol. 2, HRC.

4. Arnold to Spaatz, 4 January 1944, Report File, Box 248, Arnold Papers; memorandum, 12 December 1943, Subject File, Box 145, Spaatz Papers; U.S. Strategic Air Forces in Europe, "Planning and Organization for Large Scale Raids on Berlin," 12 January 1944, File 519.3171-1, HRC; and Spaatz to Arnold, 23 January 1944, File 168.491, vol. 2, HRC.

5. The moral aspects of strategic bombing in the European Theater of Operations are thoroughly weighed in Sherry and in Schaffer, *Wings of Judgment.*

6. Anderson Diary, entries of 27 and 29 February 1944, Box 100, Spaatz Papers; and Schaffer, *Wings of Judgment*, pp. 57 and 68 (quotation about "damn house" is from Schaffer, p. 68).

7. Grover C. Hall, Jr., to Doolittle, containing March history of 4th

Fighter Group, 6 April 1944, File GP-4-HI(FTR), HRC; and Ethell and Price, p. 13.

8. Fred Anderson to O. A. Anderson, 29 February 1944, Anderson Diary.

9. Anderson teletype conference with Giles, Vandenberg, and Hansell, 27 February 1944, Anderson Diary.

10. Ethell and Price, p. 9; and Thomas and Jablonski, pp. 264–265.

11. Anderson Diary, entry of 2 March 1944; and Eighth Air Force, "Minutes of Eighth Air Force Commanders' Meeting," 2 March 1944, File 520.141, HRC.

12. Generalleutnant Josef Schmid, "The Struggle for Air Supremacy over the Reich, 1 January 1944–31 March 1944," 1954, File K113.107-158–160, HRC; and Eighth Air Force, "Report of Operations," 3 March 1944, with weather and other statistical annexes, in Anderson to Arnold, cover letter dated 30 April 1944, File 520.331, HRC.

13. As late as January 1945, the Air Staff in Washington was concerned about test data that showed "a circular probable error of . . . H_2X bombing under conditions of 10/10 clouds [of] . . . about two miles." See Giles to Spaatz, 6 January 1945, File 168.491, vol. 5, HRC.

14. Schmid, "Struggle for Air Supremacy over the Reich"; and "Fighter Narrative of Operations," 3 March 1944.

15. Anderson Diary, entry of 3 March 1944; Schmid, "Struggle for Air Supremacy over the Reich"; and "Report of Operations," 4 March 1944, with annexes, enclosure in O. A. Anderson to Arnold, 1 May 1944, File 520.331, HRC.

16. Encounter report of 1st Lt. Nicolas Megura, 4 March 1944, in March History of 334th Fighter Squadron, File SQ-334-HI(FTR), HRC; "Bomber Narrative of Operations," 4 March 1944; and Schmid, "Struggle for Air Supremacy over the Reich."

17. Schmid, "Struggle for Air Supremacy over the Reich"; and Eighth Air Force, "Report of Operations," 4 March 1944.

18. Hall to Doolittle; and "Fighter Narrative of Operations," 4 March 1944. The 363rd Group historian reported the disappearance of the eleven aircraft as "eight miles off the French coast . . . into cloud bank." See 363rd Fighter Group History, March 1944, GP 363-HI(FTR), HRC.

19. Anderson Diary, entry of 4 March 1944.

20. Walter Grabmann, "German Air Force Defense Operations," 1956, File K113.107-164, HRC.

21. Ibid.; Schmid, "Struggle for Air Supremacy over the Reich"; "Bomber Narrative of Operations," 5 March 1944; and Yeager and Janos, pp. 26ff. Yeager claimed his first German fighter over Berlin on 4 March flying with the 357th Fighter Group. After being shot down, he evaded capture, served

for a time with the French Maquis, made it into Spain, and eventually returned to England. There he rejoined the 357th, became an ace, and soon reached the rank of captain, before returning to the United States and a distinguished career as a test pilot and battery salesman.

22. Ethell and Price, pp. 31–34.

23. "Bomber Narrative of Operations," 6 March 1944; "Fighter Narrative of Operations," 6 March 1944; and Schmid, "Struggle for Air Supremacy over the Reich."

24. Knoke, p. 148; "Fighter Narrative of Operations," 6 March 1944; and Turner, pp. 56–58.

25. "Fighter Narrative of Operations," 6 March 1944; "Bomber Narrative of Operations," 6 March 1944; O. A. Anderson to Arnold, 12 May 1944, File 520.331, HRC; and Ethell and Price, pp. 46, 179–191.

26. "Fighter Narrative of Operations," 6 March 1944; and "Bomber Narrative of Operations," 6 March 1944. Even though the Army Air Forces absorbed the Air Corps in 1942 and the latter no longer existed as an organization, the term *Air Corps* continued to be applied to a number of features of the Army Air Forces, including the song.

27. "Fighter Narrative of Operations," 6 March 1944; "Bomber Narrative of Operations," 6 March 1944; interview of Lt. Gen. Günther Rall by McFarland and Newton, 12 November 1985; "Report of Operations," 6 March 1944; and Ethell and Price, pp. 180, 182, 189.

28. "Fighter Narrative of Operations," 6 March 1944; "Report of Operations," 6 March 1944; and Schmid, "Struggle for Air Supremacy over the Reich."

29. Ethell and Price, without specifically citing their sources, give these figures as 229 killed, 29 wounded, and 411 taken prisoner for the mission of 6 March.

30. "Fighter Narrative of Operations," 6 March 1944; "Bomber Narrative of Operations," 6 March 1944; Ethell and Price, pp. 180–181, 184, 187; and Jarrell, p. 58.

31. Arnold to Spaatz, 7 March 1944, Spaatz Diary, Box 14, Spaatz Papers.

32. Ibid.; weather annex to "Report of Operations," 6 March 1944; Field Order #483, 6 March 1944, File 519.332, HRC; and Ethell and Price, pp. 143–144.

33. "Bomber Narrative of Operations," 6 March 1944; "Report of Operations," 6 March 1944, including tactical mission reports of bomb division commanders; Schmid, "Struggle for Air Supremacy over the Reich"; and Knoke, p. 149.

34. Knoke, pp. 149–150; Ethell and Price, pp. 143–144; and Beck, p. 87.

35. See Appendix; Schmid, "Struggle for Air Supremacy over the Reich"; and Ethell and Price, pp. 179–191, 194–203. Ethell and Price's information is weakened by their failure to cite specifically the source or sources from which their information came. Other sources include Office of Air Force History, *USAF Credits;* "Bomber Narrative of Operations," 6 March 1944; "Fighter Narrative of Operations," 6 March 1944; U.S. Strategic Air Forces in Europe, "The Contribution of Air Power to the Defeat of Germany," 1945, File 519.601C, vol. 4, HRC, based on "Basic Returns of the German Quartermaster Staff"; Historical Section, German Air Force, "European Essays on the History of World War II, 1939–1945," Book 4, "Battle for Air Supremacy over Germany," pp. 115–117, unpublished manuscript, August 1946, Air University Library, Maxwell AFB, Alabama; and "Air Staff Post Hostilities Intelligence Requirements on the German Air Force," File 519.601B-4, Sec. IV I, vol. 2, Appendix 3, HRC.

Probably the best source for German military personnel losses in World War II is the *Deutsche Dienststelle* in Berlin, where records help determine pension claims, but its information is not available to foreigners.

36. "Report of Operations," 6 March 1944; and Schmid, "Struggle for Air Supremacy over the Reich."

37. "Report of Operations," 6 March 1944, Intelligence Annex.

38. Field Order Number 488, Eighth Air Force R-66-E, 8 March 1944, File 519.332, HRC; "Report of Operations," 8 March 1944; O. A. Anderson to Arnold, 12 May 1944, File 520.331, HRC; and Ardery, p. 168.

39. Schmid, "Struggle for Air Supremacy over the Reich."

40. "Report of Operations," 8 March 1944; and "Fighter Narrative of Operations," 8 March 1944.

41. Hall, p. 91; and Bradley interview.

42. Letter to McFarland and Newton from Gerhard Kroll, 13 September 1988, containing Kroll's letter to Jerry Crandall, 19 June 1969, which includes this account of the 8 March 1944 mission.

43. Ardery, pp. 173–174; and Bradley interview.

44. Jarrell, title page; Hall, pp. 124–125, 129–130.

45. "Report of Operations," 8 March 1944; Schmid, "Struggle for Air Supremacy over the Reich"; and Appendix.

46. Anderson Diary, entries of 6 and 8 March 1944.

47. "Report of Operations," 9 March 1944; O. A. Anderson to Arnold, 13 May 1944, File 520.331, 8 March 1944, HRC; "Fighter Narrative of Operations," 9 March 1944; Schmid, "Struggle for Air Supremacy over the Reich"; and Hall to Doolittle.

48. "Fighter Narrative of Operations," 9 March 1944; "Report of Operations," 9 March 1944; and Schmid, "Struggle for Air Supremacy over the Reich."

49. Schmid, "Struggle for Air Supremacy over the Reich," p. 189.

50. Hinsley et al., 3:318.

51. Schmid, "Struggle for Air Supremacy over the Reich."

52. Doolittle to Kepner, 11 March 1944, with commendation, File 544.02, HRC.

53. Spaatz to Arnold, 11 March 1944, Box 14, Spaatz Diary; and Arnold to Spaatz, 24 April 1944 and 10 May 1944, File 168.491, vol. 5, HRC.

54. Schmid, "Struggle for Air Supremacy over the Reich."

55. "Comments and Opinions by High-ranking German Officers and Industrialists," 16 May 1945, File 519.045, HRC; and "The Birth, Life, and Death of the German Day Fighter Arm," 1945, File 168.6005-82, HRC.

56. Ungar to McFarland, 18 October 1988; Kroll to Newton and McFarland, 13 September 1988, with a letter from Kroll to Crandall, 19 June 1969 and chronology of his flying career; and Knoke, pp. 152–158.

57. Richmond to McFarland, 12 November 1988; Hall, pp. 80–81, 85–86, 99–101; and Hall to Doolittle.

58. "Fighter Narrative of Operations," 11, 15, 16, 18, 19, 20, 21, 22, 23, and 29 March 1944; and Schmid, "Struggle for Air Supremacy over the Reich."

59. Grabmann, "German Air Force Defense Operations."

60. Spaatz may have been responsible for the 30-day rest and recuperation idea. As he explained to Arnold, it was a better idea than simply allowing crews or individuals to return to the United States after they finished a tour, "where they lose all sense of identity with a unit . . . I feel most strongly that we will get the maximum total service by returning most of them to their own units after a suitable period of rest and recuperation." See Spaatz to Arnold, 12 April 1944, Folder 226 "Bomber Command—Great Britain," Arnold Papers.

61. "Minutes of Eighth Air Force Commanders' Meeting," 22 March 1944.

62. Giles to Spaatz, 16 March 1944, and Eaker to Arnold, n.d. (March 1944?), File 168.491, vol. 5, HRC. The best scholarly account of the 25 March meeting is Rostow.

63. See Webster and Frankland, vol. 1, pt. 3; and Craven and Cate, vol. 3. McFarland and Newton have authored a chapter on the Army Air Forces in Europe in World War II in a soon-to-be-published anthology on strategic bombing for the Office of Air Force History. This chapter places the transportation and oil campaigns in concise perspective.

64. The material in this and subsequent paragraphs is generally based on McFarland.

65. Ibid., p. 198; and interview of Kepner by Bruce C. Hopper and Charles A. Foster, 15 July 1944, VIII Fighter Command, File 524.0581, HRC.

66. "Fighter Narrative of Operations," 6, 8, 9, 15, 16, 18, 19, 20, 21, 22, 23, 24, 27, 28, and 29 March 1944. The Germans did not rise to challenge the Berlin raid of 22 March, claiming weather prevented any reaction. The Americans, who engaged in widespread strafing that day, contended that the weather was no impediment to flying.

67. Kepner to Kindelberger, 4 April 1944, File 168.6005-3, HRC; and "Fighter Narrative of Operations," 30 March 1944.

68. Anderson to Doolittle, 29 March 1944, File 508.432D, HRC; Hinsley et al., 3:320; and McFarland, pp. 199–200.

69. Arnold to Eisenhower for Spaatz, 7 April 1944, File Operation #135, Box 44, Arnold Papers. In this same file is a message from Arnold to George Marshall, same date, in which Arnold made the same pitch.

70. Giles to Spaatz, 8 April 1944, File 168.491, vol. 5, HRC.

71. Kepner interview, 15 July 1944; Generalleutnant Josef Schmid, "Aerial Warfare over the Reich in Defense of Vital Luftwaffe Installations and Supporting Services, 1 April 1944–D-Day (6 June 1944)," File K113.107-160, HRC; and "Air Staff Post Hostilities Intelligence Requirements," Sec. IV I, vol. 2, Appendix 3.

72. Kepner was apparently referring to the delay in hitting transportation targets in France because of Churchill's fear of the political ramifications of French casualties as a result of bombing and strafing. Roosevelt finally on 11 May backed Eisenhower and Tedder in their desire to attack transportation targets in France and Belgium as well as Germany. That settled the matter. See Rostow, pp. 50–51.

73. Grabmann, "German Air Force Defense Operations"; and Kepner interview, 15 July 1944.

74. Richmond to McFarland, 12 November 1988; and McFarland, p. 199.

75. Grabmann, "German Air Force Defense Operations."

76. McFarland, pp. 202–203; "Fighter Narrative of Operations," 28 May 1944; Kepner interview, 15 July 1944; and Schmid, "Aerial Warfare over the Reich in Defense of Vital Luftwaffe Installations."

77. Schmid, "Aerial Warfare over the Reich in Defense of Vital Luftwaffe Installations."

78. McFarland, p. 201.

Epilogue

1. Quoted in Ferguson, "Big Week," in Craven and Cate, 3:56.

2. Hansell to Giles, 9 April 1944, File 168.161-2, January-June 1944, HRC. Hansell summarized the major air components of the OVERLORD plan in this detailed letter.

3. Walter Grabmann, "German Air Force Defense Operations," 1956, File K113.107-164, HRC; Galland, *First and the Last*, pp. 270–271; and "Historical Study of Air Support by the Eighth Air Force for the Land Invasion of Europe," 2–16 June 1944, File 168.6005-72, HRC.

4. Galland, *First and the Last*, p. 271; and "Interrogations of General Christian and Oberst Grieff, GAF Operations Staff," File 519.601B-4, Sec. IVA, pt. 6, HRC.

5. Galland, *First and the Last*, p. 274.

6. Interview of Kepner by Bruce C. Hopper and Charles A. Foster, 15 July 1944, VIII Fighter Command, File 524.0581, HRC.

7. Galland, *First and the Last*, p. 271; "Air Operations Over the Invasion Front in June 1944," 8th Abteilung, 27 August 1944, translated by A.H.B. 6, Air Ministry, 24 June 1947, File 512.612 VII/32, HRC; "The Birth, Life, and Death of the German Day Fighter Arm," 1945, File 168.6005-82, HRC; and "ULTRA: History of U.S. Strategic Air Force Europe vs. German Air Force," June 1945, pp. 201–202, Special Research History Number 13 (SRH-013), National Security Council, RG457, National Archives.

8. Galland, *First and the Last*, pp. 279, 292–293; and "ULTRA," p. 205.

9. Grabmann, "German Air Force Defense Operations." The authors have a chapter on strategic bombing by the Army Air Forces in Europe during World War II in a forthcoming anthology on the history of strategic bombing to be published by the Office of Air Force History, in which they describe the post-OVERLORD operations.

10. Extract from Cable No. FWD 13657, 3 September 1944, Eisenhower to Arnold, File 519.553-2, HRC.

11. The source for these statistics is Freeman, *Mighty Eighth War Diary*.

12. Maurer Maurer, *Air Force Combat Units of World War II* (Washington, D.C.: Office of Air Force History, 1981), pp. 35, 68–69, 119, 231–32, 234–36, and 239. The DUC to the 357th Group was in part awarded for a mission in June 1944.

13. Generalleutnant Andreas Nielsen, supplemented and completed by Generalmajor Walter Grabmann, "Anglo-American Techniques of Strategic Warfare in the Air," 1957, File K113.107-183, HRC; Ferguson, "Winter Bombing," in Craven and Cate, 3:11; Paul F. Henry, "William E. Kepner: All the Way to Berlin," in Frisbee, p. 169; and Kepner interview, 15 July 1944.

14. Jarrell, p. 15.

BIBLIOGRAPHIC ESSAY

The primary sources for the peacetime and wartime history of the United States Air Force and its predecessors lie mainly in the U.S. Air Force Historical Research Center at Maxwell Air Force Base, Montgomery, Alabama. This site is historic in its own right, as scene of a Wright Brothers flying school and, in the 1930s, as the location of the Air Corps Tactical School, where the strategic offensive doctrine employed by the U.S. Army Air Forces was developed. The richness of these sources for both military and civil flight is quickly apparent when one takes the time to examine the Center's index files. For the American part of this study, for example, the authors were for a time overwhelmed with reports, memos, letters, orders, specialized studies, and files of the Air Staff, U.S. Strategic Air Forces in Europe, Eighth Air Force, Fifteenth Air Force, Ninth Air Force, and subordinate commands such as VIII Bomber Command and VIII Fighter Command. The Arnold Operational Letters—communications between the Air Staff in Washington and senior commanders of the numbered combat air forces in the field, such as the Eighth—are a treasure trove of personal and organizational information, and part of this collection, apparently, is not found elsewhere.

While the monthly unit histories of squadrons and groups vary in content and value and are often thin and pedestrian, they contain nuggets of useful information for the persistent miner. The narratives and supporting documents, such as mission and encounter reports, base histories, and aerial victory claim statements, often provide revealing vignettes and can add color and immediacy to an account of operations. Scholars have neglected them. While the papers of major commanders of the American forces that operated over Europe are found elsewhere than the Historical Research Center, there are exceptions. At the Center, for example, are the correspondence and other papers of William E. Kepner, who commanded VIII Fighter Command when its men and planes played the lead parts in the drama of the struggle for air superiority.

To be found at the Center are a number of oral history interviews, part of a continuing program centered at Maxwell to encapsulate the reflections of the famous and a few of the ordinary who served with the U.S. Air Force and its predecessors in and between the wars of the twentieth century. Some of these have restrictions for the average researcher; some have none. Many contain historical detail and the subject's perspectives that may not be available elsewhere. For this study, for example, a postwar oral history interview with Barney M. Giles, who was chief of the Air Staff in those crucial and climactic months before OVERLORD, shed light on the controversial changes of command in Army Air Forces leadership in Europe in December 1943. It helped to clarify these changes and relate their effectiveness to the great air battles soon to follow in 1944. The authors discovered in the Center's files documents concerning the participation in these battles of the Women's Army Corps personnel assigned to U.S. Strategic Air Forces in Europe and some of its subordinate commands. These women did not fly in the bombers or fighters, but like male support personnel they contributed in significant ways to the prime American mission—the winning of air superiority. Their efforts are worth much more than the few paragraphs the authors have allotted them. Scholars must now examine in detail their contribution.

The authors intended this book to reflect both German and American perspectives and experience. They might not have undertaken it had it not been for the existence of a corpus of studies and supporting documents on the Luftwaffe's prewar and wartime experiences written by various senior Luftwaffe commanders and staff officers. Called the Karlsruhe Collection, after the city where the writers and translators assembled, it is one of the Historical Research Center's most important and neglected collections. The studies, a few of which have been published, are in German and English; the supporting documents have not been translated into English. These are not loose and incomplete records captured from the Germans, but detailed accounts based on personal recollections and on Luftwaffe records that survived the war. Among these studies, for example, is a comprehensive examination of German flight training from the "camouflaged" efforts of the Weimar era through the prewar and wartime training of the Luftwaffe. This study, with its supporting documents, is stark in its revelations of the incredible failures of that training, which contributed to the downfall of an elite force, once considered the world's finest. In contrast, the historical records of Army Air Forces training at the Historical Research Center reveal a fairly consistent improvement in the face of the problems of a mushrooming force. These records include studies undertaken by the various training commands and training bases, with statistical analyses and other supporting documents. Aside from the three-decade-old section in volume 6 of the official history, *The Army Air Forces in World War II*, at the time of this writing no scholarly study focusing on training has yet to appear. However, Dominick Pisano's soon-to-be-published history will fill this vacuum.

The Karlsruhe Collection includes some revealing moments in which Luftwaffe brass reacted to one another and to crises, such as the campaign for control of German skies that had come to be waged over the sacred soil of the Reich itself and finally over the capital. But the authors did not have to rely for the big picture and its component parts solely on the Karlsruhe Collection. Another critical source stemming from captured German records and prisoner-of-war interrogations was a study of the Luftwaffe ordered by the Army Air Forces' Air Staff in 1945 to examine operations, training, supply, personnel, and doctrine. The latter aspect proved especially enlightening. Like the Karlsruhe Collection, the Air Staff study contains thousands of pages of text and supporting documents. The holdings of the Historical Research Center have been microfilmed and the Office of Air Force History at Bolling Air Force Base maintains copies of these microfilms, but they are solely for the use of its staff.

The papers of three of the most influential American commanders in the campaign for air superiority are to be found in the Manuscript Division of the Library of Congress in Washington. The well-arranged papers of Henry H. Arnold, Ira C. Eaker, and Carl A. Spaatz, it almost goes without saying, are indispensable to any study of Army Air Forces operations. Yet for all their usefulness, they have to be supplemented from other sources in the case of several important episodes, such as the 1943 change-of-command controversy and disagreements over implementation of ARGUMENT and the Berlin "Verdun" strategy in 1944. The bulk of James H. "Jimmy" Doolittle's papers was not available to the authors during preparation of this book. Essential documentation concerning General Doolittle, however, was found in the Arnold Operational Letters, minutes of Eighth Air Force staff meetings, and the testimony of contemporaries during European operations—found at the Historical Research Center or in the papers of such luminaries as General Spaatz and the war diary of Frederick L. Anderson, who commanded the VIII Bomber Command in 1943 and then the operations of the U.S. Strategic Air Forces in Europe. Anderson's papers are at the Hoover Institute, Stanford University.

Autobiographies and memoirs by the key American and German figures in the campaign for air superiority are few, strangely so in the American case. Spaatz, Eaker, Giles, Kepner, and Anderson did not leave them, for whatever reasons. Doolittle, the only surviving American commander upon whom this book focuses, is currently working on his autobiography. In terms of biographies, the American commanders have thus far been poorly served by scholars. The biography of Arnold by Thomas M. Coffey, as well as his biography of Curtis LeMay, the biography of Spaatz by David R. Mets, the biography of Doolittle by Lowell Thomas and Edward Jablonski, and the biography of Eaker by James Parton are useful in presenting the basic facts of their careers and some insights into their personalities, but they are not critical, in-depth studies of these most influential airmen. They seem to have as their basic motivation the glorification of their subjects, whatever documentation undergirds each book. The same can be said for Dewitt S. Copp's two studies of various of these figures. The closest to a scholarly biography of any of them is Richard Greene Davis's soon-to-be published book on Spaatz (by the Office of Air Force History), a critical and scholarly work. While concentrating on Spaatz's World War II career, it also examines to some extent his early life and pre–World War II career. The only current full-scale critical, scholarly biographies of Olympian U.S. Army Air Forces figures are Martha Byrd's study of Claire L. Chennault, which was of fringe aid to the authors' book and Phillip S. Meilinger's work on Hoyt S. Vandenberg. On the German side, the wartime deaths of Ernst Udet and Hans Jeschonnek and the postwar suicide of Hermann Göring to escape the sentence of death imposed at Nuremberg precluded any memoir in these cases. Josef Kammhuber survived the war and was one of the architects of the West German air force, but wrote no memoir. Erhard Milch survived a Nuremberg-imposed jail sentence and his testimony at the trial supplied data for the Karlsruhe Collection, but he too left no memoir. Josef Schmid, commander of the main air defense tactical force against daylight attacks in 1943 and 1944—I Fighter Corps—wrote a monograph for the Karlsruhe Collection on that air defense based on his memory and the war diary of I Fighter Corps, but wrote no memoir. The most celebrated and indeed the most useful postwar German memoir of the air war by a high-ranking official was that of Adolf Galland, in its German and somewhat truncated English versions. His interrogations as a prisoner of war and other writings add to the body of information from a very important German perspective. There are a number of biographies of Hermann Göring. By far the most scholarly and the best is R. J. Overy's work. He puts the "Iron Man" in the context of the complicated developments of a Luftwaffe beset by increasing problems, not the least of which had resulted from Göring's own incompetency and his romantic World War I notions of how the Luftwaffe should have functioned. Milch is the subject of a biography by David J. C. Irving that examines the erratic course of the Luftwaffe from the standpoint of a more competent staff officer, Erhard Milch, if a man with his own set of flaws. Yet to appear are equally valuable biographies of other of the Luftwaffe's highest ranking officers.

Post-battle histories of American fighter and bomber groups that took part in the battles for air superiority over Europe are fairly numerous and growing. They add some nuances and drama to the general saga of these battles, but often are pedestrian and formularized, written by amateurs, some of whom were assigned the duty. Now and then someone with talent wrote one, such as the classic *1,000 Destroyed* by the journalist-turned-intelligence-officer Grover C. Hall, Jr., of the 4th Fighter Group, most valuable for its lively characterization of Army Air Forces fighter pilots. An example of a superior "amateur" history of a heavy bombardment group that flew in some of the battles for the sky over Europe is Allan Healy's chronicle of the 467th B-24 Group. On the German side there is a dearth of such histories, largely because of the destruction of many of the records of Luftwaffe tactical groups and the lack of an immediate late war or postwar impetus to write unit histories, in contrast to the American itch. Histories of both German and American tactical units are underway, researched and written by professional historians with a zest for the job. A recently completed example is the history of the 303rd B-17 Group of the Eighth Air Force by Kenneth P. Werrell, a leading scholar of air power.

Memoirs of American pilots and bomber crew members, particularly pilots, who flew from England and Italy in the campaign for air superiority, abound. They vary widely in historical value. The fighter contingent is well represented by the memoirs of Richard Turner and Charles "Chuck" Yeager, both of whom flew in the decisive battles over Berlin of early March 1944. The bomber crews have two outstanding examples of the genre, one by Philip Ardery, a B-24 pilot who flew with the Eighth Air Force, and by John Muirhead, a B-17 pilot who served with the Fifteenth Air Force. The latter's is the most literate memoir of all, with the same combination of realism and poetic sensitivity as found in the poetry of Randall Jarrell, who served only in the stateside Army Air Forces, but whose "Death of the Ball Turret Gunner" is one of the most celebrated and anthologized of all American war poems. German memoirs, again, are fewer in number. A classic memoir, often cited by historians of the air war, is Heinz Knoke's, valuable not only for its account of operations, but also for its reactions of an individual to Luftwaffe training. Knoke gave and received blows in the battles of "Big Week" and Berlin. The authors of this book interviewed or exchanged correspondence with several surviving German and American veterans of the battles for air superiority. They all contributed to this book as they contributed their courage, in some cases their freedom, and sometimes their blood to those mighty endeavors.

Specialized monographs or histories of subjects that form the background of the air war in Europe and particularly the campaign of 1943–1944 for air superiority are numerous, both from scholars and popularizers and some in between. If all books but two on the air war of World War I were to vanish, those two remaining would give the reader a clear picture of the aerial aspect. By scholars, one of these is Richard P. Hallion's *Rise of the Fighter* and the other Lee Kennett's *A History of Strategic Bombing*. The best history of the Luftwaffe, among several fine ones, is Williamson Murray's *Luftwaffe*. Odds on the definitive history of the U.S. Army's air arm between the world wars is Maurer Maurer's *Aviation in the United States Army, 1919-1939*, by one of the senior and most knowledgeable scholars on the history of Army flight. His long-time colleague and equally knowledgeable scholar, Robert Frank Futrell, has the definitive work on the evolution of air doctrine in the U.S. Air Force and its predecessors, *Ideas, Concepts, Doctrine*. Participant and historian Haywood S. Hansell, Jr., has given an insider's perspective on the development of doctrine at the Air Corps Tactical School in the 1930s, the development of war plans based on that doctrine, and the implementation of that doctrine, in several books. No first class scholarly history of the Eighth Air Force has yet appeared, or of the Fifteenth for that matter, so in the meantime the encyclopedic and anecdotal works of Roger A. Freeman on the former must fill the vacuum until either the scholarly study of Kenneth Werrell or of another scholar sees the light of print some day. There is no critical, in-depth history of "Big Week," but participant and historian Glenn Infield has a useful popular book on the subject. The popular historians Jeffrey Ethell and Alfred Price have a critical, in-depth book on the daylight mission of 6 March against Berlin that scholars will find hard to improve on. There is little else, popular or scholarly, on the climactic Berlin missions of 6, 8, and 9 March. The thorough examination of the moral issue of strategic bombing in books by Ronald Schaffer and Michael S. Sherry have been and will be challenged, but will not be superseded. As both summations and analyses, anthologies on air superiority and strategic bombing from the Office of Air Force History will add depth to the knowledge of these subjects.

The official U.S. Air Force seven-volume history of the U.S. Army Air Forces in World War II remains the starting point for any specialized study of the United States in the air war. It is, however, aging, having been 30 years since the last volume was published. The official history requires revision and updating. Essential to any specialized study of strategic bombing by the Army Air Forces in World War II are the various reports of the U.S. Strategic Bombing Survey. Its examination of the European situation seems to bear out the authors' theme of the overriding importance of the possession of air superiority. David MacIsaac's scholarly monograph on the history of the Survey must be read in conjunction with its reports.

SELECTED BIBLIOGRAPHY

Andrews, Allen. *The Air Marshals: The Air War in Western Europe.* New York: William Morrow, 1970.

Ardery, Philip. *Bomber Pilot: A Memoir of World War II.* Lexington: University Press of Kentucky, 1978.

Arnold, H. H. *Global Mission.* New York: Harper, 1949.

Arnold, H. H., and Eaker, Ira C. *Army Flier.* New York: Harper, 1942.

————. *This Flying Game.* New York: Funk and Wagnalls, 1938.

————. *Winged Warfare.* New York: Harper, 1941.

Atkinson, J. L. Boone. "Italian Influence on the Origins of the American Concept of Strategic Bombardment," *Air Power Historian* 4 (July 1957): 141–149.

Ayling, Keith. *Bombardment Aviation.* Harrisburg, Pa.: Military Service Publishing Co., 1944.

Bailey, Ronald H. *The Air War in Europe.* Alexandria, Va.: Time-Life Books, 1979.

Bartz, Karl. *Swastika in the Air: The Struggle and Defeat of the German Air Force, 1939–1945.* Trans. Edward Fitzgerald. London: Kimber, 1956.

Baumbach, Werner. *The Life and Death of the Luftwaffe.* New York: Coward-McCann, 1960.

Beck, Earl R. *Under the Bombs: The German Home Front, 1942–1945.* Lexington: University Press of Kentucky, 1986.

Bendiner, Elmer. *The Fall of Fortresses: A Personal Account of the Most Daring and Deadly Air Battles of World War II.* New York: Putnam's, 1980.

Berenbrok, H. D. [Cajus Bekker]. *The Luftwaffe War Diaries*. Trans. Frank Ziegler. New York: Ballantine, 1966.

Bilstein, Roger E. *Flight in America, 1900–1983: From the Wrights to the Astronauts*. Baltimore: Johns Hopkins University Press, 1984.

Bishop, Cliff T. *Fortresses of the Big Triangle First: A History of the Aircraft Assigned to the First Bombardment Wing and First Bombardment Division of the Eighth Air Force from August 1942 to 31st March 1944*. Bishops Stortford, Eng.: East Anglia, 1986.

Blanco, Richard L. *The Luftwaffe in World War II: The Rise and Decline of the German Air Force*. New York: Messner, 1987.

Bledsoe, Marvin V. *Thunderbolt: Memoirs of a World War II Fighter Pilot*. New York: Van Nostrand Reinhold, 1982.

Bove, Arthur P. *First Over Germany: A Story of the 306th Bombardment Group*. San Angelo, Tex.: Newsfoto, 1946.

Bowman, Martin W. *Castles in the Air: The Story of the B-17 Flying Fortress Crews of the U.S. 8th Air Force*. Wellingborough, England: Patrick Stephens, 1984.

Bowyer, Chaz. *Guns in the Sky: The Air Gunners of World War Two*. New York: Scribner's, 1979.

Boylan, Bernard. *Development of the Long-Range Escort Fighter*. Maxwell AFB, Ala.: USAF Historical Studies, 1955.

Boyle, Andrew. *Trenchard: Man of Vision*. London: Collins, 1962.

Brereton, Lewis H. *The Brereton Diaries*. New York: William Morrow, 1946.

Brodie, Bernard. "The Heritage of Douhet." *Air University Quarterly Review* 7 (Summer 1953): 147–159.

Bullock, Alan. *Hitler: A Study in Tyranny*, abridged ed. New York: Harper and Row, 1971.

Byrd, Martha. *Chennault: Giving Wings to the Tiger*. Tuscaloosa: University of Alabama Press, 1987.

Callender, Alvin Andrew. *War in an Open Cockpit*. West Roxbury, Mass.: World War I Aero Publishers, 1978.

Chamberlain, Peter, and Gander, Terry. *Anti-Aircraft Guns*. New York: Arco, 1975.

Chennault, Claire L. *Way of a Fighter: The Memoirs of General Claire Lee Chennault*. New York: Putnam, 1949.

Christy, Joe. *P-38 Lightning at War*. New York: Scribner's, 1978.

Churchill, Winston S. *The Hinge of Fate*. Boston: Houghton Mifflin, 1950.

Clayton, Aileen. *The Enemy Is Listening*. London: Hutchinson, 1980.

Coffey, Thomas M. *Decision over Schweinfurt: The U.S. 8th Air Force Battle for Daylight Bombing*. New York: McKay, 1977.

———. *HAP: The Story of the U.S. Air Force and the Man Who Built It, General Henry H. "Hap" Arnold*. New York: Viking, 1982.

——. *Iron Eagle: The Turbulent Life of General Curtis LeMay.* New York: Crown, 1986.

Colby, C. B. *Headlines in Bomber Plane History.* New York: Coward-McCann, 1960.

Comer, John. *Combat Crew: A True Story of Flying and Fighting in World War II.* New York: William Morrow, 1988.

Cooper, Matthew. *The German Air Force, 1933–1945: An Anatomy of Failure.* London: Jane's, 1981.

Copp, Dewitt S. *Forged in Fire: Strategy and Decisions in the Air War over Europe, 1940–1945.* Garden City, N.Y.: Doubleday, 1982.

Crabtree, Stephen. "The Luftwaffe and the Defense of Germany: The Development and Deployment of the German Air Defense Fighter Forces in the Second World War." M.A. Thesis, Southern Illinois University, 1972.

Craven, Wesley Frank, and Cate, James Lea, eds. *The Army Air Forces in World War II.* Vol. 1, *Plans and Early Operations, January 1939-August 1942.* Chicago: University of Chicago Press, 1948.

——. *The Army Air Forces in World War II.* Vol. 2, *Europe: TORCH to POINTBLANK, August 1942 to December 1943.* Chicago: University of Chicago Press, 1949.

——. *The Army Air Forces in World War II.* Vol. 3, *Europe: Argument to V-E Day, January 1944 to May 1945.* Chicago: University of Chicago Press, 1951.

——. *The Army Air Forces in World War II.* Vol. 6, *Men and Planes.* Chicago: University of Chicago Press, 1951.

Cuneo, John. *Winged Mars.* Vol. 1, *The German Air Weapon, 1870–1914.* Harrisburg, Pa.: Military Service Publishing, 1942.

——. *Winged Mars.* Vol. 2, *The Air Weapon, 1914–1916.* Harrisburg, Pa.: Military Service Publishing, 1947.

Davis, Albert H., et al., eds. *The 56th Fighter Group in World War II.* Washington, D.C.: Infantry Journal Press, 1948.

Davis, Richard Greene. *The Bomber Baron: Carl Andrew Spaatz and the Army Air Forces in Europe, 1942–1945.* Washington, D.C.: Office of Air Force History, forthcoming.

De Seversky, Alexander P. *Victory through Air Power.* New York: Simon and Schuster, 1942.

Doolittle, Jimmy, with Beirne Lay, Jr. "Daylight Precision Bombing." *Impact*, Book 6, *Bombing Night and Day: The Two-Edged Sword.* New York: James Parton, 1980.

Douhet, Giulio. *The Command of the Air.* Ed. Richard H. Kohn and Joseph P. Harahan, trans. Dino Ferrari. Washington, D.C.: Office of Air Force History, 1983; reprint of 1942 edition.

Drake, Francis Vivian. *Vertical Warfare.* Garden City, N.Y.: Doubleday, 1943.

Dubuque, Jean H., and Gleckner, Robert F. *The Development of the Heavy Bomber, 1918–1944.* Maxwell AFB, Ala.: USAF Historical Studies, 1951.

Dunn, William R. *Fighter Pilot: The First American Ace of World War II.* Lexington: University Press of Kentucky, 1982.

Eisenhower, Dwight D. *Crusade in Europe.* Garden City, N.Y.: Doubleday, 1948.

Emerson, William Richard. *Operation Pointblank: A Tale of Bombers and Fighters.* Colorado Springs, Colo.: U.S. Air Force Academy, 1962.

Ethell, Jeffrey, and Price, Alfred. *Target Berlin: Mission 250, 6 March 1944.* London: Jane's, 1981.

Faber, Harold, ed. *Luftwaffe: A History.* New York: Times Books, 1977.

Finney, Robert T. *History of the Air Corps Tactical School, 1920–1940.* Maxwell AFB, Ala.: USAF Historical Studies, 1955.

Fletcher, Eugene. *Fletcher's Gang: A B-17 Crew in Europe, 1944–45.* Seattle: University of Washington Press, 1988.

Flugel, Raymond R. "United States Air Doctrine: A Study of the Influence of William Mitchell and Giulio Douhet at the Air Corps Tactical School, 1921–1935." Ph.D. diss., University of Oklahoma, 1965.

Frankland, Noble. *The Bombing Offensive against Germany: Outlines and Perspectives.* London: Faber and Faber, 1965.

Fredette, Raymond H. *The Sky on Fire: The First Battle of Britain, 1917–1918, and the Birth of the Royal Air Force.* New York: Holt, Rinehart and Winston, 1966.

Freeman, Roger A. *The Mighty Eighth: Units, Men and Machines. A History of the U.S. 8th Air Force.* London: Jane's, 1986.

———. *Mighty Eighth War Diary.* London: Jane's, 1981.

———. *Mustang at War.* Garden City, N.Y.: Doubleday, 1974.

Frisbee, John L., ed. *Makers of the United States Air Force.* Washington, D.C.: Office of Air Force History, 1987.

Futrell, Robert Frank. *Ideas, Concepts, Doctrine: A History of Basic Thinking in the United States Air Force, 1907–1964.* 2 vols. Maxwell AFB, Ala.: Air University Aerospace Studies Institute, 1971.

Galland, Adolf. "Defeat of the Luftwaffe: Fundamental Causes." *Air University Quarterly Review* 6 (Spring 1953): 16–36.

———. *Die Ersten und die Letzen: Die Jagdflieger im zweiten Weltkrieg.* Darmstadt: F. Schneekluth, 1953.

———. *The First and the Last: The Rise and Fall of the German Fighter Forces, 1938–1945.* New York: Henry Holt, 1954.

————. *The Luftwaffe at War, 1939–1945*. Trans. D. Dunbar and I. Dunbar. Chicago: Regnery, 1972.

Girbig, Werner. *Six Months to Oblivion: The Eclipse of the Luftwaffe*. Trans. Richard Simpkin. London: Ian Allan, 1973.

Goodson, James A. *Tumult in the Clouds*. New York: St. Martin's, 1983.

Goralski, Robert, and Freeburg, Russell W. *Oil and War: How the Deadly Struggle for Fuel in World War II Meant Victory or Defeat*. New York: William Morrow, 1987.

Greenfield, Kent Roberts, ed. *Command Decisions*. New York: Harcourt, Brace, and Co., 1959.

Greer, Thomas H. *The Development of Air Doctrine in the Army Air Arm, 1917–1941*. Washington, D.C.: Office of Air Force History, 1985; reprint of USAF Historical Study No. 89, 1955.

Gurney, Gene. *The War in the Air: A Pictorial History of World War II Air Forces in Combat*. New York: Crown, 1962.

Hall, Grover C. *1000 Destroyed: The Life and Times of the 4th Fighter Group*. Montgomery, Ala.: Brown Publishing, 1946.

Hallion, Richard P. *Rise of the Fighter Aircraft, 1914–1918: Air Combat in World War I*. Annapolis, Md.: Nautical and Aviation Publishing Co., 1984.

Hansell, Haywood S., Jr. *The Air Plan that Defeated Hitler*. Atlanta: Higgins-McArthur/Logino and Porter, 1972.

————. *The Strategic Air War against Germany and Japan*. Washington, D.C.: Office of Air Force History, 1986.

Harris, Arthur T. *Bomber Offensive*. New York: Macmillan, 1947.

Hawkins, Ian. *Munster: The Way It Was*. Anaheim, Calif.: Robinson Typographics, 1984.

Healy, Allan. *The 467th Bombardment Group: September 1943-June 1945* (privately printed in 1947).

Heflin, Woodrow Agee, ed. *The United States Air Force Dictionary*. Maxwell AFB, Ala.: Air University Press, 1956.

Hess, William N. *P-47 Thunderbolt at War*. Garden City, N.Y.: Doubleday, 1977.

Higham, Robin. *Air Power: A Concise History*. New York: St. Martin's, 1972.

Hinsley, F. H., et al. *British Intelligence in the Second World War: Its Influence on Strategy and Operations*. 3 vols. New York: Cambridge University Press, 1979–1988.

Hudson, James J. *Hostile Skies: A Combat History of the American Air Service in World War I*. Syracuse, N.Y.: Syracuse University Press, 1968.

Hurley, Alfred F. *Billy Mitchell: Crusader for Air Power*. New York: Franklin Watts, 1964.

The Illustrated Encyclopedia of Twentieth-Century Weapons and Warfare. 24 vols. New York: Columbia House, 1978.

Infield, Glenn, *Big Week: The U.S. Air Force vs. the Luftwaffe.* New York: Pinnacle Books, 1974.

Irving, David John Cawdell. *The Rise and Fall of the Luftwaffe: The Life of Field Marshal Erhard Milch.* Boston: Little, Brown, 1973.

Jablonski, Edward. *Airwar.* Garden City, N.Y.: Doubleday, 1971.

———. *Flying Fortress.* Garden City, N.Y.: Doubleday, 1965.

Jackson, Robert. *Fighter: The Story of Air Combat, 1936–45.* New York: St. Martin's, 1980.

———. *Fighter Pilots of World War II.* New York: St. Martin's, 1976.

Jacobs, W. A. "Strategic Bombing and American National Strategy, 1941–1943." *Military Affairs* 50 (July 1986): 133–139.

Jarrell, Randall. *Little Friend, Little Friend.* New York: Dial, 1945.

Johnson, Robert S. *Thunderbolt.* New York: Rinehart, 1958.

Jones, H. A. *The War in the Air.* Oxford: Clarendon, 1937.

Kelsey, Benjamin S. *The Dragon's Teeth?: The Creation of United States Air Power for World War II.* Washington, D.C.: Smithsonian Institute Press, 1982.

Kennett, Lee. *A History of Strategic Bombing.* New York: Scribner's, 1982.

Killen, John. *The Luftwaffe: A History.* London: Muller, 1967.

Knoke, Heinz. *I Flew for the Führer: The Story of a German Airman.* London: Evans Brothers, 1953.

Koch, Horst-Adalbert. *Flak: Die Geschichte der Deutschen Flakartillerie, 1935–1945.* Bad Nauheim, West Germany: H. H. Podzun, 1954.

Kohn, Richard H., and Harahan, Joseph P., eds. *Air Interdiction in World War II, Korea, and Vietnam: An Interview with Earle E. Partridge, Jacob E. Smart, and John W. Vogt, Jr.* Washington, D.C.: Office of Air Force History, 1986.

———, eds. *Air Superiority in World War II and Korea: An Interview with Gen. James Ferguson, Gen. Robert M. Lee, Gen. William Momyer, and Lt. Gen. Elwood R. Quesada.* Washington, D.C.: Office of Air Force History, 1983.

———, eds. *Strategic Air Warfare: An Interview with Generals Curtis E. LeMay, Leon W. Johnson, David A. Burchinal, and Jack J. Catton.* Washington, D.C.: Office of Air Force History, 1988.

Kurowski, Franz. *Der Luftkrieg über Deutschland.* Düsseldorf: Econ-Verlag, 1977.

Lee, Asher. *The German Air Force.* London: Duckworth, 1946.

LeMay, Curtis. *Mission with LeMay.* Garden City, N.Y.: Doubleday, 1965.

Loomis, Robert D. *Great American Fighter Pilots of World War II.* New York: Random House, 1961.

Lucas, Laddie, ed. *Wings of War: Airmen of All Nations Tell Their Stories, 1939–1945*. New York: Macmillan, 1983.

McCrary, John R., and Scherman, David E. *The First of the Many: A Journal of Action with the Men of the Eighth Air Force*. London: Robson Books, 1981; reprint of 1944 edition.

McFarland, Stephen L. "The Evolution of the American Strategic Fighter in Europe, 1942–1944." *Journal of Strategic Studies* 10 (June 1987): 198–208.

MacIsaac, David. *Strategic Bombing in World War Two: The Story of the United States Strategic Bombing Survey*. New York: Garland, 1976.

Maurer, Maurer. *Aviation in the United States Army, 1919–1939*. Washington, D.C.: Office of Air Force History, 1987.

———, ed. *The U.S. Air Service in World War I*. 4 vols. Washington, D.C.: GPO, 1978–1979.

Meilinger, Phillip S. *Hoyt S. Vandenberg: The Life of a General*. Bloomington: Indiana University Press, 1989.

Mets, David R. *Master of Airpower: General Carl A. Spaatz*. Novato, Calif.: Presidio Press, 1988.

Michie, Allan Andrew. *The Air Offensive against Germany*. New York: Holt, 1943.

Middlebrook, Martin. *The Schweinfurt-Regensburg Mission*. New York: Scribner's, 1983.

Mitcham, Samuel W. *Men of the Luftwaffe*. Novato, Calif.: Presidio, 1988.

Morrison, Wilbur H. *Fortress without a Roof: The Allied Bombing of the Third Reich*. New York: St. Martin's, 1982.

———. *The Incredible 305th: The "Can Do" Bombers of World War II*. New York: Duell, Sloan, and Pearce, 1962.

Morrow, John H. *German Airpower in World War I*. Lincoln: University of Nebraska Press, 1982.

Muirhead, John. *Those Who Fall*. New York: Random House, 1986.

Murray, Williamson. *Luftwaffe*. Baltimore: Nautical and Aviation Publishing Co., 1985.

Nalty, Bernard C., and Berger, Carl. *The Men Who Bombed the Reich*. New York: Elsevier-Dutton, 1978.

Nielsen, Generalleutnant Andreas. *The German Air Force General Staff*. Maxwell AFB, Ala.: USAF Historical Studies, 1959.

Obermaier, Ernst. *Die Ritterkreuzträger der Luftwaffe*. 2 vols. Mainz: Hoffmann, 1966.

Office of Air Force History. *USAF Credits for the Destruction of Enemy Aircraft, World War II*. USAF Historical Study No. 85. Maxwell AFB, Ala.: Office of Air Force History, 1978.

Overy, R. J. *The Air War, 1939–1945*. New York: Stein and Day, 1980.

——. *Goering, the "Iron Man."* London: Routledge and Kegan Paul, 1984.

Parrish, Thomas, ed. *The Simon and Schuster Encyclopedia of World War II.* New York: Simon and Schuster, 1978.

Parton, James. *"Air Force Spoken Here": General Ira Eaker and the Command of the Air.* Bethesda, Md.: Adler and Adler, 1986.

Peaslee, Budd J. *Heritage of Valor: The Eighth Air Force in World War II.* Philadelphia: Lippincott, 1964.

Piekalkiewicz, Janusz. *The Air War, 1939–1945.* Trans. Jan van Heurck. Harrisburg, Pa.: Historical Times, 1985.

Price, Alfred. *Battle over the Reich.* New York: Scribner's, 1974.

——. *Luftwaffe Handbook, 1939–1945.* New York: Scribner's, 1977.

Rostow, W. W. *Pre-Invasion Bombing Strategy: General Eisenhower's Decision of March 25, 1944.* Austin: University of Texas Press, 1981.

Rumpf, Hans. *The Bombing of Germany.* Trans. Edward Fitzgerald. New York: Holt, Rinehart, and Winston, 1962.

Rust, Kenn C. *Eighth Air Force Story.* Temple City, Calif.: Historical Aviation Album, 1978.

Saundby, Sir Robert H.M.S. *Air Bombardment: The Story of Its Development.* New York: Harper, 1961.

Saward, Dudley. *Victory Denied: The Rise of Air Power and the Defeat of Germany, 1920–1945.* New York: Watts, 1987.

Schaffer, Ronald. "American Military Ethics in World War II: The Bombing of German Civilians." *Journal of American History* 67 (September 1980): 318–334.

——. *Wings of Judgment: American Bombing in World War II.* New York: Oxford University Press, 1985.

Schlaifer, Robert, and Heron, S. D. *Development of Aircraft Engines and Fuels.* Boston: Harvard University Graduate School of Business Administration, 1950.

Sherman, William C. *Air Warfare.* New York: Ronald Press, 1926.

Sherry, Michael S. *The Rise of American Air Power: The Creation of Armageddon.* New Haven: Yale University Press, 1987.

Shores, Christopher F. *Duel for the Sky.* Garden City, N.Y.: Doubleday, 1985.

Sims, Edward H. *American Aces in Great Fighter Battles of World War II.* New York: Harper, 1958.

Speer, Albert. *Infiltrations.* Trans. Joachim Neugroschel. New York: Macmillan, 1981.

——. *Inside the Third Reich.* Trans. Richard and Clara Winston. New York: Macmillan, 1970.

Spick, Mike. *Fighter Pilot Tactics: The Techniques of Daylight Air Combat.* New York: Stein and Day, 1983.

Stafford, Gene B. *P-38 Lightning in Action*. Warren, Mich.: Squadron/Signal Publications, 1976.

Stokesbury, James L. *A Short History of Air Power*. New York: William Morrow, 1986.

Strickland, Patricia. *The Putt-Putt Air Force*. Washington, D.C.: GPO, 1975.

Suchenwirth, Richard. *Command and Leadership in the German Air Force*. Maxwell AFB, Ala.: USAF Historical Studies, 1969.

Taylor, John. *A History of Aerial Warfare*. London: Hamlyn, 1974.

Terraine, John. "The RAF in WWII: Lessons for Today?" *Journal of the Royal United Services Institute for Defence Studies* 130 (December 1985): 10–14.

Thomas, Lowell, and Jablonski, Edward. *Doolittle*. New York: Da Capo, 1982.

Thompson, Robert. *The Royal Flying Corps*. London: Hamish, 1968.

Time-Life Books, eds. *The Luftwaffe*. Alexandria, Va.: Time-Life Books, 1982.

Toliver, Raymond F., and Constable, Trevor J. *Fighter Aces of the Luftwaffe*. Fallbrooke, Calif.: Aero Publishers, 1978.

Turner, Richard. *Big Friend—Little Friend: Memoirs of a World War II Fighter Pilot*. Mesa, Ariz.: Champlin Fighters Museum Press, 1983.

Ulanoff, Stanley M. *Fighter Pilot*. Garden City, N.Y.: Doubleday, 1962.

United States Strategic Bombing Survey. Report No. 1. *Summary Report (European War)*. Washington, D.C.: GPO, 1945.

———. Report No. 2. *Overall Report (European War)*. Washington, D.C.: GPO, 1945.

———. Report No. 2a. *Statistical Appendix to Overall Report (European War)*. Washington, D.C.: GPO, 1945.

———. Report No. 3. *The Effects of Strategic Bombing on the German War Economy*. Washington, D.C.: GPO, 1945.

———. Report No. 4. *Aircraft Division Industry Report*. Washington, D.C.: GPO, 1947.

———. Report No. 6. *Junkers Aircraft and Aero Engine Works, Dessau, Germany*. Washington, D.C.: GPO, 1947.

———. Report No. 7. *Erla Maschinenwerke GmbH, Heiterblick, Germany*. Washington, D.C.: GPO, 1947.

———. Report No. 8. *ATG Maschinenbau, GmbH, Leipzig (Mockau), Germany*. Washington, D.C.: GPO, 1947.

———. Report No. 9. *Gothaer Waggonfabrik, AG, Gotha, Germany*. Washington, D.C.: GPO, 1947.

———. Report No. 10. *Focke Wulf Aircraft Plant, Bremen, Germany*. Washington, D.C.: GPO, 1947.

————. Report No. 11. *Messerschmitt AG, Augsburg, Germany (Overall Report, Part A, Part B, Appendices I, II, III)*. Washington, D.C.: GPO, 1947.

————. Report No. 12. *Dornier Works, Friedrichshafen and Munich, Germany*. Washington, D.C.: GPO, 1947.

————. Report No. 13. *Gerhard Fieseler Werke GmbH, Kassel, Germany*. Washington, D.C.: GPO, 1947.

————. Report No. 14. *Wiener Neustaedter Flugzeugwerke, Wiener Neustadt, Austria*. Washington, D.C.: GPO, 1947.

————. Report No. 15. *A Brief Study of the Effects of Area Bombing on Berlin, Augsburg, Bochum, Leipzig, Hagen, Dortmund, Oberhausen, Schweinfurt, and Bremen*. Washington, D.C.: GPO, 1947.

————. Report No. 40. *Civilian Defense Division—Final Report*. Washington, D.C.: GPO, 1947.

————. Report No. 53. *The German Anti-Friction Bearings Industry*. Washington, D.C.: GPO, 1947.

————. Report No. 59. *The Defeat of the German Air Force*. Washington, D.C.: GPO, 1947.

————. Report No. 60. *V-Weapons (Crossbow) Campaign*. Washington, D.C.: GPO, 1947.

————. Report No. 63. *Bombing Accuracy, USAAF Heavy and Medium Bombers in the ETO*. Washington, D.C.: GPO, 1947.

Verrier, Anthony. *The Bomber Offensive*. New York: Macmillan, 1968.

von Renz, Otto Wilhelm. *Deutsche Flugabwehr in 20 Jahrhundert*. Frankfurt: E. S. Mittler, 1960.

Watry, Charles A. *Washout: The Aviation Cadet Story*. Carlsbad, Calif.: California Aero Press, 1983.

Watts, Barry D. *The Foundations of U.S. Air Doctrine: The Problem of Friction in War*. Maxwell AFB, Ala.: Air University Press, 1984.

Webster, Charles, and Frankland, Noble. *The Strategic Air Offensive against Germany, 1939–1945*. Vol. 2, *Endeavour*. London: Her Majesty's Stationery Office, 1961.

Werrell, Kenneth P. *Eighth Air Force Bibliography: An Extended Essay and Listing of Published and Unpublished Materials*. Manhattan, Kan.: Sunflower University Press, 1981.

————. "The Strategic Bombing of Germany in World War II: Costs and Accomplishments." *Journal of American History* 73 (December 1986): 702–713.

Whaley, Barton. *Covert German Rearmament, 1919–1939: Deception and Misinterpretation*. Frederick, Md.: University Publications of America, 1984.

Wilson, Donald. "Origin of a Theory for Air Strategy." *Aerospace Historian* 18 (Spring 1971): 12–14.

Wynn, Humphrey. *Prelude to Overlord: An Account of the Air Operations which Preceded and Supported Operation Overlord, the Allied Landings in Normandy on D-Day, 6th of June 1944.* Novato, Calif.: Presidio, 1984.

Yeager, Chuck, and Janos, Leo. *Yeager: An Autobiography.* New York: Bantam Books, 1985.

Credit Lines

Grateful acknowledgment is made to the following for permission to reprint copyrighted material:

Photographs are courtesy of the United States Air Force Historical Research Center, Maxwell Air Force Base, Montgomery, Alabama; Raymond F. Toliver; William R. Lawley, Jr.; Mary Gill Rice; and the Smithsonian Institution's National Air and Space Museum.

Selections from *Those Who Fall* by John Muirhead. Copyright © 1986 by John Muirhead. Reprinted by permission of Random House, Inc.

Extract taken from *I Flew for the Führer* by Heinz Knoke, reproduced by kind permission of Unwin Hyman Ltd. Copyright © 1953 by Heinz Knoke.

Selections from *Bomber Pilot: A Memoir of World War II* by Philip Ardery. Copyright © 1978 by Philip Ardery. Reprinted by permission of Philip Ardery and University Press of Kentucky.

Reproduced by permission of the Smithsonian Institution Press, selections from *The Dragon's Teeth?: The Creation of United States Air Power for World War II*, by Benjamin S. Kelsey, page 69. Washington, D.C. 1982.

Selections from "The Evolution of the American Strategic Fighter in Europe, 1942–1944," by Stephen L. McFarland. Copyright © by *Journal of Strategic Studies* 1987. Reprinted by permission of Frank Cass Publishers.

Selections from *Yeager: An Autobiography* by Chuck Yeager and Leo Janos. Copyright © by Chuck Yeager and Leo Janos. Reprinted by Bantam Books, a division of Bantam, Doubleday, Dell Publishing Group, Inc.

Selections from *Target Berlin: Mission 250, 6 March 1944* by Jeffrey Ethell and Alfred Price. Copyright © by Arms and Armour Press, 1981.

Selections from *Little Friend, Big Friend* by Randall Jarrell. Reprinted by permission of Mary von S. Jarrell.

Index